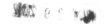

AMERICAN BIKER

The History, The Clubs, The Lifestyle, The Truth

by
Bill Hayes

Foreword by
U.S. Senator (Ret.) Ben Nighthorse Campbell

P R O D U C T I O N S

www.flashproductionsllc.com

First published in 2010 by Flash Productions, LLC. P.O. Box 34, Birmingham, MI 48012-0034 U.S.A.; flash@flashproductionsllc.com.

On the front cover:
Main: Charlie Brechtel
Inset: Bill Hayes

On the back cover:
Top: (*Left to right*) "Earthquake," Boozefighters MC; "Knuckles," Vagos MC; "Ghost," Boozefighters MC
Photo by Bill Hayes.

Center: "Spike," President, Hessians MC, MCOC
Photo courtesy of Randall Wilson/Guerrilla Docs.

Bottom: Jim Elrite, Hells Angels MC
Photo by Jennifer Thomas.

ISBN: 978-0-615-37595-3
Library of Congress Control Number: 2010936913

Editor: Jennifer Thomas
Designer: Jennifer Thomas

Printed in the United States of America.

To find out about more of our books, join us online at:

FlashProductionsLLC.com
AmericanBikerTheBook.com
TheOriginalWildOnes.com
BIKERTRUTH.com

Roaring down the interstates, we don't hold on for our lives;
rather, we hold on to live life.

—Cole Bieler,
Attorney, MC Member, and American Biker;
On the way to Sturgis

Contents

Contents

Preface

In 2005, filmmaker Randall Wilson released *American Biker*: a documentary film that finally—honestly—bared the absolute guts, soul, and personality of the motorcycle culture.

The clinical nuts and bolts history was there, too, but it wasn't wrapped in journalistic sterility; it was presented through the eyes, words, and passion of those who had created it—and those who proudly live it hard and fast each day.

I am honored to be one of those people.

And I was especially honored when Randall asked me to continue his passion by writing *American Biker,* the book. To use my *own* half-century of intimacy with the motorcycle culture to unleash "The History, the Clubs, the Lifestyle, the Truth." To unlock some heavy doors into the inner circle of this culture: doors to a vicarious wonderland for those on the "outside," and a multi-level badlands oasis for those on the "inside."

It is with love and respect to Randall and to this way of life that I present *American Biker,* the book.

Acknowledgements

A lot of people on the "inside" made this book possible...
through their stories, their photos, their friendship, and their inspiration.

Special thanks to...

(in some semblance of alphabetical order by various parts of their names!)

Keith "Bandit" Ball
Cole Bieler (always on the "Incredible Journey")
Steve Boyd (ya know, the Black Guy)
Charlie Brechtel (translating brotherhood into music...
and yes, that's him on the cover!)
"Buttnaked"
Ben Nighthorse Campbell
George Christie
Miles Davis (Om Tat Sat)
Sandy Dell
Jim Elrite (He *is* "that guy"!)

Flint a.k.a. "Zippo"
"Sweet William" Fritsch (the badass)
John "Ghost" Wagner
Kara Grace and Troy
John "Rogue" Herlihy
Paul Jamiol (a great guy, despite our political differences)
"Knuckles" and Teri (the most real biker couple on earth)
Jeff "EZJ" Kraus and Debbie
Gene Long (Editor's note: I'm Not Stephanie!)
Lou and Bill, Chosen Few MC
Evie Loutfy of ImagiCom Media (for her unending support and guidance!)
Lompico Lyle
Dave Nichols
Lee Nolan
Jim Owens
Robert "Ripper" Patrick (yes, that Terminator 2 guy)
Wendell Perry and "Bart at Large"
"Popeye," VNVMC
Beverly Roberts (a lady who really "gets it")
Bill Rodencal (the guy with the greatest job in the world!)
Michael Schacht and Markus Karalash
"Shadow"
Tom "Old School" Skoglind
J.J. Solari (possibly the funniest and most offensive man in the universe)
"Spike," HMC MCOC
Michael Stein
David Tootell (a true brother!)
Billy Warlock
Amy White (The Wicked Bitch)
Randall Wilson (I hope this does your film justice!)
Yuriko (a truly tough adventurer)

And to Jennifer Thomas, my editor and my everything...

Foreword

Nothing instills the concept of freedom more than the American Biker.

The birth of this American icon (as opposed to its predecessor, the "motorcyclist") began on July 4, 1947, in Hollister, California. That date, coincidentally, was the date I took my first ride on my older cousin's war-surplus 1942 WLA Harley-Davidson, only a two-hour drive from Hollister.

In the half-century (plus a few years) of riding these two-wheeled steeds, I am convinced that modern day bikers are kindred spirits to the adventurous Americans, from the mountain men era through the cowboy and Indian days. How else can one explain the similarity of dress, ornamentation, and lifestyle that is so common? Fringe, beads, eagles, horses, bears, leather, and silver were all symbols of the brotherhood of people who made our nation great. Their character exemplified personal responsibility and patriotism as well as independence and courage—qualities in men and women that are still admired to this day.

There is a calling that perhaps only bikers hear. Often maligned by government and stereotyped by Hollywood, it is a calling that is felt but not explained.

American Biker is the culmination of countless hours of research and interviews as Bill Hayes and Randall Wilson—through words and images—document the people who are called "American Bikers."

—Ben Nighthorse Campbell,
U.S. Senator, Retired

Introduction

The Feral Brotherhood of the American Biker

Recently, a major motorcycle publication featured a negative review of a book about the biker culture. The reviewer complained that it was filled with "all the same tired clichés: the last of the cowboys, the last of the outlaws, the only true patriots, the last independent spirits, etc., etc. All of which makes for great storytelling, even if few of the stories are true."

He adds:

> *I'm sorry, but after 35 years of riding, I've never met the archetypical; "lone scooter tramp" who lived by his wits on the road year round, footloose and fancy free. Everybody I've been privileged to meet has had jobs, lives, homes, kids, and obligations. The common thread that bound them all together was motorcycling. It was their chosen hobby and many have stuck with it for a long, long time. That's what a "biker" is: someone who rides year in, year out, mile after mile because it's what they enjoy. Everything else on the subject is extraneous sidebar fluff, hardly worth mentioning.*

Well, this called for some serious reflection.

And a serious drink.

We've all known this guy—guys like this reviewer. The guy who always carries an ironed handkerchief to neatly mop and organize his mucus, never simply wiping his nose on his sleeve or the pant leg of his Levis like the rest of us. The guy who complains that the music is too loud. The guy who actually makes it a point to go out and buy new underwear, long before his mother, girlfriend, or wife does it out of some primal survival instinct or simple hygienic obligation.

In "35 years of riding" this guy has never met a scooter tramp who "lived by his wits on the road year round, footloose and fancy free"?! He really has been spending far too much time wiping his nose and buying underwear.

In *my* "35[-plus] years of riding" I've met *plenty* of individuals who have lived on—and *for*—the road. People who have lived just for riding that bike. Sure, I've also met those with "jobs, lives, homes, kids, and obligations." They, of course, are in the majority; but I'm glad I haven't been so insulated from the real world that I haven't also met those who have forsaken (and in a lot of cases, lost) *everything* in order to live the life of a two-wheeled nomad—several of whom have shared their stories in this book. I've encountered many who have given up— or never even accepted—"normal" life in order to live out an existential biker existence.

Many died young. Many drifted into all kinds of strangeness. Many grew as strong and proud as the bikes they rode. But *all* true bikers I've met have accepted the strengths and risks of this lifestyle, fallen in love with its aura, and made a successful and satisfying lifetime commitment to it—some while still doing fine in the "jobs, lives, homes, kids, and obligations" department. Each person's outcome has ultimately depended on the choices he or she made, of course; and each journey represents a tangible and true component of the American Biker.

Our fastidious reviewer talked about "motorcycling" as being merely a "chosen hobby."

Collecting stamps is a "hobby."

Building plastic model airplanes is a "hobby."

Pasting up decoupage murals of babies and kittens is a damn "hobby"!

Seriously loving the biker culture—on all of its levels—is *a way of life.*

The definition of a "biker" that our pristinely underweared reviewer enlightens us with is that it is someone who simply "rides year in, year out, mile after mile." Anything beyond that, he tells us, is "extraneous sidebar fluff, hardly worth mentioning."

That statement alone warranted another shot of Cuervo.

All the tales of adventure don't count?

All the "interesting" characters—the wild personalities and how they intertwine around one another and society—are "fluff"?

Anything beyond a sterile recognition of hardbutts climbing up on some transportation vehicles and riding "mile after mile" is "hardly worth mentioning"?

The incredible social and cerebral connection between so many people and these unique machines just doesn't register with this mope. He obviously lives (figuratively and probably literally) inside of one of those smothering full-face helmets, with no peripheral consciousness whatsoever.

The American Biker is a hell of a lot more than someone who simply rides motorcycles as a "hobby."

It's obvious.

It's obvious to respected political leader Ben Nighthorse Campbell, who distinguishes the enormous differences between the "motorcyclist" and the "biker."

It's obvious to Randall Wilson who produced *American Biker,* the film: the best, most real, most truthful biker documentary on record.

It's obvious to legendary men like Peter Fonda who (sorry, Mr. Reviewer) *do* accurately still equate the American Biker to the cowboys and other folk heroes of our country.

It's obvious to *anyone* who has ever seen—or more importantly, been a *part* of—a long, loud line of big bikes rolling down the interstate together. Riding like that produces a *feeling.* A feeling experienced in the *soul*—not just in whatever tiny lame synapse controls the "hobby" urge that drives one to engage in things like assembling a plastic model of a big, fast airplane that the "hobbyist" could never be intimately connected to in any real way.

The people in this book; the descriptions of their lives and adventures; the looks into times, events, and eras that twisted our society; the sometimes bent panoramas that occur not just *on* two wheels but also *around* the entire lifestyle may even frighten fragile people like our reviewer.

But so what?

There has never been anything fragile about the American Biker. There never will be. That's the truth—no apologies.

Our reviewer friend looks at folk-hero depictions of the American Biker as simply "great storytelling, even if few of the stories are true."

¡Más tequila, por favor!

I can't think of *any* real biker who has ridden for *any* length of time who doesn't have a heavy dossier of stories. True stories. Stories about the people, the places, the runs, the events, the machine—and how all of that has affected their lives. Not to mention stories about the history of the lifestyle and its legendary personalities.

All of this may be "hardly worth mentioning" to those who spend a lot of time tidying up their bodily secretions. But it means virtually everything to those of us who feel so comfortable and alive within the feral brotherhood of the American Biker.

AMERICAN BIKER

Chapter 1

Risk Is for the Elite

Fences, Fonda, & Fear in Hooterville

The mythology of a biker is like being a cowboy.
There's no fences on the highway.

—Peter Fonda;
Interviewed in *American Biker*, the film

Fonda was right.

There are no fences.

Not for us.

In 1969, Fonda *became* "Captain America" when he rolled out on his chrome-heavy Panhead, searching for the hard-pumping heart of this country in the seminal film *Easy Rider*. Any mainstream social "fences" left even partially standing in the crazed wake of the 1960s culture storm were about to be crushed entirely.

Those years were a high and wild time. You bet your ass. A lot was said, done, attempted, accomplished, failed, celebrated, and regretted.

And the late-'60s served as a telling bridge in the evolution of the American Biker. With no subtlety whatsoever, the twisted '60s linked the four major eras that define this lifestyle: The "Birth of the American Biker" in the post-World War II 1940s; the late '50s / early '60s' chopper-and-"growing club force in Oakland" years; the post-peace-and-love Vietnam period; and the still-unfolding twenty-first-century "star power" years.

More than just a tongue-in-groove chronological link, the late '60s provided iconic examples of just what this lifestyle has been, done, and stood for throughout its entire existence.

For all the high-volume in-your-face running amok that went on in the '60s, the truth is that most of the citizenry remained in a low-profile, nine-to-five, missionary-position existence. The "silent majority" was indeed both. While the most visible "social fences" had been torn down and scattered by psychedelic drugs; the skinned-alive torment of the Vietnam War; the British music invasion; Woodstock; and a re-energized biker culture fueled by men like Sonny Barger and his Hells Angels—only the most wild and restless of the pack dared make the choice to be *truly* different, in a permanent way-of-life sense.

That kind of risk is always for the elite.

And when it comes to wildness, restlessness, and risk, bikers have always been way out in front. Few restraints or guardrails inhabit the soul of a true biker. No fences have *ever* lined their highway.

When *Easy Rider* hit the drive-ins and "walk-ins," it proved to be more than just a "biker flick"; little in the '60s media was that simple. Barger himself once referred to the film as a "Western," and it *was*—if only in its wandering, seeking tone. It was also a low-brow "chopper opera," a high-brow "exercise in existentialism," and more: A trip down the fenceless highway that everyone wishes they could take. A trip that only a select few actually do. *Easy Rider* became a symbol that transcended—even as it linked—the eras before and after it.

An undiluted freedom-lust is instinctive in nearly every human being. But having the balls to give in to this lust—regardless of the consequences (as the cinematic ghosts of Captain America and his partner, Billy, can attest)—is a matter of choice.

Folk heroes have always given in to it. That's what makes them folk heroes. From the dime novels that celebrated the Old West's gunslingers to the slick high-tech media productions of today, the rebel and his cause have universal appeal.

For those on the "inside"—the ones who actually *do* what the media tries so desperately to portray—the rebel elicits kinship pride and self-assurance.

For those on the "outside," the rebel is full of power and intrigue. From the mystery of what drives him to his pure abandon-fed ability to act on that drive—he evokes fantasy, envy, and respect.

And fear.

Someone who is so passionately driven—someone to whom consequences are just an unfortunate detail—usually commands a wide berth.

Easy Rider's introduction of a motorcycle into this mix of legends, truths, and tales heated the fantasies, envy, and pride to their flashpoint. The big bike, like no other tool of the folk-hero trade, combined abject power with abject freedom.

> *If there's a religious or spiritual component here,*
> *it's between me and my God.*
> *Maybe God doesn't exist until you hit about*
> *a hundred miles an hour.*

—"New York Myke,"
Owner, San Diego Harley-Davidson;
Interviewed in *American Biker,* the film

From the gunslinger's Colt .45 to the swashbuckler's sword to the rum runner's galleons to James Dean's lead-sled Merc—muscle and romance have always ignited whatever instrument each particular rebel has used to further his particular cause. But the motorcycle is unique. It's a hell of a lot more accessible than a three-masted schooner; easier to "soup up and strip down" than a hot rod; and stylishly less ominous than an out-and-out weapon. Yet it remains an instrument obviously not designed to be enjoyed by just anyone. The same goes for the lifestyle that accompanies it.

There is the mystery. *There* is the explosive mating of envy and fear.

The American Biker is a figure who could (and does) live right next door. He—or she—works with you. Other folk heroes, or *anti*-heroes, are simply not this real.

Most people never actually *knew* Billy the Kid or *worked with* Doc Holiday. They never met a pirate either. And the Sal Mineo / James Dean–style "juvenile delinquents" of the uncomfortable old black-and-white movies were dismissed by the mainstream as shadowy figures in some distant "concrete jungle"—far removed from their own familiar tree-lined avenues: tranquil mirrors of the neighborhoods they saw every week on *Leave It To Beaver* and *Father Knows Best*.

Motorcycles and the people who ride them are *not* remote and distant. And *that* little fact is what intensifies the emotions. Gunslingers, pirates, and giants were seldom seen roaming the public highways within spitting distance of Plymouth station wagons. Brooding, angst-ridden teenagers weren't flung into the backseat with Wally and "The Beave." But the American Biker, at every stage of development, has always been this close.

And the media has done everything possible to drive this unnerving point home.

Right after California's Hollister "incident" in 1947 (compounded a short time later by the infamous Riverside event of '48) is when the media began to instill the ice-edged fear of bikers into "normal, God-fearing humanity." A very close-to-home threat was indelibly gouged into the once-smooth, unblemished suburban skin along Main Street, U.S.A. If *they* could take over towns like Hollister and Riverside, why couldn't the same thing happen in the Anderson's Springfield, the Cleaver's Mayfield, or even Mayberry and Hooterville?! A descending horde of savages, drooling over Betty in that tight Angora sweater. Or worse: your own virginal daughter asleep in the fragile safety of her bedroom, in Yourtown, U.S.A.?

Peaceful men like Jim Anderson, Ward Cleaver, and Sheriff Andy Taylor were always so cerebral and psychologically inspiring with their insightful and serene thoughts and emotions. They invariably saved the day when tribulations threatened to disrupt life behind television's white picket fences. But wait— a new species-mix of humankind was on the loose. The media introduced "marauding bikers": bloody battalions who were always ready to meet peace and compromise with whip-chains and switchblades; ready to crush the likes of Jim, Ward, and Andy like mealworms under the heels of their gore-encrusted boots.

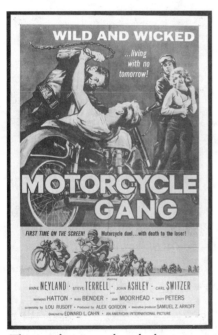

The media introduced the concept of "marauding bikers."

And while the media has indeed played upon the public's fear, no one can deny the element of truth inherent in this scenario. Certainly, there is a giant, two-fisted difference between a person who enjoys the buffered comfort of white picket fences and a person who enjoys— *demands*—no fences at all. So while the media may have *exploited* the sheer force of the biker world over the years, they haven't necessarily exaggerated it. The misperception lies in *how* the force is directed.

No one roaming *outside* those prim fences need barge his way back in just to bully Beaver's dad or his soft-core buddies for cheap thrills. Enough *real* thrills can be found on the fenceless side of things. And that—once again—is why this lifestyle is chosen.

In the real world, the basic biker attitude pretty much boils down to: "Hey, even if you live next to me, your desire to remain behind your nicely arranged boundaries is your business; the fact that I don't have any is mine. If we can keep it like that, everything's cool."

In truth, it's virtually impossible to exaggerate the "sheer force" of the biker culture—especially when it comes to consistency and tradition. In the '60s, the American Biker not only rolled over those shattered fences, but was able to rise above the unchecked weirdness that flattened them in the first place.

No one else did that.

This "rising" is a high-flying example of just what this lifestyle has done, been, and stood for—long before and long after the '60s.

Ultimately, the entire hippie culture—the social slice that dominated the headlines and the cult of personality of the era—was seen as a confused and searching minority whose loud voice was shrill, and incited primarily by mind-altering chemicals. The "straight" world didn't fare much better: From the bullets in the brains of the Kennedys to the extremes of George Wallace to the bewilderment of Lyndon Johnson to the smarminess of Richard Nixon to Mayor Daly's Gestapo in Chicago '68—disasters and taints pervaded the expectedly staid halls of American cornerstone politics.

But nothing inconsistent derailed the American Biker.

The passion that launched the World War II veterans through the fences of the post-war years has been as unstoppable as a Hellcat tank-killer at full speed in its power to unleash true wildness, restlessness, and risk. While the pop culture of the '60s drifted in and out of fads and "latest crazes," and the elected officials thrashed like drowning monkeys to escape the muck and mire of a quicksand war—bikers remained bikers. The thick leather of the World War II bomber jackets never changed; the basic mechanics of the machine that began in a Milwaukee shed in 1903 remained constant; and the instinctive freedom-lust never wavered. The American Biker had a history—and a future—that was steel-solid, tempered in pride and tradition.

When Fonda and Dennis Hopper followed Kerowac's advice and put their *Easy Rider* bikes "on the road," a contradictory dynamic was fittingly added to the '60s. Most of the decade had been dedicated to an allegedly peaceful and utopian "gently floating" way of life. The day-to-day existence of the high-profile sub-culture was mobilized by groovy little VW bugs and microbuses with brightly colored happy flowers painted randomly around the universal peace sign. It was all too beautiful.

The bikes, though, were different.

They are always different.

While the '60s fringe sub-culture permeated the plotline of *Easy Rider,* the undeniable undercurrent was that the bikes represented a constant—a constant that dated back to the '40s and that would remain long after the paisley shirts, the bell bottoms, the Strawberry Alarm Clock, and the "beads and Roman sandals" were gone.

The fact is that a big Harley is a big hammer that can be wielded— in both real life *and* the media—in a variety of big ways. It swung in late 1953 when Brando and Lee Marvin rode in with *The Wild One.* It swung crazily and hard as the motorcycle exploitation flicks of the early '60s shook the nitro of "the biker fear quotient."

But one thing is certain: hammers are almost never swung softly. That's not their purpose.

The fact that Fonda and Hopper didn't go in search of America in an oval-windowed bug or a chartreuse van was a pretty good gut-check for the entire love-in culture.

So were *Easy Rider's* final scenes.

The "feelin' groovy" non-stop drift dance that was the '60s came to a screeching halt in the movie's closing frames—just as it finally did at the Rolling Stones concert in Altamont, just months after *Easy Rider's* release.

The common denominator of big motorcycles—and the culture that goes with them—in both of these landmark events means something. It means that these bikes and the people who ride them— who *live* for them—are not part of an idealized world that is insulated from the harsher aspects of humanity. It would be nifty if all of life's complexities could be understood and solved simply with one of Ward Cleaver's knowing and wise looks—like helping the Beaver overcome the searing pain of yet another Little League loss.

But sometimes it takes more.

The World War II veterans who had seen just about every imaginable horror and inhumanity came home and found a natural outlet for their shredded emotions and smoldering psyches. Twisting the throttles of their Harleys, Indians, and other big bikes supplied them the mental thunder to attempt to clear their heads. The small California towns of Hollister and Riverside may not really have been "taken over"—held captive, as the media would report—but neither were they Kiwanis Club pancake breakfasts.

They were *gatherings* of bikers.

Gatherings, runs, rallies. Growing group camaraderie. Get-togethers like these—by way of sheer numbers and a certain slash of attitude—helped to establish "The Image": one of the most powerful personality portraits this country has ever seen. When this image found its way into a well-publicized 1951 short story, "Cyclist's Raid," and subsequently onto the big screen in *The Wild One,* the protagonists weren't on horses or in Studebakers. They were on motorcycles—acting strong and taking risks.

Strength is appealing; not everyone has it. Risks are appealing—almost erotically; few take them. The individuals who do *are* different.

Special.

Envied.

Feared.

And while these individuals may indeed be your next-door neighbors, and while the accessibility of the machine is as simple as going out and buying one, a dicey chasm lies between mainstream society and the *genuine* biker lifestyle. A deep moat, housing more than a few briny surprises, separates the two. It's so easy to look at the castle walls; it's so difficult to get inside.

Sure, here in the warm glow of the enlightened twenty-first century, when sunny Sunday afternoons roll around, a long line of bikes parked outside a bar or roadhouse (or even a "clean, well-lighted" restaurant) no longer signals the immediate fear of trouble or intimidation. Many straight establishments openly encourage biker business with "Hogs and Hot Link Sundays!" or "Blues 'n' Bikes Weekend!"—festive afternoons when bikers are especially courted, but curious families in minivans are just as welcome. Dads and Moms who have never ridden a motorcycle are a normal sight at Sturgis, Daytona, and other major runs, casually strolling the streets with their kids.

There is no denying that the term "American Biker" has broadened. The cross-section of Harley owners has grown. It's become cliché to mention things like "doctors and lawyers ride Harleys" and that "as expensive as these motorcycles are, you won't find any bums or riff-raff riding them anymore." All of that may be true—to an extent.

But there is a deeper level to the lifestyle.

And it is *here* where the briny creatures in the moat have bigger teeth. Where the pure and dedicated to the lifestyle—the folk-heroes and anti-heroes, the ones who generate the most fear and envy—exist.

We have inherited a myth, if you would,
of something that's truly unique to America.
We've invented French fries, we've invented Corvettes,
but we've also invented the motorcycle clubs…
and we've given this to the world.

—Bill Kennedy,
Kennedy's Custom Cycles;
Interviewed in *American Biker,* the film

When the serious and structured motorcycle clubs began to form in the mid-1940s, it was for a reason. The outlet that the war vets needed to regain some semblance of peace in their young lives revolved around the strong bond of a distinct camaraderie, one that fit just perfectly on a machine that symbolized wildness, restlessness, and risk.

And—most importantly—the freedom they had fought for.

The freedom many of their brothers had died for.

The war was tough. So were they.

So are big motorcycles.

In contrast to the creased and uniformed pre-war "riding clubs," the post-war motorcycle clubs were much more than mediums for social events, or groups of people to gather with on sunny weekends in those clean, well-lighted places. They became brotherhoods; the same kind of brotherhoods that grew in the trenches of war when men's very lives depended upon their trust, love, and respect for one another.

This brotherhood essence is the core of the biker lifestyle; the veins where the blood runs a deeper red, much closer to the heart.

But each level is important, and fundamental to the whole of the American Biker. Inherent to free living is freedom of choice. It is totally up to the individual just how deeply he or she wants to dig into this lifestyle. The sunny Sunday afternoons are available to everyone. But some things you may encounter en route are not.

Say, for example, you've just enjoyed a "biker day" in Northern California's South Bay area and you are cruising home along I-280. You might notice a motorcycle club's clubhouse just off the Interstate. This is *not* a place that is open to the public. You need an invitation to enjoy the festivities *here*.

Similar establishments exist all around: in Fort Worth; in upstate New York, right off the Hudson River; in L.A.; in Miami; in Detroit. They exist in virtually every major city in America, as well as small towns and many foreign nations.

You need an invitation to enjoy the festivities at a place like this.

The large, established motorcycle clubs represent the love and respect the members have for one another, which is not given or taken lightly. In the club world, it is not a case of changing hats for the weekend; it is a case of dedication that is as permanent as a full-back tattoo.

One day a co-worker asked me:
"When you ride your motorcycle and go to these events,
do you dress up like those motorcycle people?"
"No," I replied simply,
"I dress up like you *people when I come downtown to work."*

—Cole Bieler,
Attorney and MC Member

But all riders—from those who change the hats, to those with the committed eternal ink—are integral to the flow that courses through the deep tributaries to the American Biker.

At the end of *Easy Rider,* both Captain America and Billy are blasted off their bikes by elements of the very heartland they set out to find. The first true bikers—the World War II vets—exemplified that freedom always comes at high risk. This concept is timeless to *any* true biker, whether in the dust of Hollister in '47; the streets of Oakland and 'Berdoo in the '60s; the family sunshine of new-century Daytona; or in the brotherhood warmth of a private clubhouse.

If this risk—if this taste of freedom—comes at too high a price, well, maybe that's why so many prefer to remain on the "safe" side of those fences.

After all, risk *is* for the elite.

Chapter 2

Fired with Desire

From Indians to Crockers to Riding with Ghosts

*From the beginning, I always rode a custom-type
motorcycle—never a stock motorcycle.
It was always altered to fit my personality.
I look at them as works of art, in a sense—
because they're an extension of yourself.*

—George Christie,
President Emeritus, Ventura Hells Angels;
Face to Face with George Christie

Were the bike and the biker ever two separate and distinct entities? Did the two *gradually* meld into a package deal, mutually dependent upon one another to complement and supplement The Image, only after years of mechanical evolution had transformed the machine into a legend-heavy beast and years of social evolution had developed its rider into a folk hero?

No.

That's not how it happened.

Any instrument that has enough voltage to project a soul will connect *immediately* in an ethereal way with an artist or operator destined to lay hands on it.

The motorcycle fits this criterion.

And the "destined" artist or operator must be possessed of a similarly charged and ethereal soul.

The true biker is.

The brightest emotional sparks ignite instantaneously and the strongest bonds are locked in quickly. The first time Stevie Ray Vaughan or Eric Clapton felt the neck of a six-string, for example, they undoubtedly felt a connection—*something*. No, they couldn't make the thing talk yet—maybe they hadn't even picked a string—but somewhere deep inside, surely they knew that the guitar was *them*. A brush in the hands of Pablo Picasso became an extension of the painter's emotions, long before it created true magic from a wet pallet. Ansel Adams certainly sensed that his eye would become his camera lens. These kinds of feelings are not learned; they simply *are*.

The motorcycle and its rider are made for one another in a way that has little to do with something as mundane as mankind needing another mode of transportation.

Two entities with the same electricity.

One.

Okay.

But whoa, back to earth for a second here.

Admittedly, of course, some utilitarian elements *did* go into the creation of the motorcycle.

The motorcycle really became the vehicle
that put Americans and Europeans on wheels.
Its competition at that time was not the automobile;
it was the horse.

—Ed Youngblood,
Motorcycle Historian and Author;
Interviewed in *American Biker*, the film

True enough. But especially in America, the practical aspects proved to be secondary. Right from the starting gate, this was all about something else.

It was about freedom.

It was about excitement and passion.

It was about living more dangerously.

It was about *really* living.

It was about being different.

It's telling that the first motorized vehicle to ever cross America from coast to coast was a motorcycle. In 1903, the same year that Harley-Davidson was being born in its manger-like setting, George Wyman crossed the U.S. on his California "motor bike." And Wyman didn't *have* to make this trip—he *wanted* to.

"During the previous summer I had made the journey on a California motor bicycle to Reno, Nevada," Wyman wrote in his journal. "And I knew that crossing the Sierras, even when helped by a motor, was not exactly a path of roses. But it was that tour, nevertheless, that fired me with desire to attempt this longer journey—to become the first motorcyclist to ride from ocean to ocean."

Bikers have been "fired with desire" ever since.

These inner flames have cut through gender, race, and socio-economics.

In 1915, Effie Hotchkiss and her mother stoked the feminine fire when they became the first women to match Wyman's cross-country feat, rolling from New York to San Francisco—from the first of May, on into July—on Effie's sidecar-equipped three-speed V-twin.

"Decent roads would be non-existent for most of the way, there would be deserts to cross, high mountains to climb, lack of water, no repair shops, no this and no that," reported Effie in her journal. "Some things there would be, such as wild animals, wilder Indians, probably floods, maybe cyclones and other off-hand acts of God...I would not have missed it for the world."

This desire—this fire—has scorched America's cultural fast lane throughout every period in this country's industrial history. Becoming one with the *soul in the metal* has helped a lot of people soar over some particularly full bogs of humanity-induced ugliness: things like world wars, racism, and cultural chaos.

The 1960s experience in the Northern California Bay Area was like swimming blind in a tight warm-water vat packed with sharks; piranhas; and soft, friendly, busty mermaids. You could either sink, swim, be ripped to shreds, satisfy some serious fantasies, or all of the above.

Tobie Gene Levingston founded his all-Black biker club, the East Bay Dragons, right as the Oakland-'Frisco feeding frenzy began to unfold. His book, appropriately titled *Soul On Bikes,* describes how the riders' bond with the bike provided the ability to transcend even the most wildly explosive of situations.

"Unity. That's what I love most about the motorcycle set," writes Levingston.

> *Hell, even the vibes we got from the cops (and this is*
> *pure speculation on my part) felt constructive...You hear a lot*

about white club racism, police brutality, and range wars. But when the chips were down, all the pettiness flew out the window…We were all brothers watching each other's backs. That part felt good. Maybe the white birds and the black birds could fly together after all.

The motorcycles, the riders—fired with desire.

In the mid-'60s, the late Hunter Thompson wrote the classic epic *Hell's Angels: The Strange and Terrible Saga of the Outlaw Motorcycle Gangs.* Thompson's ultimate purpose and effects can be endlessly debated, but no one can argue his being wholly consumed by the machine he became intimately familiar with:

The lever goes up into fourth, and now there's no sound except wind. Screw it all the way over, reach through the handlebars to raise the headlight beam, the needle leans down on a hundred, and wind-burned eyeballs strain to see down the centerline, trying to provide a margin for the reflexes…But with the throttle screwed on there is only the barest margin, and no room at all for mistakes. It has to be done right…and that's when the strange music starts.

For all true bikers, the fiery soul in motorcycle metal *defines* intensity in human passion. It launches one through planes of existence—spiritual sprints into a cosmic ether.

American author Miles Davis has spent years rolling over every inch of the vastness of India on two wheels. He has absorbed the heat, the dust, the beauty, the horror, the mysticism, the crowds, and even the intricate belief system of that ever-churning country. He has absorbed it all just as he has absorbed the soul of his bike:

My serendipitous discovery of India's ancient lore in 1968 marked the genesis of a long adventure of the soul, a journey towards the yoga of inner realization. Later in India, the revelation of motorcycle yoga dawned upon me when I found that two wheels can transport me in solitary bliss to secret hidden places where yogis still meditate alone; to holy spots that were long ago forgotten by the Hindu masses.

The sacred and immortal wisdom of Bhagavad Gita kick-started this adventure in spirit. Indian-built Vespas, Royal Enfields, and Jawas transported me there. For the motorcycle yogi, the journey of one thousand miles begins with first gear. With a twist of the throttle and the Name of God vibrating to the beat of the pistons, the lone rider finds moto-ecstasy in his heart of hearts. Can the spinning wheels of the motorcycle free us from the karmic cycle of samsara? That rests in the intent and purpose of The Ride.

May He who pervades each atom guide your way along the path of dharma.

Om Tat Sat.

—Miles Davis,
Author, *Motorcycle Yoga: Meditative Rides through India*

But beyond the fire-driven—spirit-driven—desire of Miles is an incredible and very real resolve. In his book, *Motorcycle Yoga,* he writes:

It has been a journey of meditative bliss on two wheels, a good day and a great ride. So good, in fact, that if I am called from this world here and now, I would leave entirely fulfilled and satisfied.

George Wyman and Effie Hotchkiss may not have referred to their early-twentieth-century odysseys as "journeys of meditative bliss," exactly; but it's certain that they were. No other machine satisfies this wanderlust obsession so deeply.

But just as the Tin Man needed an oil-can fix before he could trundle off to Oz to get his heart, the heart *and* soul of motorcycle metal required a fair amount of nuts, bolts, and engineering before the true wizardry began.

The year 1885 was interesting in the U.S.A. and beyond: lots of zings and landmarks. The first successful appendectomy was performed; an invention called the "roller coaster" was patented; Mark Twain's *Huckleberry Finn* was published; Grover Cleveland became president; the Statue of Liberty arrived in New York; the first Dr. Pepper was poured; Ulysses Grant died; "Gabby" Hayes was born. Meanwhile, in Germany, Gottlieb Daimler invented the first internal-combustion engine-powered vehicle. His was a single-cylinder, two-wheeled "conveyance" that had two other wheels installed as outriggers to keep the thing upright.

Daimler's creation led to the first "production motorcycles" being manufactured on a very limited basis in America as well as Europe; he and his partner, Wilhelm Maybach, began selling foreign licenses for the engine in 1887. More of the world was introduced to this new invention at the Paris World's Fair from 1886 to 1889.

Most of the bikes constructed in the U.S. at that time consisted of small gasoline engines mounted on bicycle frames. But other configurations of mechanical genius (and not-so-genius) were being wrenched, welded, and wired both before and after Daimler's first internal-combustion putt.

A steam-powered bike, developed in 1867 by a man named Sylvester Roper, was one of those ideas that just never quite caught on in a mass-marketing sense. But hey, that didn't stop the production of another steam bike, the Austin, in 1868. Or Rollin Abell from trying the concept *yet again* in 1901, manufacturing a steamer called—what else?—the Abell.

Sure, these bikes produced smoke, but unfortunately not that sweet smell of overwhelming success. While in many circles, intense heat between one's legs is considered a good thing, out-and-out coal-burning boiler-straddling is another story all together. And let's just say (risking insensitivity here) that there was probably a *reason* Mr. Roper died of a heart attack while riding one of his "hot" bikes in 1896.

The steam may have eventually cleared, but there was no lack of other hazy ideas, concepts, and trials fogging up the path to what has been called by many, the "perfect vehicle."

For example, in 1895, nearly a century before Mazda popularized the hum-whir of a rotary engine, Sumpter Battey patented a rotary engine for a motorcycle. And, sure, the bike was called the Battey. The Riotte motorcycle was also produced that year, running on kerosene.

In 1897 George and Earl Holley built a single-cylinder three-wheeler. They started the Holley Motor Company in 1899 to build engines, and started producing motorcycles around 1901. (Their true fame, however, came much later as their Holley carburetors became as integral to the world of '60s hot rods as cool shift knobs and Ed Roth Rat Fink decals.)

The Gearless, seen in 1905, used a shaft drive and had a variable friction tranny. The Electra of 1913 was an electric bike—ninety years before the final bunch of EV1s (GM's failed electric car) were removed from the roads and crushed. The 1909 Royal had an exhaust system that ran through the frame tubes.

But legends don't pop up or refine their R&D overnight. Quick fixes and fast-food engineering are for fads, weak pop singers, bad artistes, splash actors, and government programs.

After Dorothy and the bunch applied those first squirts of oil to the Tin Man's joints, a lot of creaks and groans were heard before he hit his metallic stride and acquired his heart.

As the world of motorcycle development began to unkink and hit *its* stride, searching for *its* heart and soul, every step along that particular yellow brick road ultimately led toward Harley-Davidson: the towering Emerald City that came to represent the mechanical essence of the American Biker.

But it took a while.

According to the All-American Transportation Museum in North Carolina, prior to 1913, the U.S. was home to over 120 manufacturers of motorcycles.

A lot of creaks and groans were heard before Harley-Davidson hit its metallic stride.

George Wyman's cross-country mount, the California, was made by the California Motor Company of San Francisco (est. 1901). In 1903 the Consolidated Manufacturing Company in Toledo, Ohio, bought the rights to the motorcycle and later made the Yale California.

The Feilbach Limited, produced from 1904 to 1914, was used by the Milwaukee Police Department, right in Harley-Davidson's backyard.

Other bikes included the Yankee, Whipple, Tourist, Barber, Breeze, Flying Merkel, Excelsior, Comet, Crouch, Pansy, Patee, and Manson.

The Bi-Auto-Go, built in 1913, was one of the weirdest. Looking at it (in the Owl's Head Transportation Museum, Maine) is uncomfortable; it's like looking at an old snapshot of an aging Cyclops—an ugly mutant creature with bad balance. Constructed by Scripps-Booth, the thing had an aluminum car-like body with doors, a 323-cubic-inch eight-cylinder engine, and outrigger wheels that would retract at speed. Described by some as a "two-wheeled car," the beast weighed in at 3,200 pounds— more than two full-grown camels put together.

Between 1913 and 1920 the number of American motorcycle makers was cut like piled bait. The few survivors included Bayley-Flyer, Ace, Cleveland, and Pope.

Harley-Davidson was *also* there—ready to become king.

Ready to become the royal essence that millions would gladly worship; the image they would gladly tattoo all over their bodies.

Ready to become the first "immunity idol": a totem that could— if found and used properly—nearly guarantee survival from the mainstream.

Ready to be imitated by just a shitload of excuse-bearing lookalikes: "I really love my Kawasaki Vulcan / Honda Shadow / Yamaha Roadstar (insert wannabe-bike here)…it's so much more dependable than a Harley…and it *sounds* like a Harley…and it has a shaft drive… and a radiator…and from a distance, people can't tell the difference."

Yes, they can.

And everyone knows it.

If there is one man in this world who has a true dream job, it's Bill Rodencal. His job description as the Factory Restorer / Conservator of the Harley-Davidson Motor Company and Museum must include things like "shaman, master mechanic, metal immortalizer, and resurrector of two-wheeled souls." He takes rusted relics, barn-dwellers, and the neglected elderly, and he carefully—and lovingly— massages youth back into them.

Fueling the Madness

by Bill Rodencal

"What is it about these old bikes—specifically Harley-Davidsons—that fuels your madness?"

It's a question that I'm often asked, and to be honest, it's something I've never really stopped to dissect. But I can draw on two specific factors that I'm positive helped plant the seed for me.

Like most kids of my generation, I was completely in awe of Evel Knievel, and I was glued to the television every time he attempted to haul his XR750 Harley-Davidson over a dozen buses. It then became a feat that all the neighbor kids would try to replicate with their Schwinn Sting-Rays over garbage cans.

The other "planting of the seed" was my brother. After finishing college, he purchased a slightly used 1972 Harley-Davidson Super Glide. He'd ride up in the summers from Chicago with his buddies; drop in for dinner; and off they would go. The whole neighborhood shook as they rode in, and all the neighbors hated it.

I thought it was great!

I truly believe that the DNA make-up of men makes us inherently love all things mechanical. The only variable is that some love the latest, greatest technology and others lean towards a simpler approach.

I am of the latter.

I have always had a love for old things. From cars to airplanes to boats to houses to guitars to radios—there is something about days gone by that really speaks to me. These old things truly "fuel the madness."

By madness, I mean: just what is it that makes a person take perfectly good hard-earned money and turn it into a pile of rusty metal? For me, it's because in my mind's eye I see what that item was long ago. Just what work went into the design and construction of it—the materials that made it up—all very different, yet so basic compared to what is used today. No plastics, composites, or carbon fibers; just steel, rubber, and leather.

Bill Rodencal, "resurrector of two-wheeled souls."

I also take it as a personal challenge to take something that too many people think is way past the point of no return and bring it back to the glory it once radiated when new.

The magnitude of the project is often underestimated, in many ways, by the individual undertaking it—the time element as well as the economics.

The payoff in the end?

First, there is selfish personal satisfaction—a moment of Zen with an object that has been long inanimate and is now reincarnated.

The second is the moment that life is breathed into the engine, when it once again comes alive after decades of silence.

The final payoff is to share the rebirth of this "time capsule," in hopes of inspiring and educating individuals to become the next generation of enthusiasts in the world of motorcycling!

—Bill Rodencal,
Factory Restorer, Harley-Davidson Motor Company

But while Harley-Davidson was surviving the American motorcycle manufacturer purge of the late teens / early 1920s, the Indian Motorcycle Company was still there, too; and in relation to Harley-Davidson, Indian came first.

In 1901, in Springfield, Massachusetts, a bicycle manufacturer named George Hendee teamed up with engineer Oscar Hedstrom, and the mechanical roots of the American Biker and The Image underwent its absolute·raw germination; like a wet, pumping implant of a live, beating heart into the Tin Man—a celebration of machine and being as one.

Even the naming of the firm laid important roots. In honor of the company being the first major American "motor-driven cycle" manufacturer, homage was extended to America's main symbol of a proud heritage: the Indian. Of course that was in 1901, long before the political-correctness cult would have screamed like scalped palefaces over George and Oscar's ugly insensitivity of using a name that had anything even remotely to do with American ethnicities; even in the most positive sense. (Take the "Racial Mascots Act," proposed by California assembly member Jackie Goldberg in 2002, calling for an absolute ban on schools using Native American team names, including "Redskins, Indians, Braves, Chiefs, Apaches, Comanches, or any other American Indian tribal name.")

Ironically, the shift in U.S. values and priorities over the last hundred years or so by the country's socio-political swingers exemplifies how the consistent beat of the American V-twin and the true American Biker is all about tradition. It always has been and always will be about a simpler time. A time when the definition of the word "normal" wasn't up for debate. A time when elected lawmakers who consider themselves the safety police and morality marshals would have been considered either a bad, cheap beer–induced joke or the outtake scribbling from a young George Orwell's notebook.

But thankfully, the Indian motorcycle *was* created—and *named*—in a simpler time. (And I'm sure it would add to Ms. Goldberg's horror and outrage to know that from 1907 to 1911 "Apache" motorcycles were also made here in the good ol' U.S. of A.)

But by the 1930s, Indian was having management struggles. Both Hendee and Hedstrom had long since retired, and the company was sold to the automobile manufacturer and chemical-paint giant, DuPont. Indian fell into the hands of diversified clinical *business* rather than singular personal *passion*.

For Indian, the fire-driven desire was no more.

Meanwhile, Harley-Davidson had been founded two years after Indian, in 1903—a date so many know as readily as their own birthdays. Walk around any major motorcycle event and ask when William Harley and the Davidson boys kicked things off in that sacred 10-by-15-foot shed, and you'll have a pretty good shot at getting the right answer (even if it takes some mathematical back-engineering by those quarter-million or so who traveled to the land of Packers, beer, and brats for the weeklong Harley 100th Anniversary celebration in 2003).

True, William Harley and Arthur Davidson were ostensibly just trying to come up with a vehicle that could get them to their favorite fishing hole a little more conveniently. But again: the simple utilitarian "tool" aspect of the motorcycle was overshadowed by that *passion*. Walter and William Davidson—along with local resident, marine engine and carburetor specialist Ole Evinrude—joined the team and a big switch was thrown, one that would jolt generation after generation with an irresistible spark.

Apart from their *individual* fires and desires, Indian and Harley took fire of another type when they were both used extensively in World Wars I and II. The bikes' war use was an important factor in their respective demise and success.

As early as 1916, motorcycles were being recognized as a pretty good military weapon—mainly because of their functional similarity to the horse. They were used by U.S. forces to pursue Mexican rebel Pancho Villa as he carried out raids along the crazed terrain of the Tex-Mex border.

Pancho Villa also rode a motorcycle: an Indian.

World War I expanded the use of motorcycles, again taking advantage of their spiffy mobility. But the war was a suffocating drain on Indian, as the company starved its domestic dealers in favor of throwing all its resources into its quest for war profits.

And when motorcycles were again used heavily in the theatre of World War II, it was Harley-Davidson who negotiated the most favorable government contracts.

Just five years after D-Day, Indian found itself owned by the British firm that manufactured the Royal Enfield. "Real" Indians, according to purists, were no longer made after 1953; the few produced in the years immediately following were essentially Royal Enfields with the Indian name.

So as Indian weakened in the post-WWII years, Harley-Davidson gained muscle. One of the main reasons for this was that the four founders—William Harley and the Davidson brothers: Arthur, Walter, and William—kept their enthusiasm and fire alive for the machine that they had created.

And that fire never died.

It never will.

The king *still* reigns.

Today, Indian purists also have a lot to say about the latest two incarnations of the hallowed name. From 1999 to 2003 "Gilroy Indians" were produced in Gilroy, California (the "garlic capital of the world," just a clove's throw from Hollister); first with S&S engines, and then in 2002 using the new Powerplus 100ci engine.

In 2003 the Gilroy Indian surrendered to bankruptcy.

In 2006 *another* company—England-based Stellican Limited—took over the Indian name and their HQ was set up in Kings Mountain, North Carolina. They have big plans for a very big name.

Again.

Of course, there was *another* American V-twin that had a driven soul and an especially fast hook into the seductive image. Founded in the speed mettle that winds through the guts of the American Biker, Al Crocker and the namesake bike he created in 1936 gave both Indian and Harley-Davidson a wild run for their money—literally.

Today, surviving Crockers are more than just relics: they are legends to be worshipped by those who understand and appreciate the engineering in these machines. They were (and *are*, perhaps) the ultimate American V-twin. The price tags on vintage Crockers are steep, ranging well into six figures. Art and timelessness get their price.

Rising intact from the dead is also pretty impressive. According to some, it has only been done once. Crocker may be a reasonably legitimate number two.

After extensively studying the mind and machine of Albert Crocker, Michael Schacht and Markus Karalash set out to honor both with a new life. In 1997 the pair revived the Crocker Motorcycle Company. But they didn't just exhume the name and slap it on a modern machine; Crocker's design didn't need updating. Using the *exact* specifications developed by Al in his Los Angeles factory in the 1930s, Michael and Markus began producing authentic Crocker parts, rolling away the stone to a golden age and a golden motorcycle.

Michael and Markus describe the story of Al and his machine in near apostolic reverence:

Crocker: The Man, The Machine, and The Legacy

by Michal Schacht and Markus Karalash

Crocker: The Man

Albert Crocker's life may seem unremarkable at first glance. In many ways, he lived and died like most Americans, with some daring moments and many years of hard work. Why then, is Al Crocker's name well-known to motorcycle enthusiasts, especially to connoisseur collectors? He is considered a legend—a hero—for the standards that he set; the moving art forms that he developed using chromium, aluminum, and steel; for the races he won and for his associations with famous motorcycle companies and people throughout his life. He is also renowned for taking on, and besting, the big-name motorcycle manufacturers of his time.

Al Crocker was born in 1882. After receiving his engineering degree from Armour Institute (part of Northwestern University), his first employment was at Thor Motorcycle— the motorcycle division of Aurora Automatic Machine Company—where he engineered new products. Although an engineer, he loved riding and racing. He competed in and won many endurance contests, riding the famous "White Thor."

While racing, he met Oscar Hedstrom and Charles Hendee of Indian Motorcycle. A close friendship developed, which evolved into a full-time position at Indian for Al Crocker.

In 1924, Al married Gertrude Jefford, his co-worker at Indian's Denver, Colorado, branch and the widow of former bike racer Eddy Hasha. Al also took over the Indian dealership in Kansas City, Missouri, which functioned as distributor for several Midwest states.

When the West Coast beckoned Al Crocker, he sold the Kansas City operation to "Pop" Harding and bought Freed, an established Indian dealership.

Al Crocker and [foreman] Paul Bigsby must have spent many of their off-hours designing and developing their own bikes; for in 1931, they turned the racing world on its ear when they introduced their dirt-track racers. The first reviews were absolute raves, recounting how "two American-built night speedway racing engines swept the boards...9 first places and 3 second spots out of 12 starts."

Al also invented the Crocker 30–50 cubic-inch single-cylinder speedway bike, which was the bike of choice for many of the best riders on the Pacific Coast when speedway racing was at its height.

At the debut race, Al Crocker made a brief appearance. His quiet, down-to-earth personality is evident in the following coverage of the event:

The call came suddenly for the builder; for Al Crocker who was in the pits...[He] came to the microphone. His speech was short, brief; just the sort of thing that the situation called for...He was glad that [the bikes] were good... They would be better.

In the mid-1930s, Crocker and Bigsby began to realize another dream: to build a heavyweight, high-performance, overhead-valve V-twin motorcycle.

The great Crocker V-twin was definitely the best motorcycle produced in this country at that time.

On the road, nothing else could catch it.

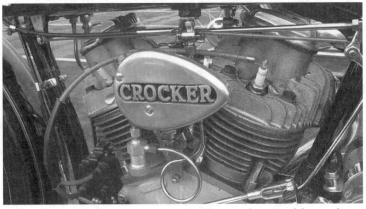

The great Crocker V-Twin: Nothing else could catch it.

Crocker: The Machine

The machines Al Crocker invented were well ahead of their time in design and function. His bikes were visually pleasing, as Crocker seemed to have a perfect eye for form and balance, for color and simplicity. They were such great examples of fluidity of design that they seemed to be moving, even in still photos.

The innovative styling was equally matched by record-breaking performance.

When the first Crocker road machines blasted onto the scene in 1936, it astonished the motorcycling community and "single-handedly caused Harley-Davidson and Indian more grief than any event up to the British motorcycle invasion of the 1950s" (Iron Horse, *April 1979, p. 32*).

When the first road test results were released, showing cruising speeds of 90–100 mph, the Crocker became an overnight success. Orders for the Crocker Twin exceeded all expectations. It had to be the best motorcycle produced in North America at that time, and riders wanted it.

The Crocker was built heavy-duty for maximum performance; custom-tailored to the individual rider's order; and built in Al Crocker's own facility. Each buyer could choose color, degree of chrome trim, and even gear ratio and displacement!

So confident was Crocker of this magnificent machine that he offered to refund the full purchase price to any buyer who was beaten by a rider on a factory stock Harley or Indian.

No refund was ever given.

Crocker: The Legacy

Despite the success of and demand for Crocker's bikes, the recession of the time made it increasingly difficult to produce vehicles in small quantities. Sadly, this financial reality forced Al Crocker to abandon production of his machines.

Although fewer than one hundred Crockers were built, motorcycle aficionados will not forget them. They serve as a challenge to today's manufacturers: proof that a classic American V-twin can be both fast and graceful.

Nor will Al Crocker be forgotten. He is remembered as the genius who created America's first "superbike."

—Michael Schacht and Markus Karalash,
Revivers of the Crocker Motorcycle Company

Crocker owners are a rare and envied breed. One such man was Jack Lilly.

Jack Lilly was all biker. He needed speed, strength, and freedom— *and* the proper tool to make all three work as one. His choice was the Crocker.

After Crocker ceased production, Jack and his friend "Red Dog" Dahlgren dreamt of acquiring the old factory, along with the parts and everything else that went with it. It was a dream that was never able to forge quite enough reality (or money) to once again put a key into the doors that Al Crocker locked for good at 1346 Venice Blvd. in Los Angeles.

Still, the fact that Jack Lilly rode—and more importantly, genuinely *loved*—his Crocker motorcycles opens the history books even further, revealing even more rich layers in the groundwork of the American Biker.

Jack Lilly rode—and loved—*his Crocker.*

With the aid of a friend, a stranger, and an L.A. motorcycle dealer named George Beerup, Jack was able to sell one of his old speedway bikes—a Rudge—and acquire a Crocker.

The friend was George Manker; he allowed Jack to take over payments on his near-new Crocker. The stranger who bought Jack's Euro Rudge was a guy who just happened to walk into the bike shop when all the "high-level" negotiations were taking place. He overheard the wheeling and dealing and decided that he'd like to buy Lilly's bike. The stranger was named "Wino Willie" Forkner: the man who eventually founded the Boozefighters Motorcycle Club in 1946; the man the entire 1947 Hollister incident and the subsequent Birth of the American Biker revolved around.

Whether it was due to the tight-knit world of bikers in those times, or the war, or simple fate, or all three—Jack, Manker, and "Red Dog" would *all* eventually become members of Wino's legendary club.

In the late 1990s, as Jack was approaching eighty years of age, the Boozefighters MC arranged for him to be reunited with his most beloved Crocker. Jack had owned three; his favorite was the one brought to him in pristine restored shape: serial #103. It was a motorcycle he hadn't seen in fifty years. The surviving bike was owned by renowned collector Daniel Statnekov, and—strictly by coincidence—when #103 was rebuilt, it was painted green and white, the colors of the Boozefighters MC.

When Jack sat on that bike again after all those years, he wasn't an eighty-year-old man—he was young and strong. He was one of "the original wild ones," with a smile and a *knowing* that his experiences had helped to shape this lifestyle. The scenes that he could play over and over in his memory would make most of us wince, cringe, cry, laugh, and give vital body parts to have been a part of them—just as he was a part of that bike. A soul in the metal.

When Jack died several years later in 2005, it seems assured that some of his final thoughts were about his beloved Crocker:

Jack Lilly's "last ride" on his old Crocker.

"Jack's wife, Anne, told me that one of the last things Jack whispered was that he needed to call his good friend JQ and tell him something," Boozefighter historian Jim "JQ" Quattlebaum told me emotionally after Jack's death. "I'll never know for sure what it was, but I'll bet it had something to do with the exciting visit he'd just had from Michael [Schacht], who came to visit and give him a Crocker t-shirt.

"And probably, for me to tune into the History Channel as he was being honored with pictures of himself as a young man on his 1939 Crocker #103.

"I'll be watching that documentary tonight with mixed emotions."

The evolution of the motorcycle and the men and women who ride them is a single intoxicating gestalt. It's impossible to separate the components; impossible to separate the soul in the metal from the soul in the flesh of the complete American Biker.

It's kind of like all those weird stories and myths that circulated around the 1943 "Philadelphia Experiment," in which a Navy ship was allegedly made invisible as an experiment in weaponry. But something went very wrong there; horror stories emerged about grisly fusions of flesh and metal.

That's *not* what we're talking about here.

No.

There's nothing wrong at all, here in the biker world—a society that feeds upon a *healthy* fusion. In *our* metal, and in the most aware and vital wetness of our brains, it really *is* all one. And ultimately, it extends far beyond the bike and rider.

The bike, as George Christie said, is "an extension of yourself."

This *fusion* is what drove the "originals" to build and ride these things in the first place—to create the perfect mechanical storm to augment the quick-freeze maturation the WWII vets had just endured, trapped in blood-run trenches or gunning their way through shrapnel skies in the ball-turret bellies of B-24s and B-25s.

This *fusion* is what shot juice into the major clubs in the late '50s / early '60s.

This *fusion* is what provided an antidote, when abrasive civilians and lame-ass sedans just didn't do it for the forgotten heroes of Vietnam.

And this *fusion* is what inspires, and will continue to inspire, motorcycle riders—"bikers"—now and in the future. Because there will always be people who inherently understand, and *feel*, the soul in the metal.

I damn sure do.

The ride from Williams, north into the Grand Canyon, is a pretty straight shot. As you roll along Arizona State Route 64 and U.S. Highway 180 you run more or less parallel with the old-time locomotive and Western train that has steamed up its sixty-five miles of track with a fair amount of regularity since 1901. That train has boasted passengers like Teddy Roosevelt, John Muir, William Howard Taft, FDR, Ike, and Clark Gable. And their ghosts might still take an occasional ride along these rails; because the whole atmosphere of this ride is one of looking over your shoulder. Not at danger, but at times gone by.

This is a good ride to do alone. Just you and your bike. And it doesn't matter what time of day or night. Each time is perfect.

The morning is *my* favorite, for the always-heavyweight reason that it's a beginning. Another beginning.

But the mid-day works, too, in a very sensual way. The relative warmth of Williams becomes the cool of the Canyon as you climb, and you feel every degree of the change without the plastic benefit of climate control and multi-directional heat or A/C dashboard ducts. It's a lot like real sex—straight-ahead sex that doesn't need the peripheral zip of acrobatics and devices.

Most of the wildlife is in at mid-day, of course; but you're out, and you're as much a part of that wildlife as they are, and you sweat and shiver and are as close to nature as the deer and the cats and the raccoons and all the rest. But you're faster, and that handy opposable thumb has allowed your kind to build that machine and to control it (though that control *could* be up for debate, as you pretty much give in to the wishes of that bike just as much as it responds to your twists, turns, and push).

Sundown is also just right. If you make it into the Canyon directly at sunset, another sexual metaphor about the perfect climax to the day can be used. Riding up a road like this two-lane as sunset nears will bring tears and a shadowy kind of melancholy that has an expensive and vintage taste to it. You're aware that those old railway tracks are just off to your left. You think of those on the passenger lists, and how their adventurous spirits are undoubtedly still roaming this countryside. Those presidents—Teddy, Taft, FDR, and Ike—they were all tough guys; three of them intimately involved with war, one of them a future Chief Justice. Muir was a survivalist. Clark Gable was what every red-blooded boy and man of that era wanted to be. Gable's pictures, side by side with Carol Lombard, hang on the walls of the rough-and-tumble bar at the Oatman Hotel where they honeymooned, 187 miles to the west.

As you ride alone toward the ever–mysteriously erotic five-thousand-foot-deep mouth of the earth, you look over the other shoulder, and there is the Ghost Rider; the transparent rush that you've seen so many times in magazines. But here he is. And another ghost appears.

Dave Mann took the ideal of the American Biker to artistic perfection. But there were times when he seemed *too* perfect; too socially symmetrical. Is this lifestyle really *that* good?

A ride like this answers that question.

At night, the road isn't just dark; it's a complete vacuum for anything but the purest form of solitude and melding of rider and bike. The danger can shoot from the almost one-dimensional blackness at any time. Things with yellow eyes that glow in the headlight beams don't want to be run into, and you don't want to run into *them*—together creating a seriously chaotic recipe that could boil over quickly; leaving you sprawled and broken in the back-wall off-road tundra where you'd be something's lunch months before any human discovered enough of you to shovel into a bag.

But I'm no stranger to blackness and solitude on a bike. I've been there before. Many times. That exact black vacuum enveloped me on California State Route 371 the night I left Anza, headed back to the coast—the last time I ever saw or spoke with Jack Lilly. Jack's Anza home was not far from the city of Riverside, where the second of the infamous "biker riots" put Jack and his brother Boozefighters into the klieg lights of American post-war media.

Jack was always laughing, or at least smiling. His tales about this lifestyle were always pure fun. He spoke of all the adventures with Wino Willie Forkner. He spoke of all of those WWII vets who were picking up life's pieces on the barstools at the All American Café in Los Angeles, consciously or unconsciously creating the most bare-knuckled lifestyle ever in America's social flow. Every tale, truth, and yarn was another strong and clear vein pumping dark, rich blood through the body of the American Biker.

I was headed for the Canyon and I was thinking of Jack. It was too dark to see Mann's Ghost Rider now, but I knew he was there. I could feel him. I could feel the old folklore myths, too. Pecos Bill, John Henry, and Paul Bunyan—all given a chunk of the credit for "digging" this 277-mile hole in the ground up ahead.

Those are cute stories. Fine. And there are myths surrounding the American Biker, too. But these men and women weren't the product of hopeful and vicarious fantasy. They were—*are*—real. The only fantasies in the lives of the Jack Lillys of the world revolve around others wishing they could live the same way: with the open, smiling recklessness to ride with understanding ghosts anytime— and all the time. Twenty-four hours a day.

And that hasn't changed.

It's just pre-dawn. Route 64 takes me east out of the Canyon and back down in elevation to the junction at Cameron. It's warmer here, so the leathers come off. I know they'll go back on during the climb south up into Flag. In the twelve-thousand-foot shadow of Humphrey's Peak, I begin to turn it on. I haven't seen a cop other than a forest ranger since Williams, and I really don't care much anyway. If he can stay with me, more power to him.

Jack told me a story about how he once got jailed for speeding on his Crocker. It was a story of humor (naturally), not tinged with the abrasion and sick rust that has made the modern conflicts between cops and bikers anything but funny.

The sun coming up on my left just brought the Ghost Rider back into view…and Jack on that Crocker…and Gable with that smile and that suaveness…and all the rest. I appreciate the company, of course.

But then again, I was never really alone.

Chapter 3

The Real History of This Lifestyle

No Revisionism Allowed

> *Sure, we want to go home.*
> *We want this war over with.*
> *The quickest way to get it over with*
> *is to go get the bastards who started it.*
>
> —General George Patton

The evolution of the American Biker is encircled by four particularly thick growth rings in the cross-cut of this country's industrial history.

The World War II years and those immediately following served as the wide and fertile canal for the Birth of the American Biker.

Phase Two came in the late 1950s and early '60s with the charisma of Sonny Barger. The cornerstones to the Red & White empire were laid, and along with them came at least a *vision* of the potential and influence of the motorcycle clubs and their brotherhood.

Rebel Without a Cause hit the theaters, and its cool abandon grabbed the nation's youth by the throat. Creative-juice-infused "choppers" eclipsed basic, stripped-down "bobbers" as the bikes of choice. This era's clubs made themselves much more visible.

Phase Three was the Vietnam War period, including its impotent and unsatisfying end. The Vietnam aftermath reinforced and expanded on everything "biker" that had occurred in the first two eras: the need for camaraderie; the need to reject rigid parameters and rules; a desperate need for cleansing; and a simple, respectful enjoyment of the image in general.

Phase Four arrived with the twenty-first century. The new millennium blew in, amidst the freaks hiding under dusty beds in fear of Y2K, or butchering themselves in the name of God for a ride on a comet. This fourth growth ring oozed some pretty lush sap into the biker world, as the ever-expanding cable and satellite networks made stars and household names of a lot of motorcycle folks who in another time would probably have just shared a lot of cheap, simple nights in garages with friends—a Bud in one hand, a wrench in the other, a bike in pieces on the floor...and a whole lot of slurred opinions as to what to do with all three.

Exploding TV exposure has also brought biker *history* to a much wider public: our lifestyle in high-def.

But popularity, renewed awareness, and big ratings aside—let's make sure that there is no "revisionism" in *this* history.

What happened, happened.

And World War II did indeed happen.

And it provided *the beginning*.

War produces many casualties. Along with cut-down lives and limbs are serious economic repercussions. After the *first* World War, the domestic motorcycle manufacturing firms were rendered pretty lean. The companies that *did* survive were having a tough time reorganizing their customer base; a base that had been drained of normal living by the craziness and life-mixing elements of war.

The "sport" of motorcycling had long been centered around the racing side of things, but the post-WWI years were left void of any serious racing structure.

The Motorcycle Manufacturers and Allied Trade Association (MM&ATA) got involved in some regrouping efforts in 1920, and racing within specified parameters returned to the motorcycling community. In 1924 the MM&ATA morphed into the American Motorcyclist Association (AMA). The AMA became the main racing sanctioning body and eventually promoted the huge Gypsy Tours: statewide, good-clean-fun, jamboree-picnic soirées, which proved to be the ground-seeds for events like the Sturgis Rally.

Racing led to a certain degree of camaraderie and the formation of certain types of clubs. But motorcycling, in general, always did. Long before the wars and the AMA races and the wingdings, there *were* motorcycle clubs, of sorts: groups who socialized and rode together.

But World War II was about to bend the social metal.

Realities—and attitudes—would change.

The veterans who rolled home from the scattered fronts of World War II were not really in the mood for doing much "within specified parameters"—or being "sanctioned" by anyone or anything that had even the slightest nauseating stench of officiousness.

They'd had enough of that.

Hell, everyone who was in the Boozefighters was a veteran,
and we all came back with the same thing in mind:
"Jesus, now we can kind of play and do hairy things
and nobody's shootin' at our ass…!"
That made a hell of a difference in life.

—"Wino Willie" Forkner,
Founder, Boozefighters Motorcycle Club;
Interviewed in *American Biker,* the film

The clean sweaters, three-point hats, and shirts and ties that outfitted the early "riding clubs" weren't a big hit either. The mud and gore of war has a way of making its own stark fashion statement.

To the returning vets, the motorcycle made a statement, too.

The war had been over for five years or so when my own family moved to Long Beach, a major port town of Southern California.

Both my uncle and my dad had been in the Big One. The man across the street had, too. He had served in the Navy and was actually *in* Pearl Harbor when that particular horror erupted. He didn't like to talk about it much, but every now and then, with the help of some Pabst that my dad and uncle always had in the ice box, we'd get a "history lesson."

"That wasn't a good place to be," he'd understate. "It all happened so quick…pure hell."

My dad had been in the Navy, too, but he'd spent most of the war on a submarine, and then they sent him to Panama. He said there wasn't much action there, but we still have his photo albums with old black-and-white snapshots of young native kids, naked with rifles. We have his pictures of the shrunken heads and stacks of skulls that were all over the jungle there. We have pictures of the big iguanas they ate.

My uncle had been in the infantry, on the front lines.

"Not much to talk about," he'd always say.

We knew better, but that's all he ever gave. He had other ways of expressing what went on overseas.

My uncle had owned motorcycles before the war, so as soon as he came home he got another one. He wound up with three: two Harleys and an Indian. Once the two families moved to Long Beach, my dad would borrow one of my uncle's and we'd all take off on rides. The two of them would shoot pool in places like Joe Jost's down on Anaheim Street while I sat in the big-backed booths and sneaked sips out of my dad's schooner of Pabst.

Sometimes my uncle and I would go for rides alone. Up into Signal Hill or down by the Pike amusement park or out to the waterfront in San Pedro. He'd always stop for a drink somewhere, usually at a place that had another bike or two parked outside.

I think I was about six or seven when we went this bar (he always called them "joints") in San Pedro (he always just called it "Pee-drow"). He always said that the waterfront was one of the toughest areas in Los Angeles, but he liked to go down there because he liked to look at the ships that were all around Terminal Island.

Well, inside the bar, two young guys started giving my uncle a bad time. I don't know what started it, but one of the guys took a swing at him. My uncle was in his snug leather jacket. He was tall and slender, and in that leather he looked like a god. He was, to me.

It took only half-a-second for him to push me out of the way, and he decked that first guy so quick I didn't even see it. But I sure saw the second guy when he reached for a pistol in his belt.

My uncle saw him, too.

Before the guy could draw the gun, my uncle shattered a brown beer bottle right across his face. It made a real mess of the guy, but my uncle didn't even flinch. He ordered another beer. While he drank it, a big Cadillac ambulance showed up and took what was left of the second guy away. The cops came and picked up the first.

"Stupid sumbitches!" my uncle called them, smiling as we watched the ambulance pull out toward Gaffey Street.

We left the bar in silence and got on his "sickle" and headed home. He was walking me over to the house when I told him how good a fighter I thought he was. "That wasn't fighting," he told me. "That was just playing around.

"Normandy…Omaha Beach…*that* was a fight," he said.

That's all he said.

Years later, the man across the street died. I remember going to a nursing home to see him in those last years. He was frail and thin, and I couldn't help getting choked up. To me he was such a tough guy… a true hero. He may have gotten old, but that didn't diminish what he and his entire generation did. They were *still* tough guys.

My dad died at a young age of a heart attack. He went out with a beer in his hand, sitting comfortably on the beach in Oceanside. Today they would have cited him for violating the "NO ALCOHOL ON THE BEACH" law before allowing the coroner's wagon to take him away.

My uncle rode right up until the day he died. I remember helping him lift his bike up one time when he had dropped it. He was well into his seventies by then, and he wanted to make sure I didn't tell my aunt that he'd dropped the bike.

"She'll have a conniption fit!" he said.

Fit or no fit, he would have kept riding. *All* those guys kept riding. They—the essence of what they did and the memories they left—started this ride. Every time I fire up my bike, I think of them. And that's the absolute truth. This lifestyle didn't begin by accident. It was centered around the most precious gift of all: Freedom.

It still is.

The story of the 1947 Gypsy Tour in Hollister has been told nearly as many times—and with as many variations, speculations, gyrations, explanations, and palpitations—as the chronicles of the Kennedy assassination. To get to the truth of it all, however, doesn't require the microscopic reverse-viewing of a fuzzy 1960s 8-mm film. It doesn't require trying to scrounge up medi-speak information from a nearly half-century-old autopsy. And it requires no tangential measurements from a grassy knoll or a high building window.

No.

We have the words, visions, and remembrances of those who were actually there.

But right from the initial drippings of the boozy avalanche this event triggered, many in the media have ignored the vicious gang of facts that might puncture their excitement dinghies, submerging the whole sensationalistic shebang.

And some *pre*-Hollister facts are important as well, the most important being that the returning WWII vets needed two things: brotherhood and thrills. The spit-shined and flat-ironed social cycling groups from before the war were like pissy light beer to those who had cultivated a bit more powerful of a taste.

So it's no surprise that the clubs that came *after* the war were not in the same serene-swishy ilk as bird-watching societies or canasta klatches. Hell, no.

Post-war motorcycle clubs had three main purposes: to ride motorcycles, to race motorcycles, and to do a lot of drinking—before, during, and after the rides and races. All in the company of the friends you loved and trusted the most.

It was simple, direct, and to the point.

Wino Willie Forkner founded the Boozefighters Motorcycle Club in 1946 at his favorite hangout, the All American Café *(bar!)* at 1143 East Firestone Blvd. in Los Angeles (near what is now the city of South Gate). He had "left" *(been kicked out of)* the 13 Rebels Motorcycle Club because he drank too much—even for *them.*

When the Fourth of July rolled around in 1947, the Boozefighters rode to Hollister—ostensibly for the Gypsy Tour and its accompanying races. But more and more, events like that were becoming just destinations to ride to for some fun. The formal activities were secondary.

The Boozefighters had a strong presence, mainly due to the never-low-profile personality of Wino Willie. The club had expanded to three chapters: Los Angeles, San Pedro, and San Francisco. Members from all three were in Hollister, along with members of other clubs, like the Market Street Commandos, the Top Hatters (formed in Hollister that same year and still thriving today), the 13 Rebels, and the P.O.B.O.B.s (the Pissed Off Bastards of Bloomington—generally recognized as the first evolutionary stage of the Hells Angels Motorcycle Club).

The Sharks were another club to come out of post-WWII.

At that time, the small town of Hollister had a population of about 4,500. It also had twenty-seven bars within its city limits. That body-to-liquid ratio probably contributed to the fact that "a good time was had by all."

Eyewitnesses all corroborate the stories that there *were* a fair amount of drunks, as well as the riding of a few bikes (like those of Boozefighters Jim Cameron and Gil Armas) through the open doors of bars like Johnny's. The main street was essentially used as a corral for some interesting "precision riding maneuvers." And it *was* a fact that Boozefighter "Red Dog" Dahlgren did get himself thrown in jail; however, his infamous "jailbreak" was nothing more than Wino and some of the boys going down there to see if they "could bail the poor bastard out."

Was there some "action and excitement"? Sure. But was there a dark descent into the bowels of a two-wheeled hell, the likes of which no civilized American had ever seen before? *Was* the Birth of the American Biker really centered around leather-jacketed thugs doing burnouts atop stacks of mangled corpses that used to be the gentle population of the quaint town of Hollister—the bikers' mouths still dripping with the ripped and shredded flesh from the mayor's daughter's thighs?

Not exactly.

The idea of "gangs" of bikers "taking over" towns for the sheer and randomly sadistic purpose of "terrorizing its citizenry" was the sickly slick media flash that came out of all this.

But there's no argument that this specter creates a truly haunting fear.

It's a fear of helplessness. And it's damned frightening. And like a lot of frightening stuff—exploitation sells.

First, there was the July 21, 1947, edition of *LIFE* magazine: A *San Francisco Chronicle* photographer named Barney Peterson staged what is arguably the most famous and most discussed photograph in motorcycle history. While the *Chronicle* ran a variation of the photo, it was *LIFE* magazine that drew the public's attention and induced labor for the Birth of the American Biker.

Page 31 of that historic *LIFE* issue (which also featured a piece on flying saucers) was a giant full-page shot of this goofy drunken character, whose name was never formally known (although other books and publications have speculated), sitting on a bobber surrounded by broken and scattered beer bottles.

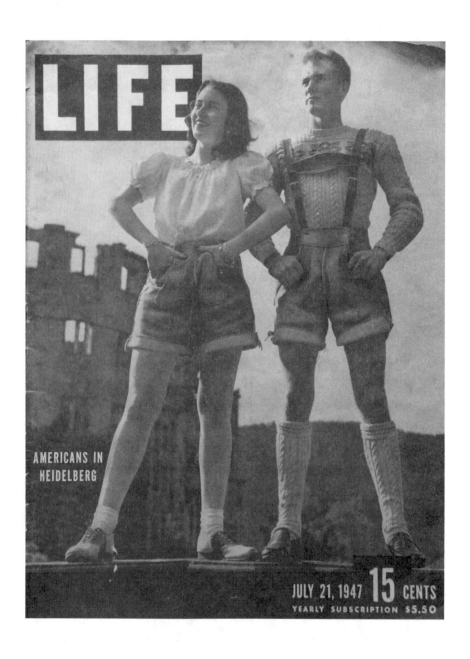

LIFE

AMERICANS IN
HEIDELBERG

JULY 21, 1947 **15** CENTS
YEARLY SUBSCRIPTION $5.50

CYCLIST'S HOLIDAY

He and friends terrorize a town

On the Fourth of July weekend 4,000 members of a motorcycle club roared into Hollister, Calif. for a three-day convention. They quickly tired of ordinary motorcycle thrills and turned to more exciting stunts. Racing their vehicles down the main street and through traffic lights, they rammed into restaurants and bars, breaking furniture and mirrors. Some rested awhile by the curb (*above*). Others hardly paused. Police arrested many for drunkenness and indecent exposure but could not restore order. Finally, after two days, the cyclists left with a brazen explanation. "We like to show off. It's just a lot of fun." But Hollister's police chief took a different view. Wailed he, "It's just one hell of a mess."

The caption read:

CYCLIST'S HOLIDAY
He and friends terrorize a town

On the Fourth of July weekend 4,000 members of a motorcycle club roared into Hollister, Calif. for a three-day convention. They quickly tired of ordinary motorcycle thrills and turned to more exciting stunts. Racing their vehicles down the main street and through traffic lights, they rammed into restaurants and bars, breaking furniture and mirrors. Some rested awhile by the curb (above [referring to the photo]*). Others hardly paused. Police arrested many for drunkenness and indecent exposure but could not restore order. Finally, after two days, the cyclists left with a brazen explanation. "We like to show off. It's just a lot of fun." But Hollister's police chief took a different view. Wailed he, "It's just one hell of a mess."*

—*LIFE* magazine, July 21, 1947

Of course, the photo was staged and the report exaggerated. But that didn't matter. *This* is what set the fear in motion. *This* is what broke the water and began the birth.

And then the American Biker took on a "life" of its own.

On the hype-heels of the 1947 *LIFE* piece, a short story was published in a 1951 issue of *Harper's* magazine by a writer named Frank Rooney. The story was entitled "Cyclist's Raid," and the theme of bikers *taking over a town* was formalized as a genre, which was to become as common as Western gunfighters staring each other down at high noon.

A short time later, *The Wild One* put The Fear on the big screen, and bikers were branded for good.

The fear was heavy and the brand was deep. Completely counter to the lightheartedness of the event itself.

The media had succeeded.

Exploitation.

Not only did Peterson *set up* the photo by gathering busted-up beer bottles and getting some random dupe to sit on the bike, but *LIFE* compounded it with their wacked-out commentary.

Just the first line of the photo caption shows how some things never change. Like that media hunger for big numbers. In 1947, *LIFE* was attributing an unnamed club as having *four thousand* members. No club at that time had anywhere *near* four thousand members. The Boozefighters had about sixty: roughly twenty in each of their three chapters.

Jump ahead fifty-eight years to the 2005 Hollister Rally, after which the local newspaper, the *Hollister Free Lance*, reported a story about the *possibility* of "a confrontation between rival motorcycle clubs, the Mongols and the Hells Angels":

Police "Dodge an Atomic Bomb" at Rally

...a tense situation Saturday evening had cops out in full force when a group of between 20 to 30 Mongols showed up and walked through the downtown event arena—several hours after nearly 300 Hells Angels rode through town, followed by about the same number of Hells Angels supporters, according to Hollister Police Chief Jeff Miller.

—Erin Musgrave;
Hollister Free Lance, July 5, 2005

The "atomic bomb" reference is one thing, but the idea that a specific group—*any* group—of *six hundred* motorcycles could ride together through the Hollister Rally at any one time is as wacky as imagining Gamera, the giant Japanese sci-fi flying turtle,

53

landing belly-up on Runway 30 of the San Jose International Airport at noon singing a Tohoku-ben version of "Jimmy Crack Corn." And just how *were* the three hundred "supporters" recognized? Funny hats like Rotarians? Or maybe they had their faces painted with their "team's" colors like Raider fans in the "Black Hole"?

You've got to hand it to the media for consistency, though: six decades and they haven't missed a beat.

In 1998, writer Mark Gardiner gathered eyewitness accounts from people who were actually in Hollister in 1947. Some interviews appeared soon after in *Classic Bike* magazine; these interviews in their entirety can be found in *The Original Wild Ones: Tales of the Boozefighters Motorcycle Club.*

The words of Gus Deserpa (the only human clearly seen in the *LIFE* photo, other than the drunk on the bike) tend to take the journalistic zip out of words like "terrorize" and "raid":

Gus Deserpa revealed the truth about *LIFE*'s photo in *American Biker,* the film.

I was a projectionist by trade. I worked at the Granada Theater, which was on the corner of Seventh and San Benito. I would have got off work around eleven p.m. My wife came to pick me up and we decided to walk up Main Street to see what was going on.

I saw two guys scraping all these bottles together that had been lying in the street. They positioned a motorcycle in the middle of the pile.

After a while this drunk guy comes staggering out of the bar, and they got him to sit on the motorcycle and started to take his picture.

I thought, "That isn't right," and I got around against the wall where I'd be in the picture, thinking that they wouldn't take it if someone else was in there. But they did anyway. A few days later the papers came out and I was right there in the background.

They really weren't doing anything bad, just riding up and down, whooping and hollering, not really doing any harm at all.

This alternate photo supports Gus's testimony that Peterson's photo was staged.

The Boozefighters MC and The Wild One's *role in the Birth of the American Biker are commemorated on a mural outside the famous Johnny's Bar, above.*

Below, Karen Kramer (Director Stanley Kramer's widow) sits atop the Wino Willie tribute bike while interviewing BFMC members for Sony Picture's DVD re-release of The Wild One.

In one of the crowd-heavy corners of Johnny's Bar during the 2005 Hollister Rally, a middle-aged biker was bellyaching to anyone who would listen about how, here he was, "sharing a few cold ones" with a couple of the last remaining "wild ones" from '47, and how "so many of the new riders—*these kids*—don't have a clue as to who these guys are and how all of this really started!"

One of the old-timers just smiled.

"Don't worry, brother," he said. "It's the same way with the freedom we fought for in World War II. Lots of folks just take shit for granted."

He smiled again and took another slow drink of his beer. His hands were steady—something you wouldn't expect from a man his age. But something you *would* expect from a man like *him*.

"*We* know who took care of business in that war…and *we* know who started all this motorcycle stuff. Just look around…look at all these people…look at all these *chicks!* Listen to the sound of all those bikes." He raised his glass. "Look, man, everyone's having a hell of a good time, just like we all did in '47. And by God, we're all still *free*!

"That's all the glory *I* need."

Chapter 4

Clubs

The 3-Piece Patch, The Big Four and More, Jesus Gets His Colors

Survival Tip #28

When dealing with an injured member of a motorcycle gang, do not cut their "colors", the leather or jean jacket emblazoned with the gang logo. For instance, if a member has a broken arm, maintain traction if possible and slip the arm from the jacket. Motorcycle gang members would rather endure the pain of moving a fractured arm than have their [colors] cut. Although this practice is not medically accepted and no protocol or medical text will endorse this action, your survival may depend on it.

—From *When Violence Erupts: A Survival Guide for Emergency Responders*

Anything that is "by invitation only" is special.

Anything that is only consummated after long periods of developing—and *proving*—trust, love, and respect is often considered thicker than blood.

The pre-war "riding clubs" were about, well, *riding* together.

The *motorcycle clubs* that came after were—and *are*—about so much more. They're about *living life together.*

Pretty much everyone knows that the "one-percenter" label really started gathering steam in '47 after Hollister. The AMA talked about something like "Ninety-nine percent of all motorcyclists being fine, upstanding folks, while it's only one percent that cause all the trouble."

Fuck 'em. A lot of clubs and guys that just wanted to race and have fun, without being held down by a bunch of rules, turned the AMA's negative comments into a positive; they actually dug the label. One percent of anything is rare and special!

I've seen some members of some clubs wear the AMA logo patch upside down on their cuts as a symbol of protest against the organization's rejection of them. Other clubs simply say: "One percent means the best of the best."

Club member "JQ" "toasts" the AMA by wearing their patch upside down.

Any way you look at it, these clubs are definitely *rare and special. They live up to the rep.*

—"Tom," on the street;
Interviewed at *Horse* magazine's "Smoke Out" 2008,
Cottonwood, AZ

The major motorcycle clubs in America—some of which have extended around the world—are not casual coalitions that you can simply "join" by filling out a form and sending in a year's worth of dues. A member doesn't *join;* a member *evolves* into a brother. If all goes well, he earns his patch.

The word *"earns"* is significant.

So is the 3-piece patch.

"Outlaws," "one-percenters," clubs with numbers, clubs with clout, clubs with high profiles, clubs with long histories, or clubs with any combination of these heavy attributes are *usually* wearers of the 3-piece patch. (Two notable exceptions within the big boys are the Sons of Silence and the Vagos; both wear variations on the theme.)

Defined in general, the 3-piece patch consists of a top "rocker" that names the club, a center patch of the club logo, and a bottom rocker indicating the club or club chapter's home territory. Somewhere in or around the array is the designation "MC": Motorcycle Club.

The 3-piece patch is a holy trinity. More than a simple identifier, it is a coveted brand. It's the proud window into a soul of commitment—of *brotherhood.*

And the path to that patch—like everything else that counts in this lifestyle—has a long legacy.

The intense closeness the WWII vets shared led to another aspect of the clubs that remains solid within the traditional base: the process by which someone enters the brotherhood.

The "hang around" period is the beginning. A newcomer who already has at least *some* degree of friendship and trust with *some*one in the club is allowed to share in *some* of the peripheral activities so that the club members (or "patch holders") can get to know him.

If a feeling of dedication and brotherhood indeed develops, the newcomer may be invited to become a "prospect"—a prospective member of the club. A prospect is usually allowed to wear at least a portion of the club's colors—for example, just the lower "rocker" and/or the "MC" patch.

At this stage, the prospect's degree of dedication and bottom-line desire to be part of the club is truly exposed—and tested.

> *I remember the first time I was ever invited to a party at an actual clubhouse of a major club. The first thing you see, after the fence is opened, is that sign that says "Members and Invited Guests Only." I had a couple of friends there, but I was scared shitless anyway.*
>
> *But it was cool...I didn't do anything stupid, and everyone treated me cool and we all had a good time.*
>
> *The main thing I kept thinking, though, was that this was so damn real! This wasn't one of those stupid movies, or a story in one of the biker magazines. I mean, I've read those magazines and I'll be honest: I think a lot of the time maybe the stuff in there is kind of fantasy shit. No one really rides like that, drinks like that, has chicks like that. But, damn—here it all was!*
>
> *But you could tell the guys who had been doing this for a long time. They looked tough, yeah—but not mean. They were just so sure of themselves, so comfortable in there. You could tell that the younger members and prospects were just trying to keep up.*
>
> *I kept wondering, how many of them will really make it?*
>
> —"East Coast Ghost";
> Interviewed at Daytona, 2009

The prospecting period—the time it takes to prove oneself—varies. Requirements vary, too. It depends upon the club. It depends upon the individual.

What never varies is that by the time a full patch is earned, both the club and the member know damn good and well where each one stands.

Earning the Patch

by John Janovetz

I read the book about the Boozefighters prior to "hanging around" with the local chapter in my area. Later I became a prospect.

Many of the stories in the book tell of the Boozefighters' adventurous spirit; traveling the countryside, living with a come-what-may attitude. I ride with the same spirit.

In June of 2008, I was a prospect at Chapter 64's annual Pig Party in Bowie, Texas—a three-day affair of camping, games, food, and creekside fun.

The Pig Party's turnout was as good as the weather. Although I didn't get to involve myself in too much of the fun, my sponsor, "Scrappy," made sure I did meet some influential Boozefighters.

One of the Boozefighters I'll never forget was "Flamer." Flamer is our Missouri rep, and the charter holder and president of his chapter.

All during the Pig Party, Flamer and Scrappy sent me on different tasks: find my bike, find my trailer, find a green pen, find such and such Boozefighter...

But there was one task—I found out—that would set my head reeling.

It sounded simple at first. Flamer said, "Get me a beer."

Now earlier, Scrappy had told me that I couldn't "patch out" until I got Flamer's signature—which is virtually impossible.

But then Flamer said, "You bring me this beer—to my home—and I'll sign it."

I asked him, "Where do you live?"

"In Kansas City, Missouri."

"Really? Okay!"

Actually, I wasn't worried. It sounded like a good chance for me to go on a long haul—see what's out there and challenge myself on the open road.

A month went by, and in July I received some vacation time from work. I was really champing at the bit to ride. I told Scrappy that I wanted to go get my beer signed by Flamer. Scrappy made the necessary phone calls and all was set.

Early Friday morning I made my way north, stopping only for fuel and fluids. It was about a six-hundred-mile trip one way. The last hundred miles were a little rough, as I came into Kansas City at rush hour on my slammed 2002 Softail Standard.

I found Flamer's home with no problem as I made my way round the Interstate. As soon as I saw his house, my kickstand was down and I was lying under a shade tree with that feeling you can only earn by doing a high-speed long haul. I was reeling in the pain and satisfaction of going the distance. I figured that many others probably would have stopped and thrown in the towel.

Flamer has an unmistakable laugh. I can pick it out of a crowd anytime. When he arrived home on his Dyna Wide Glide, he laughed and gave me a big hug.

"You doing all right?" he asked.

"Yeah," I answered, with a little questioning of my sanity.

"You got that beer?" Flamer asked.

I nodded, smiling.

He told me to put it in the freezer.

Flamer invited me into his house. He and his wife, "Blush," introduced me to their family. Blush asked if I needed anything to drink as she was preparing dinner.

In the living room, Flamer pored over picture albums full of Boozefighters parties and stories. He had plenty of hair-raising tales of late-night dashes for last call and beer-buying.

After a dinner of Blush's fried chicken, Flamer asked me if that beer was cold yet. It was. I gave it to him, and he cracked it open, tilted his head back, and finished it off in no time. Blush took our pictures holding the holy can that had traveled so far.

We talked into the night, and Flamer eventually gave me the beer can as I was getting ready to turn in. Signed in a green marker, it simply read, "Flamer."

It was before dawn the next morning when I started getting ready for the ride back home. But looking outside, the good weather I'd heard predicted the day before was wrong.

It was raining and cold.

I hadn't prepared for rain. Blush offered me an extra leather jacket. We all said our goodbyes and I headed south in the rain.

Luckily the wet weather didn't last that long.

At dawn, I was southbound on the Kansas Turnpike near the city of Bazaar. With just enough moonlight and approaching sunrise, I was able to see the surrounding hills—there were no cars, no lights, no buildings, or landmarks. The dark blue hills were barely visible—cresting like waves as I rode into Cassoday, Kansas.

I was all alone.

It was my moment, and that's why I love riding. And it made getting that signature all the more sweet.

—John Janovetz,
BFMC Chapter 63, Watauga, Texas

America has many motorcycle clubs. Some are limited to specific regions; others extend through multiple states or even into foreign countries.

Lots of variables go into why some clubs are more well-known than others; why some have grown, in both membership and influence, while others remain relatively small and quiet.

For the most part, these reasons are considered "club business." In other words, it's *no one's business but the club's* as far as just how much publicity, popularity, growth, and exposure they want to encourage. The right kind of high-profile *positive* publicity can make life easier for everyone. But notoriety can backfire badly and cinch the negative-perception noose just that much tighter, branding certain clubs with an especially hot iron.

Just as Las Vegas has "handicappers" who have set themselves up as experts in the art of rating and charting the best and biggest in sports; there are those who routinely examine the who's-who and "scoreboards," reflecting the day-to-day wins, losses, and movement within motorcycle clubs. They've even come up with their own unique leaderboards.

But these handicappers aren't sipping low-rent scotch and puffing on bundled cigars in a casino back room somewhere along the Strip.

No.

These handicappers wear badges. They sit in city, county, state, and federal offices. They head up organizations that always seem to have "OMG" somewhere in their group's acronym: Outlaw Motorcycle *Gang*.

With a rating criteria presumably based on membership population, national and worldwide influence, longevity, notoriety, fame, infamy, and just good old generally perceived ferocity—these keepers of the score have come up with a "Big Four," which have remained at the top of that board for a very long time.

But there's another important component to this rating scale; a component that extends out and sweeps like a heavy sea net, sucking in and pulling out everything in its wide path. According to the FBI and north-of-the-border's Criminal Intelligence Service Canada, the criteria that makes the Big Four the Big Four is that these clubs have a large enough national impact to be prosecuted under the federal Racketeer Influenced and Corrupt Organizations (RICO) statute.

As we'll see, this is a statistic with a hefty degree of weight.

In alphabetical order, the Big Four clubs are the Bandidos, the Hells Angels, the Outlaws, and the Pagans.

The Bandidos started in the South, riding out of Texas. The Angels began in the West, in Southern California. The Outlaws emerged from the Illinois heartland. Maryland and the East was the first home of the Pagans. Every corner of this country has contributed its seed to the club lifestyle.

If you drew lines on a map connecting the birthplaces of the Big Four, you'd come up with a rough diamond shape; coincidently, the shape of choice for most of the small "1%er" patches worn by many clubs.

That diamond-shaped patch on the cut of a Bandido is gold, trimmed in red: not-so-coincidently the same proud colors shared by the United States Marine Corps. Bandidos founder, the late Donald Eugene Chambers, served in Vietnam as a Marine.

Chambers established the club in 1966, and according to the United States Department of Justice, since then, they have become "one of the two largest OMGs operating in the U.S." (the HAMC being the other) and "in thirteen other countries."

As to *exactly* where the Bandidos first called home, news sites have credited the cities of Houston, San Antonio, and Galveston all with having been the spawn-point of Chambers' "Bandido Nation." These hit-and-miss "facts" exemplify once again the media inaccuracies that surround the origins and inner workings of the major clubs (and plenty of other clubs, too, for that matter). There have been no shortage of journalists-in-heat who have stepped on their own sensitive appendages in an effort to make a name for themselves, cash-in quick, or even install themselves—for a variety of reasons, I suppose—into a world they don't belong and/or know anything about.

And the Bandidos have certainly had their share of media coverage—both positive and negative.

The upside is found in one of the most compelling biker-lifestyle interviews ever recorded, when longtime Bandido and Shreveport Chapter "P" (President) Jim Owens opened up to our cameras for the *Bikers: The Inner Circle* DVD series. Like a wise old guidance counselor and spiritual advisor, Jim rationally and patiently discussed how feuds, territorial wars, and infighting between the clubs undermine this way of life. He explained how the real enemy of this lifestyle is comprised of sources on the *outside*—namely the bureaucracy that seeks to legislate the biker world out of existence. He discussed the laws that close so many doors on our freedom:

In the Bikers: The Inner Circle *DVD, Bandido "P" Jim Owens discusses the "real" enemy for all bikers.*

It's all "motorcyclism"; we're all out here to help each other...Most of us club people realize that with the federal government and the law, we're going to be just like the Indians. They're gonna just take us out if we don't start working together...Even the yuppies, they need to understand...We all need to be educated...We're not too old to learn...We all need to get registered to vote...If we'll stick together, we can defeat these laws; we can stay in existence. It's not a territorial thing anymore; hell, we're all together!

In other words, maybe the clubs should start acting a bit less like the Hatfields and McCoys, and more like the unified early patriots who overturned more than just crates of tea as they fought toward a collective goal—and *against* a collective enemy!

But, as is media-common for all major clubs, every step forward in the positive pub department seems to be met with one of those tell-all roadblocks.

The most curious spike-strip thrown in the Bandidos path was a book by former member Edward Winterhalder: *Out In Bad Standings: Inside the Bandidos Motorcycle Club, the Making of a Worldwide Dynasty*. It was billed in press releases as "an exposé of the Bandidos Motorcycle Club" and a book that "for the first time, tells the true story of the members of the outlaw motorcycle clubs that are employed and have families."

I was never exactly sure what the last part meant—even after reading the book. But one thing I *was* sure of was that for 432 very long pages, I received excruciatingly detailed personal information about Winterhalder. The names of the elementary schools he attended; the color of the Pontiac he bought in 1972; the chronicle of when his daughter first rode her bicycle without training wheels... *All* that— and so very much more—was there, distractingly interspersed among Winterhalder's recollections of life in the Bandidos.

Far more caustic and damaging was Alex Caine's *Befriend and Betray: Infiltrating the Hells Angels, Bandidos and Other Criminal Brotherhoods.*

Caine wasn't a cop; he was a mercenary—an infiltrator-for-hire.

Two things about this book are especially noteworthy. One is the historical chronicling of the early Bandido days of George Wegers, a man who would eventually become the club's world president. (And by the way, Caine's history reports the birth of the Bandidos as being in San Leon, Texas—another location to add to the list.)

Second was Caine's report of what went on in the hours before the Laughlin, Nevada, shootings in 2002; it tends to prove Jim Owens' point. Caine claims a "set-up" by law enforcement provoked the whole incident—and the subsequent feud between the Hells Angels and the Mongols: an all-too-plausible, sick scenario.

(Author's note: Far *less* caustic and damaging was Caine's 2009 *The Fat Mexican: The Bloody Rise of the Bandidos Motorcycle Club,* which focused mainly on the so-called "Massacre at Shedden" in Canada, at which Caine was not even present!)

In terms of pure notoriety and worldwide recognition, the "Big Red Machine" of the Hells Angels Motorcycle Club has been in the public's wide eye for over six decades.

The club's origin dates back to 1948 in the Fontana / San Bernardino area of Southern California, evolving in part from WWII vet Otto Friedli and his P.O.B.O.B. club: the Pissed Off Bastards of Bloomington.

One of the most interesting twists in the HAMC genesis is the coincidental use of the name "Hells Angels" by both Friedli's San Bernardino group and a different group some four hundred miles to the north, in Oakland. The Oakland group was started in the spring of 1957 by Ralph "Sonny" Barger—a man whose name has since become synonymous with so many parts of this lifestyle.

Sonny's account of what resulted all from this is one of the most compelling parts of his autobiography, *Hell's Angel*. When the two groups discovered one another in the late summer of '57, they decided to merge, structure, and organize, heading the biker world straight for the fast lane.

This was Phase Two in the evolution of the American Biker: when Barger's charisma and leadership accelerated already-set realizations about the clubs—from both the outside and the inside. The post-WWII MCs were kicked up several strong notches. A serious and long future lay ahead here.

Longtime San Jose Hells Angel Jim Elrite.

But the military roots of the HAMC are as important as Barger and Friedli, Oakland and 'Berdoo.

These roots have been highly detailed by a member of the club's Charleston, SC, chapter, in a treatise that could result only from the kind of research usually seen in master's theses or doctoral dissertations. Tracing the name, the club's red and white colors, and highlighting the contributions of WWII heroes like Irl Baldwin and Arvid Olsen, the work relates a strong history that focuses on men and events born from pure American heritage. It's well worth going to the source for a read.

It's *always* worth educating yourself in all the facets, history, and protocol of this lifestyle.

We were walking through the vendor booths. Two or three different chapters of the Red & White had booths out there selling support shirts and stuff. We were stopped at one of them when this other couple comes up. I mean, they looked like bikers and all—the guy had on a standard-issue black Harley t-shirt and the chick wore a fringed leather vest—but the woman started asking the prospect and the patch holder manning the booth some questions…some really stupid *questions.*

Sure, the only stupid question is supposed to be the one that's not asked—but there are degrees *of stupid, for Christ's sake! Here was the most prominent motorcycle club in the universe, and this broad is looking at the t-shirts and patches and stuff, asking things like: "What's the Big Red Machine?" "What's the Red & White?" "What's '81' mean?" "Is this a club or what?" "Are you from around here?"*

Damn! Everyone's got to start somewhere, but if you start out with your head that far up your ass already, you aren't giving yourself much of a chance to get educated. And you'da thought her ol' man would have apologized to the guys in the booth, grabbed her by the arm, and quietly led her away for a bit of a lesson in the most fundamental part of this entire lifestyle: Respect.

But then again, hell, maybe he *didn't know, either… that shit's just sad, man!*

—An unnamed biker;
Interviewed at Palm Springs Bike Weekend, early 2000s

The Outlaws Motorcycle Club is easily one of the oldest existing clubs in the nation—one-percenter or otherwise. The club dates back to 1935 when The McCook Outlaws Motorcycle Club was formed at Matilda's Bar in McCook, Illinois (about eleven miles west of Chicago).

Like so much of the American Biker's heritage, the village of McCook has a fitting heartland warmth to it. There's its proximity to the "Main Street, U.S.A." Route 66. There's its police statistics showing a lack of hard crime. And there's its heartland history: In 1942 the government built one of the world's largest single-building factories there to manufacture aluminum airplane skins for the WWII effort.

The original patch of the Outlaws featured a small skull; after 1954, crossed pistons were added (again demonstrating the influence of the movie *The Wild One*; Brando's patch in the film is very similar).

Anchored in the Outlaws MC are two of the finest photojournalistic chronicles of the club and biker lifestyle ever produced.

Brando's patch in The Wild One *inspired the Outlaws to add crossed pistons to their own patch.*

In 1968, Danny Lyon's *The Bikeriders* was first published. In text and in photos, Lyon—a member of the Chicago Outlaws—captured not just the wildness of the club, but the even wilder melding of the second and third phases of this lifestyle as it rolled into the Vietnam years. His words and pictures go a long way in gutting the idea that bikers *aren't* really (as alleged by our hobby-hobbled reviewer at the start of this book) *"the last of the cowboys, the last of the outlaws...the last true independent spirits."*

They were then and they still are today.

"If anything has guided this work beyond the facts of the worlds presented," Lyon says in his Introduction, "it is what I have come to believe is the spirit of the bikeriders: the spirit of the hand that twists open the throttle on the crackling engines of big bikes and rides them on racetracks or through traffic or, on occasion, into oblivion."

Truth remains truth; the real truth transcends years and even generations.

The Outlaws' 1960s era is preserved by a treasure vault of photos taken by Jim "Flash 1%er" Miteff.

Current Outlaws carry on the club's long legacy and distinctive patch.

In 2008, another treasure vault to the Outlaws—and to this entire culture—was opened when Beverly Roberts published *Portraits of Americas Bikers,* the first in a series containing long-stored photos taken in the 1960s by her father, Jim "Flash 1%er" Miteff.

Like Lyon, Miteff had been a member of the Outlaws MC. And, again like Lyon, he was a true artist with a camera. Wielding the huge, then state-of-the-art, Graflex Speed Graphic Press camera, Miteff is able to tell us—*show* us—just what this lifestyle was like forty-plus years ago. And, for the most part, what it is still like today.

And hopefully, what it always will be like.

The Pagans Motorcycle Club was formed in 1959 in Prince George's County, Maryland (adjacent to the nation's capital in Washington, D.C.), by Lou Dobkins, a biochemist at the National Institute of Health. The Pagans have been the most low-profile (in relation to the media) of the Big Four clubs.

Until recently.

On February 12, 2009, the History Channel aired a segment of its *Gangland* series entitled "Devil's Fire." Viewers were given the Pagans history as seen through the eyes of former club "P"—and bitter ex-member—Jimmy "Jimmy D." DeGregorio. You can guess how that went.

But shortly before that episode's broadcast, the book *Riding on the Edge: A Motorcycle Outlaw's Tale* by John Hall was released.

Hall's recollections had a different tone.

John Hall is a former "P" of the Pagan's Long Island chapter. His book not only lays out the club's history with love and respect, but—like the works of Lyon and Miteff—it constructs a bridge into the golden biker years of the late '60s.

"Today every department store in the country sells black Harley-Davidson t-shirts that proclaim: 'The Legend Lives On,'" writes Hall.

"But it wasn't Harley-Davidson that made 'the Legend'; it was the people who rode them…"

Along the line of respectful recollections is a poem that has circulated called a "Pissed Off Pagan's Wife," by "Mama Jackie." If you can find it, read it. It is easily one of the most intense and respectful testimonies about patch holders ever written by a woman inside the lifestyle.

Even *kids* who have grown up surrounded by club life have their own thoughts and remembrances:

> *When I was just a kid in school, I remember that I used to wear an old Army shirt a lot that had the sleeves cut off. I'd seen pictures and heard so many of my dad's stories about the Boozefighters…I went into my room with a magic marker and drew the Boozefighters emblem and rocker patches on the back of that old shirt. I was just a kid and I really didn't understand about not being able to wear colors if you weren't a real member of the club; I just wanted to be like Dad and make him proud of me.*
>
> *Anyway, I got into all kinds of trouble because of that. First of all, the teacher didn't want the word "booze" in school. But then this kid named James McCool said that the club name was "stupid," so naturally I beat him up. I was just a kid but I got suspended for three days for that!*

—Lee Nolan,
Son of Lee "Bear" Nolan

Falling in line behind the Big Four motorcycle clubs are countless others. The Department of Justice (who seems to be the law enforcement agency most concerned with the numbers) claims that "there are more than three hundred active OMGs in the United States…ranging in size from single chapters with five or six members to hundreds of chapters with thousands of members worldwide."

"Lompico Lyle" is the President of Northern California's Ghost Mountain Riders MC; his observations are shared by many patch holders:

THE CLUBZ

by Lompico Lyle

We serve no real purpose they say…a scourge on polite society say others. Some try not to look at us as we go by. Others stare in envy…or fear…or loathing!

The police and feds run our license plates and take pictures. Mothers and fathers caution their daughters to stay away from us and hope their sons don't turn out like us. We've been reviled in newspapers and TV for sixty years or more. We've been glorified and exaggerated in movies, and the government seeks ever-new techniques to eliminate us; yet still we exist.

Our houses have been broken into, our dogs shot, our wives and girlfriends roughed up and threatened, our weapons stolen and drugs planted, all to try to take away the lifestyle we love and live.

We are the butt of bad jokes and sleazy stereotypes, the ridicule of those who self-righteously put themselves above us, on pedestals of their own insecurities. And we are loved and hated alike by the very country many of us have fought for.

Who are we? We are the Motorcycle Clubs. We are the great American outlaws of the twentieth and twenty-first century. We are the bikers who have banded together with those who share our love of the road, the lifestyle, the danger, and the brotherhood.

And more than that, we are the de-facto reason why the Harley-Davidson phenomenon has come to be; why all the newbies and RUBs [Rich Urban Bikers] *own trophy Harleys in this brave new age. We are the reason Mr. Mid-life Crisis now throws his leg over his chromed-out, tricked-out Softail on the weekends and—scowling his best hard-core smirk—putts off to his local latte joint to terrify the denizens thereof.*

Who is he trying to be like? Well, it's us: the Clubs. Even if he's got it wrong, he's trying to emulate what club members have by natural selection. He's now Joe Cool. As he saunters to the counter to order his double latte frappuccino mocha, he is reveling—albeit vicariously—in the biker image that he believes is real. He's living—if only in his own mind—in our boots, trying to convince himself and everyone around him that he's a badass, hard-core biker, if not a club member.

But make no mistake: who he's trying to be like is *a motorcycle club member.*

Why? Well it began, of course, with the Hollister "riot" and the media's description of that event. It continued on with The Wild One, *and was reinforced with all those B movies of the '60s and '70s, with a little bit of charisma thrown in by the movie* Easy Rider. *We are the ones all "bikers" are trying to be like—if only for the weekend.*

Can they really be like us? Well, sure—in some ways...

They can ride the bike, and look the look. They can even join a factory-sponsored group now, and put a "patch" on their back. In short, they can come close, but without enduring the rules of the club brotherhood and without respecting those who are and have been club members. They will never be as we are, nor will they ever really understand, share the rigors, or have the love of a club.

And what about Harley-Davidson's role in all this?

In the '50s, '60s and '70s—even into the early '80s—Harley did all it could to distance itself from the rowdy, less-than-desirable image that the club members had. They even tried a Honda-style "nicest-people" ad campaign for a while. That was before Willie G. took over and recognized that what would sell *could only be the rough-and-tumble image Harley had tried for so long to refute. Realizing this, he encouraged the look, the image, and the lifestyle. He smoothed it over, modifying it to make it "acceptable" to mainstream Americans, who finally embraced it and became—at least for a little while—the American Biker.*

And now Harley, who tried so hard to pretend we didn't exist, sells t-shirts and paraphernalia with skulls and words of questionable taste, all directly related to the motorcycle clubs' original use of these symbols. Now every Tom, Dick, and Harry can pretend he's the same as us, even if he doesn't know what DILLIGAF means.

Is all this a bad thing for the clubs? Well, it can be.

When some dipshit, trying his best to portray his version of a badass biker, does something stupid, and maybe has a design or insignia of some kind on his back, then ALL CLUB MEMBERS may suffer from this unschooled individual's actions. Say what you will about the clubs, but they are quick to act when a member gets out of line. Club members usually go through the necessary hazing or prospect period for a reason. That reason is to keep the goofballs out; goofballs who could do something that might bring heat to the club.

By extension, if one guy—or maybe a group of guys— tries to start up a club, thinking it would be cool to be a club, etc., and they slap a patch on their back, then the oldest or most dominant club in the given area just might be "interested" in who these guys (or gals) are, and may want to have a word or two with them. It's not uncommon for these new clubs to "disband," after "talking" with the dominant club.

There are rules and protocol in the club world, and those thinking about becoming a club without understanding this proper protocol might want to think again. There have been enough dirt-bag clubs creating shit for the rest of us—we don't need any more!

So what am I saying here?

Just this: All bikers are not club members; but all club members are bikers. And all bikers or wannabes owe the clubs credit for the image they try so hard to portray.

It was the Clubs that began this current phenomenon of the Great American Outlaw. It was the Clubs that made The Image. It was the Clubs that stood and fought (and are fighting) for our rights as citizens and bikers. And it's the Clubs that have taken all the heat from the Law and the "Moral Majority" (which is neither) who have created this sort of "renegade" image of the biker—this rugged, independent, Marlboro-smoking "cowboy on a steel horse" that men aspire to. Even if just for a little while.

Am I down on the RUBs or weekend warriors who want to be like us? No. Because some of these people actually take the time and have the heart and the interest to become a club member. Some will endure the prospect period and be savvy enough to learn the rules, and will have respect enough for those who have gone before him (or her) to become a motorcycle club member in good standing. Some will find the brotherhood *and camaraderie of the club world and will embrace it—as it embraces him—with all its strengths and passions and trials and experiences. All its life.*

Because that's *what the club world is: it's not just a hobby—it's our* life!

So, support your local club! They are responsible for a whole lot of things the biker world is made up of today!

—Lompico Lyle,
"Prez," Ghost Mountain Riders MC;
Chairman, Monterey Bay Confederation of Clubs

Regardless of what law enforcement estimates the number of motorcycle clubs to be (again, "outlaw" or otherwise), the cutting truth is that these brotherhoods have had a monster impact on the image of the American Biker. They have touched every corner of the country and have influenced every motorcycle rider in one form or another; from things like big-run event t-shirts designed to resemble a 3-piece patch (ironically, even at runs where club members are outright prohibited, many of the "official" run shirts are styled like this), to factory-produced bikes that evoke the custom fabrications pioneered by the clubs, to everything else in between.

These clubs were not born during a decade of extreme specialization, of course. The '40s was still essentially a "general practitioner" cut in time, when most slices of the social pie weren't baked with a specific tongue in mind. "General contractors" built *everything.* You could go downtown to the "general store." Doctors in "general practice" still made house calls, treating maladies from whooping cough to heart attacks (there hadn't yet been a rush for physicians to go disease-specific and become things like nephrologists and addictionologists).

But the original clubs and the early informal groups *did* seem a bit specialized. In a way. The military veteran element and other social factors (which can be argued and debated forever) led to the most *visible* bikers back then being a de facto bunch of blue-collar white guys. With few exceptions, that little social fact didn't change much—especially in the world of actual MCs—until after 1955, when "Heavy" Evans and his Rattlers pulled up in 'Frisco and L.A. and Tobie Gene Levingston began his East Bay Dragons—a club still proudly seen on the streets of Oakland and the Bay area.

It wasn't so much that *integration* had suddenly swept through the MCs; it was more of a statement that this lifestyle—and the love of it—has nothing to do with race.

It transcends virtually everything else as well.

As the years rolled on, modernization led to a lot more serious and focused specialization within the purposes and goals of many motorcycle clubs.

The bike, the lifestyle, and the brotherhood began to bend in different directions. For some, these potent ingredients became more of a medicine than an intoxicant.

This *is* a lifestyle of risk; and risk ultimately ends up in one of two ways: you survive—enjoying every spark of lightning that you've bottled along the way—or you don't. It's a lifestyle founded on—and still based on—hard riding, hard drinking, hard living, and hard commitments.

But hard riding, hard drinking, hard living, and hard commitments take their toll. Alcohol and drugs have their effects. People fall off, or get knocked off, their bikes. They die or get crippled. Teeth, noses, ribs, knees, and knuckles suffer similar fates, both inside and outside of drinking establishments (*biker bars* are legitimately mythical yet very "real").

After a few decades or so of these realities dealing out their heat, certain portions of the brotherhood branched out into a kind of "second chance wing."

Jesus and sobriety began to wear colors.

While the motorcycle and the lifestyle became, regrettably, the way into a personal wasteland for some; it also became the way out.

Christian MCs and "clean and sober" MCs began to organize in huge numbers. Nets were thrown (particularly in the '80s and '90s) to reel in suffering souls, lives, minds, and decaying livers. In the ways of "daily living," these brotherhoods were—and are—very different from the traditional MCs. But the underlying love and "I've got your back" respect between members is the same. The machine in the middle is also the same.

"You're ridin' that big loud motorcycle, got them tattoos,
and you call yourself a Christian?"
If you only knew how many times I've heard that one!
Problem is, folks have forgotten who Jesus hung out with!
He didn't hang out with the religious people;
he hung out with drunks, prostitutes, outcasts, and outlaws.
The ones who needed Him….and still do!
Thank God Jesus died on the cross for an old outlaw like me
…and you!
"Motorcycles and Jesus—a way of life!"

—Pastor Dave "Easy" Tootell,
Bikers for Christ, Coos County

In the end, maybe the ride of the Christian clubs and the clean and sobers *is* a bit straighter; but that's *their* choice. Some of us really still enjoy those dangerous curves.

Along with the therapeutic religious and sobriety groups, motorcycle clubs have now been formed for just about every niche, target, interest, or quirk you can think of.

Dixie's Olde Thirteen MC, for example, focuses their energy on the preservation of the confederate flag.

There are clubs just for women.

Just for sober women.

Just for Black women.

There are clubs aimed at a color wheel of specific ethnicities.

There are clubs for firefighters.

There are clubs exclusively for veterans of the Vietnam War, the Gulf War, and Iraq.

Each branch of the military has its own club.

There are clubs for people of "alternative sexual persuasions."

And for people of alternative sexual persuasions with a leather fetish.

Amongst all this, there is a particular type of motorcycle club that drops a particularly heavy irony into the club mix: Cop clubs.

The scenario itself is something a political cartoonist might come up with: a panel of, say, the Road Runner and the Coyote, or maybe Itchy and Scratchy, having an uneasy beer together. Or maybe we could just pour oil and water in a glass and stare at it for awhile.

In 1947, Hollister Police Chief Fred Earl called the event in his town "one hell of a mess."

The Boozefighters said (and *still* say) that they were just having a good time.

What we have here is, yes, a slippery failure to communicate. Maybe more. Much more. The Road Runner is fast, but the Coyote has the anvil and the catapults. Itchy has the dynamite; Scratchy has the big axe. Each adversary has power and numbers at their disposal. But only *one* has the ability to close those heavy cell doors—from the *outside*.

Law Enforcement Officers (LEO) have spent many years with a litigious-based, tight-fisted interest in pursuing motorcycle clubs. But now, they, too, have *their own* motorcycle clubs.

The combination of the those two conflicting pursuits adds an interesting chaser to the brew.

Every club helps define this lifestyle.

The Clubs:
A Short Encyclopedia

In addition to the Big Four, *every* club—large or small, well-known or more obscure—helps to define this lifestyle. From the familiar, frequently seen patches, to the clubs with names like the Catahoula Cur Dogs, the Brick City Spinners, the Chrome Divas, and 667: Neighbors of the Beast MC. *All* of their adventures and histories serve to further fine-tune the definition of the American Biker.

Below is a sampling; a short "directory" (again, in alphabetical order) of some of the *other* clubs (those not considered by law enforcement to be the "top four"). These are clubs with members throughout America and beyond; clubs with long legacies; clubs I have personally interacted with from time to time; clubs that are just plain interesting. This is a list presented with the "love and respect" that permeates the club world.

But it is by no means complete. That would be an impossible task, considering many clubs' regional visibility, attrition of the old, addition of the new, and many other factors.

All clubs, listed or otherwise, have a legitimate stake in the legacy and make-up of the American Biker.

Aliens MC—This MC dates back to 1964, founded in New York by Johnny Pinstripe. Mentioned prominently in John Hall's 2008 book, *Riding on the Edge: A Motorcycle Outlaw's Tale.*

Bikers for Christ—Founded in 1990 by Pastor "Fred Z" in California, this Christian club ("ministry," actually) has a "mission" statement that exemplifies the focus of the Christian MCs: *Some wish to live within the sound of church or chapel bells; we want to run a rescue shop within a yard of Hell!!!*

Blue Knights MC—"The oldest and largest law enforcement motorcycle club in the world," according to their official history. Founded in Bangor, Maine, in the spring of 1974 by seven municipal police officers, the Blue Knights—as of July 2005, according to their own figures—have 553 chapters and almost 19,000 members in 28 countries. "Make no mistake," they say: "WE ARE THE GOOD GUYS."

Boozefighters MC—One of the most publicized clubs of all, in magazines, books, and television reports. Formed in 1946 in Los Angeles, the Boozefighters' intimate connection with the 1947 Hollister and 1948 Riverside "incidents" and the movie *The Wild One*, as well as the world-famous persona of their founder, Wino Willie Forkner, have made this six-decades-old club synonymous with the Birth of the American Biker.

Brothers of the Third Wheel—Another unique one! This all-trike club, founded in 1983 by Jim Sickler, has chapters in America as well as Europe.

Brother Speed MC—Founded in May of 1969 by three guys who'd been friends since the third grade, Brother Speed MC, according to the Department of Justice, is one of six clubs in Oregon identified as an "outlaw biker gang." The club made headlines in September of 2009 when *twenty-six* members crashed, as their pack was involved in a traffic pile-up.

Buffalo Soldiers MC—This Black MC honors the famous "Buffalo Soldiers": the name given to members of the 9th and 10th Cavalry and the 24th and 25th Infantry Regiments (comprised solely of African-Americans) formed by the U.S. military shortly after the Civil War.

Choir Boys MC—Another major law enforcement MC, named for the landmark book written by former Los Angeles PD sergeant Joseph Wambaugh. Founded in 1991, the club has members in California,

Arizona, Texas, Nevada, and South Dakota. The Choir Boys' credo demonstrates the "friction" that sometimes exists between LEO clubs and non-LEO clubs:

> *Our members do not associate with outlaw motorcycle clubs/gangs (including clubs/gangs that find it necessary to display the 1%er badge to convince others that they're "bad" and other clubs/gangs that visualize themselves as 1%er supporters). We do not participate in 1%er events and they are not invited to ours.*

Chosen Few MC—This club name poses an interesting "patchwork" for biker historians. On either U.S. coast are Chosen Few clubs with American Biker histories that are long and strong.

The Chosen Few MC of the Los Angeles, California, area dates back to the late '50s. Their one-piece patch—a cross of bones on a red oval—has become a familiar sight in Southern California for the past several decades; and their motto is compelling: *Our history is not written but lived.* (True enough, but they *do* have a compelling written

The Chosen Few MC has a compelling lived—and written—history.

history as well, as presented in Chapter 10). The history they have lived includes the rough transitioning from an all-Black MC to the "First Fully Integrated Outlaw MC."

The Chosen Few MC established on the "streets of eastside Buffalo, New York," in 1966 wears a center patch that features a classic "beatnik" (indicative of the era and area in which they were formed). This club has had more than its share of "interesting" interactions with other clubs in the northeast, but through it all has maintained an adage promoting unity: *IF WE ALL RODE TOGETHER, HOW STRONG WE COULD BE!!!*

The club name also exemplifies that jump of American motorcycle clubs beyond U.S. borders: The Chosen Few MC of France (with chapters in several neighboring European countries) claims an established date of 1988 and has for its center patch a grim reaper backed by a U.S. Confederate flag. The Chosen Few MC of Sandviken, Sweden (with a center patch that appears to be some kind of "thunderbird") claims an established date of 1972 and makes it clear that their club has "no connections to other Chosen Few MC clubs." The Chosen Few MC of Ireland has a winged skull for its center patch.

(Yet another denim piece of the Chosen Few name patchwork was seen recently on eBay.

Up for auction: one vintage Levi's vest [cut-off jacket] with the colors of the Chosen Few, a 1960s Cincinnati, Ohio, motorcycle club. A recent estate find, the original owner was a member of the club in 1968 and 1969. The vest is in good condition for its age, shows appropriate wear. The added leather piping is very brittle, has some losses, and easily breaks.

The cut went for three hundred and ninety bucks!)

Christian Motorcyclists Association—One of the oldest, largest, well-known, and visible Christian clubs; founded by Herb Shreve in 1975.

Dead Rabbits MC—A Florida-based club with one of the most interesting name histories of all: "Dead Rabbits" referring to one of the famous "gangs of New York" prominent in the 1850s.

Defiant Ones MC—Featured in Guerrilla Docs' documentary *Glory Road: The Legacy of the African American Motorcyclist,* this long-running club began in L.A. in 1958.

Devil Dolls MC—Easily one of the most unique and interesting MCs on the planet. Formed in the Bay Area (which just drips with serious MC history) in 1999, this is an all-female club, with a patch right out of a fiery Betty Page dream.

Devils Diciples MC—Established in 1967, their Los Angeles–area clubhouse remains a monument to the unchained era from which they were spawned. The word "diciples" was intentionally misspelled by the club's "originals" so there would be no confusing them for a religious group.

A patch right out of a Betty Page dream...

    An Irish MC uses the more conventional spelling—Devils *Disciples*—and claims 1979 as their formation date.

East Bay Dragons MC—A truly legendary club with a truly legendary leader, Tobie Gene Levingston. Formed in Oakland, California, in the 1950s, this Black club remains alive, well, and active. The entire history of the club can be found in Tobie Gene's book, *Soul on Bikes: The East Bay Dragons MC and the Black Biker Set.*

Galloping Gooses MC—Another classic club from the post-WWII years, having "started around 1949 or 1950" in Los Angeles with thirteen members, including founder Dick Hershberg. The MC was named for Hershberg's bike, the "Galloping Goose." Painted on the bike's gas tank was the distinctive "running finger" now seen in the club's patch.

The entire GGMC patch (which also features an outhouse) was designed by famous L.A. artist John Altoon—a nearly cult figure in the art world of the day. Descriptions of Altoon say that "this boisterous, hard-drinking, skirt-chasing man [was] plagued by bouts of depression alternating with episodes of mania that often turned destructive and ugly."

Well, okay. But the man had talent.

In 2005, the Galloping Gooses were the subject of a law enforcement "chat room" discussion about "OMGs." How could one not be impressed with this (uncorrected or edited in any way) post from an LEO named "BlueBoy"?:

> *Being in the Midwest we have a local OMG the Galloping Gooses. They have been around for many years but are slowing starting a come back after taking some of the streets with some good busts and great a court system.*

Apparently the "come back" went well: the Galloping Gooses MC (and Altoon-designed patch) are still going strong today.

Ghost Mountain Riders MC—Interviews with several members of the GMRMC were featured in *American Biker,* the film; their thoughts and comments represent those of a true, traditional MC. According to members, the club "was started in 1982, on a ridge high in the Santa Cruz Mountains. Three guys were sittin' around one drunken, smoky evening, talkin' about the ancient Indian burial grounds and the legends of the ghosts haunting the mountains. From that inspiration was born the legend of the riders from Ghost Mountain."

Gypsy MC—A club with a seriously long history. The Gypsy MC began "in a small mountain town in eastern Tennessee named Marysville" in 1932. Their first president was the venerable Lee Simerly. The Gypsy MC experienced some of the first "societal anti-biker sentiments" when they were called the "sour pickles of society." The club embraced the name and their patch has always featured the now-famous pickle on their unique gold cuts.

Gypsy Jokers MC—In 1966 Hunter Thompson referred to the Gypsy Jokers as the "number-two outlaw club in California" (second, of course, to the Hells Angels). April Fool's Day, 1956, is the date most often attributed to the San Francisco–originated club. Their current center of activity is the Pacific Northwest.

A Gypsy Jokers MC Australia also exists, bearing an "established date" of 1969, with chapters throughout "Down Under."

Hellbent MC—This club out of Sacramento, California, has in its legacy one of the most renowned figures in the biker world: James "Mother" Miles. Featured prominently in Hunter Thompson's *Hell's Angels,* the story of Mother Miles' evolution as one of the most important members of the Hells Angels MC is an epic in itself. At age thirty, he died on his bike, in a head-on wreck with a truck. His funeral procession provided one of the starkest photos ever published in *LIFE* magazine (January 28, 1966).

Henchmen MC—"The Black & Blue Crew." An MC out of Northern California that prides itself especially on its promotion of charitable events. They have a motto: *Saepe Expertus, Semper Fidelis, Fratres Aeterni* ("Often Tested, Always Faithful, Brothers Forever").

Hessians MC—Quintessentially old-school, the Hessians shot hard out of the Vietnam War era. The Hessians were founded in Southern California on March 7, 1968, by Tom Maniscalco.

Guerrilla Docs' *Hessians MC* documentary traces the club's history through the words of the members who lived it. Especially notable in the film—and real life—is the Hessians' charismatic president, Spike.

Huns MC—Another club linked with the "wild bunch" era of the '60s and '70s. The president of the Bridgeport, Connecticut, chapter was John "Rogue" Herlihy who went on become one of the most famous photojournalists in the biker world—seen and read by millions in the pages of *Easyriders*. Interestingly, Rogue's website posts a passionate letter by former Huns Captain and Treasurer "Rooster," talking about the brotherhood of the "old days" and the demise of the Huns MC in 1981, particularly the Huns' mother chapter. But Huns MC chapters currently exist in Arizona and New Mexico, crediting the founding of their club to Jessie "Scooter J" Sinka in California in the '50s.

Iron Horsemen MC—The strong early history of this club is evidenced in Wikipedia's candid reference to Iron Horsemen MC, among weighty company:

> *The Pagans, by 1965…clad in blue denim jackets and riding Triumphs, had begun to evolve along the lines of the California stereotype generated by such famous motorcycle clubs as the Boozefighters, the Warlocks…Iron Horsemen, Outlaws, etc.*

In May of 2009, members of the Maine chapter were convicted on a variety of drug-related charges in a widely publicized trial.

The Iron Horsemen MC also offers another "interesting connection" story between an American club and what has occurred abroad: The Iron Horsemen MC of Australia boasts an "established date" of 1969, having formed in Melbourne, and its patch differs greatly from its American namesake.

Iron Pigs MC—Never Let the Bastards Wear You Down is the motto of this high-profile nationwide law enforcement MC. Iron Pigs MC is a disgruntled spin-off of the Wild Pigs MC (proving that inner-club dissension can affect any and all groups; even those whose members are sworn to uphold law and order).

Jackpine Gypsies MC—Formed in 1936, this is a club to be revered for all they have done and represent. The club was founded by "Pappy" Hoel, who was instrumental in founding the Sturgis Black Hills Rally in 1938. It doesn't get any more real or genuine than this.

Jus Brothers MC—Founded in 1990 in Tracy, California, the club is now centered in the nearby Stockton area. "We have been asked about the word 'JUS' and what it means," they explain. "It's simply slang for the word 'JUST,' and since Brotherhood is the foundation of our organization, when all is said and done, we are all JUS' BROTHERS...Nothing more, and Nothing less!"

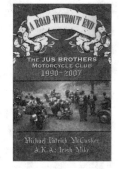

In 2008, the club's founder and first "P," Michael Patrick "Irish Mike" McCusker, published *A Road Without End: The Jus Brothers Motorcycle Club 1990–2007.*

Leather & Lace MC—Their motto of *Never ride faster than your guardian angels can fly* isn't a bad little axiom to live by. This nationwide women's MC was founded by Jennifer Chaffin in 1983; their main focus is promoting charities that benefit kids.

Lonely Ones MC—This enduring New York–based MC, established in 1967, is the subject of the song "The Lonely Ones Blues," written and recorded by premier American Biker musician Charlie Brechtel. The Lonely Ones have also been featured in *Bikers: The Inner Circle*.

Loners MC—A seriously traditional club right out of the formative California mold of MCs. Founded in February of 1973 in La Mirada, CA. (Personal author's note: this was the first MC I was ever asked to possibly prospect for, and I will always have a warm place for them in my heart.)

Midnite Riders MC—A Southern California–based, "family oriented" MC: the model for clubs that really use their time and energy for charity events and making their communities—and the image of the American Biker—better.

Glen "Professor" Pine and "Skippy," longtime members of SoCal's Midnite Riders MC.

Mid-West MC—Indiana's (and one of America's) oldest MCs, established in 1923 in the basement of John Morgan's Harley-Davidson Motorcycle Shop at 701 S. Meridian Street in Indianapolis, Indiana. The club's founder, Ralph Moore, was an active member until his death in 1977.

Molochs MC—Established in 1968, the Molochs—with their distinctive "Gold Dragon" center patch—have long been "breathing fire" along California's Central Coast.

Mongols MC—Another of the strongest and most dominant MCs; located primarily throughout western America and into Mexico. The Mongols' notoriety was "heard round the world" with the shooting that occurred between members of their club and the Hells Angels MC at the Laughlin, Nevada, River Run in April of 2002.

A lot more notoriety hit the fan in 2005 when author and undercover cop William Queen released his book *Under and Alone,* the chronicle of his covert infiltration of the club.

A different kind of notoriety hit the stands in 2008 when the club's then-international president, Ruben "Doc" Cavasos, published his controversial *Honor Few, Fear None: The Life & Times of a Mongol.* But it was a quick "fifteen minutes of (literary) fame" for Cavasos, who would soon be out of office.

On October 21, 2008, federal and local agencies executed a slew of interstate warrants, resulting in the arrests of sixty-one club members. Not only was Cavasos jailed in the operation, but former members and associates came forward with allegations of his corruption in office. Cavasos pled guilty to racketeering conspiracy, and is no longer the International President.

But the *real* impact of this particular law enforcement "mission" was the resulting ban on the Mongols colors (discussed further in Chapter 6).

And the Mongols turmoil wasn't over yet. In July of 2009—in a tense situation reminiscent of segregationist governor Lester Maddox holding his axe handle at the Georgia schoolroom door—Mayor R. Rex Parris of Palmdale, California, blocked the Mongols (even with its members patchless from the federal ban) from holding a large meeting at a motel in his town. Not only did he tell the club: "We do not want you. We will not tolerate your presence"; he built a chain-link fence around the hotel, effectively putting its owner out of business.

So much for the First Amendment.

Motor Maids—The first motorcycling organization for Women in North America. Pretty damned impressive! "In the late '30s, a young woman motorcycle enthusiast named Linda Dugeau of Providence, Rhode Island, conceived the idea that there might be a number of women who owned their own motorcycles and might be interested in becoming acquainted with one another. Linda wrote to dealers, riders, and anyone she thought might know of women motorcycle riders. After this extensive search, she compiled a list from which the Motor Maid organization was founded with fifty-one charter members in 1940." Harley-heroine Dot Robinson of Detroit was appointed the first club president.

Mount Baker MC—One of the ten oldest clubs in America; established in 1925. Formed by Harley-Davidson dealer E.L. "Pop" Place, the club is proud that "in 1931 The Mount Baker Motorcycle Club started the now famous 'Cow Bell Enduro' patterned after the famous 'Jack Pine Run' in Lansing, Michigan. The Cow Bell is held the first Sunday after Armistice Day, and has been held every year since."

Nuggets MC—Formed in 1962 at the Nugget bar in Buena Park, California, this club's original patch was a beer-drinking rabbit on a motorcycle! That made perfect sense, because what Nuggets reportedly liked to do was "fuck like a rabbit, drink beer, and ride motorcycles." Nothing wrong with all that!

Two things the club has been most proud of were their famous (but unfortunately short-lived) Death Valley runs between 1975 and 1978 and their notorious "beer truck." According to club history: "Many other club runs weren't scheduled until it was confirmed that the Nugget beer truck was available. The party didn't start until the beer truck arrived and didn't end until the beer truck left."

The Nuggets have chapters in California, Iowa, and Oregon, and they "still maintain the same values and traditions [they] had when the club was started."

Oshkosh Aces MC—Another real oldie! The Oshkosh Aces MC was formed in America's heartland in 1928. Its homespun history includes a "rebirth" in early 2000, launched by three friends who found an antique club shirt at a yard sale. The reborn club now includes some members of the original club!

Rare Breed MC—Established in 1989, the Rare Breed is a high-profile African-American MC in Southern California. Their motto is an inspiration that crosses all ethnic lines: *There is a greatness in all of us. Our goal is to leave this world in better condition than when we arrived. It is important to us that we always lend a hand to those in need. Wish us luck in our travels.*

Red Emeralds MC—"Boston's Oldest Continuous Running Motorcycle Club," established in 1964.

Rough Riders MC—A veteran-focused worldwide MC with an interesting twist: they accept non-vets possessing of the right attitude and support of vets; but with that portion not to exceed twenty percent of the club's membership.

Their wonderfully heartfelt motto: *For those who came home… for those who did not come home…for those who have yet to come home…*

San Francisco MC—The SFMC held its first meeting in November of 1904 at A. Freed's Thor Motorcycle shop on the 1400 block of Market Street near Fulton. Twelve charter members were in attendance, including: C.C. "Daddy" Hopkins, J.L. Tormey, George Payton, Joe Hollie, Harry Rockwell, and A. Freed. During the club's long history, members have included P.H. McCarthy, San Francisco's mayor during the early 1900s, and Dudley Perkins, famous hill-climber and owner of what has proven to be one of the oldest surviving Harley-Davidson dealerships in the country (est. 1914).

The SFMC was famous for their TT Racers and drill team, who were there in Hollister 1947. One of their most successful TT Racers in the '30s was AMA Hall of Famer Hap Jones, who served as president of the SFMC on two different occasions.

Satans Slaves MC—When the infamous "Lynch Report" was released in 1965, outlining all the Hells Angels' alleged "dirty deeds," *this* club got the following mention:

> On September 19, 1964, a large group of Hell's [sic] Angels and "Satan's [sic] Slaves" converged on a bar in South Gate (Los Angeles County), parking their motorcycles and cars in the street in such a fashion as to block one-half of the roadway. They told officers that three members of the club had been recently asked to stay out of the bar and that they had come to tear it down. Upon their approach the bar owner locked the doors and turned off the lights and no entrance was made, but the group did demolish a cement block fence. On arrival of the police, members of the club were lying on the sidewalk and in the street. They were asked to leave the city, which they did reluctantly. As they left, several were heard to say that they would be back and tear down the bar.

We don't know if they ever went back and tore down the bar, but we do know that the Satans Slaves' presence in America waned.

But the name did become strong throughout Europe and New Zealand (the New Zealand club lists their date of establishment as "about 1969–1970").

Although the two continents' groups reference and link to each other on websites—and both clubs spell "Satans" with no apostrophe (as in the proper name of the Hells Angels)—the two groups have different patches. New Zealand's features a bird; Europe has a skull.

Satyrs MC—Founded in July of 1954, this club is distinct and unique: It is the first motorcycle club in the U.S. founded by and for gay men.

Sisters of Scota WMC (Women's Motorcycle Club)—I'll tell ya', every time I'm at an event and members of this club show up, they definitely are noticed! The Sisters of Scota WMC was founded by Dayna Davidson, a.k.a. "Grumbles."

Soldiers for Jesus MC—One of the more predominant international Christian MCs, with chapters from the U.S. to Canada to South Africa. According to them, "We are a bunch of characters, who, by the grace and mercy of God have been delivered from some very colorful lifestyles."

Sons of Silence MC—Another heavyweight: Number Five behind the Big Four, as "rated" by a federal report entitled "The National Gang Threat Assessment for 2005."

At the same time that declaration was made, an article appeared in the *Durango Herald,* headlined: "No complaints heard about 'outlaw' group," in which club members were praised for their security work at the 2005 Labor Day run:

> *Organizers of this year's Four Corners Rally in the Rockies hired members of a so-called outlaw motorcycle club to work as security guards, a rally planner said.*
>
> *Ten of 55 security guards staffing the Labor Day weekend's biker event belonged to the Sons of Silence motorcycle club, said Berry Mullennix. Despite the group's past scrapes with the law, La Plata County Sheriff Duke Schirard said local police and Sons of Silence members "had pretty nice cooperation."*

The club was featured on the April 2, 2009, episode of the History Channel's *Gangland* series entitled "Silent Slaughter."

Top Hatters MC—A truly historical group, formed at the "Birthplace of the American Biker"—Hollister, California—during *that year:* 1947.

The Top Hatters MC still has surviving original members who continue to be active in the club; most notably the Bravo brothers, Jess and Joe. (Editor's note: Sadly, just as this book went to press, Jess Bravo passed away. The loss of him—and the history he carries—is felt throughout the entire culture.)

The Bravo brothers have provided a direct link to the Top Hatters' 1947 origin.

Tribe of Judah MM (Motorcycle Ministry)—A Christian club begun on May 11, 1980, in Houston, Texas, by Ben Priest. The club has chapters across America and in Australia, Canada, Denmark, England, Germany, Ireland, Norway, and Sweden.

Vagos MC—Another truly major club. One of the more compelling stories impacting the entire motorcycle community was the saga of the Vagos winning a nearly two-million-dollar lawsuit against the Hawthorne, California, police department in 1990 for various harassment-related indiscretions. (The Hawthorne area of Los Angeles County has always been volatile; throughout the '80s it was central to infamous California Democrat Dick Floyd's nearly religious [and unfortunately, ultimately successful] crusade to force the helmet law upon the riders of California.

The Vagos began in San Bernardino, California, in the '60s and the club continues to grow nationwide.

The Vagos MC continues to grow nationwide.

Viet Nam Vets MC (and Legacy Vets MC)—Begun in the early '80s, the VNVMC has members throughout the U.S., Canada, and Europe. Having personally attended many VNVMC events, the pure pride and patriotism for this country I've witnessed is overwhelming. Obviously the number (and lifespan) of Vietnam vets is finite, so the Legacy Vets MC was formed, made up of active duty military and of vets who have served after 1975, to "carry on the visions, principles, and traditions" of the VNVMC "well into the future."

Warlocks MC—Another important Vietnam-era club, formed as "a hope and a dream" by thirteen young sailors stationed aboard the aircraft carrier USS Shangri-la. Of the thirteen, one, "Grub," apparently had the heart— and "stick-to-it-iveness"—of a true biker, and turned the idea into a worldwide organization. Grub founded the original chapter on the outskirts of Orlando, Florida, where the mother chapter remains to this day.

The club was featured on the November 7, 2008, episode of the History Channel's *Gangland* series, entitled "Paid in Blood."

The Warlocks was formed as "a hope and a dream" in the Vietnam era.

Further documentaries about the club have been planned by biker musician and film producer Charlie Brechtel.

Wheels of Soul MC—The subject of Guerrilla Docs' *Wheels of Soul* documentary, their motto expresses a common sentiment throughout the MC world: *When we do good, no one remembers— When we do bad, no one forgets.*

Wild Pigs MC—The interesting footnote about this law enforcement club (est. 1987) is that it has spawned several spin-off clubs, including the Iron Pigs MC, the Po'g Mahon MC, and the Iron Warriors MC.

Wind & Fire MC—There are a million puns I could make about "hot bikes" and the like—but I won't! This is a club comprised of firefighters. Established in April of 1991, Wind & Fire claims a membership of "over 3,900…in 153 chapters" with "members living in 49 states and 22 countries."

X Winos MC—One of the oldest (if not *the* oldest) clean and sober MCs. Based in the Minnesota and Kansas areas, the club was established in 1977 after one of the original members-to-be was struck by lightning "after a long night of boozing."

Yonkers MC—Definitely a landmark club, in that it's recognized as *the* oldest "still-rolling" MC in America; begun in 1903 by George Eller— first as a bicycle club, later evolving into a motorcycle club.

Zodiacs MC—An African-American club established in 1973 in Kansas City, Missouri. The Zodiacs were instrumental in the foundation of the giant annual National Bikers Roundup.

From the Heartland:
A Rebirth of History and Respect

The Oshkosh Aces MC
Est. 1928

by James "Lippy" Lehndorf,
Secretary (retired), Oshkosh Aces MC

The Oshkosh Aces Motorcycle Club, Inc., began in 1928 as the Oshkosh Ace Motorcycle Club, in Oshkosh, Wisconsin. The club was formed at National Cycle, a local Harley-Davidson dealership on Ohio Street, by the proprietor, Joe Robl, along with Clarence Robl and Carl Reigh. The club held meetings in a clubhouse behind the dealership.

Over time, membership increased substantially. As with many clubs of the time, members were involved in events such as flat-track racing and hill-climbing. The club collectively received many competition trophies and safety awards over the years.

The club patches went through many transitions. Some of the early designs were simple white shirts with hand-stitching of the club name on the back, and riding pants with leather leg protection below the knees. Around the 1940s, the shirt colors changed to green with gold hand-stitching, depicting a winged ace of spades as the club insignia. There is at least one surviving example of this early-period shirt (owned by Elwyn Long, an original 1940s member and current member of the re-established Oshkosh Aces MC). It was donated to the museum at Doc's Harley-Davidson of Shawano County, Wisconsin, where it is still proudly displayed.

The original Oshkosh Ace Motorcycle Club endured until the late 1950s, when membership dwindled as individuals married, got jobs, and slowly drifted apart. For many years, the club remained dormant, surviving only as a memory in the former members' minds.

The original Oshkosh Aces made quite a fashion statement.

In early 2000, the club was resurrected by three friends who felt that the club's history needed to be carried on. The idea was born when one friend stumbled upon an early-period green club shirt in a rummage sale. "Muck," "Doc," and "Lippy," who would become the new club's President, Vice President, and Secretary, respectively, founded the modern incarnation of the Oshkosh Aces and set about building an organization once again centered around the love of motorcycles. The club is not a one-percent group; it simply focuses on the love of riding and having fun.

Since the "rebirth," the club has incorporated, and membership has increased steadily. The club holds monthly meetings and is active in several charity endeavors. The members participate in events like the Sturgis Motorcycle Rally and Daytona Bike Week, as well as weekly rides throughout the state of Wisconsin and the country.

Our membership includes active military; veterans from Vietnam and Korea; current and retired law enforcement; and businessmen, tradesmen, and professionals. The club is also proud to include some of its original members from the 1940s.

The Oshkosh Aces Motorcycle Club, Inc., is a strong supporter of our military. Each year in May, we host a benefit ride for the Intrepid Fallen Heroes Fund. All event proceeds go to the fund, which provides financial aid to the families of soldiers who have given their lives serving our country; the fund also includes the Fisher House Program, which houses families of wounded military while the soldiers are recuperating.

We ride for any positive reason.

The current Oshkosh Aces: "We ride for any positive reason."

Chapter 5

A Mixed Brew

Cops, Bikers with Badges, & A Few Words from Buddha

Law enforcement couldn't care less what you look like.
It's what you do.
If you want to be a criminal, then you're going to meet us.
If you don't do anything criminal, you'll never meet us.

—Lt. Terry Katz,
Maryland State Police

I never had any experiences with our court system
until I started riding a Harley-Davidson...
then all of a sudden it's like, "Holy shit!"

—John Gilbert,
Former Editor, *Tailgate* magazine

Believe nothing just because a so-called wise person said it.
Believe nothing just because a belief is generally held.
Believe nothing just because it is said in ancient books.
Believe nothing just because it is said to be of divine origin.
Believe nothing just because someone else believes it.
Believe only what you yourself test and judge to be true.

—Buddha

Sometimes it's personal.

It was a perfect Sunday morning. Most summer days in Southern California are everything they're supposed to be. And Pacific Coast Highway is everything *it's* supposed to be, as it lays a fast, straight edge along the shoreline side of "Surf City": the "OC" community of Huntington Beach.

I was southbound on my hot-rod FXR, passing the Goldenwest Street intersection. I had salt air, an early sun, and no reason to speed.

Right along this stretch is where Martin Milner and George Maharis met Hob the Surf God in their *Route 66* Corvette in that classic TV series' coolest episode. Right along this stretch is where the Golden Bear nightclub stood from 1964 to 1986; rocking the beach with acts like Neil Young, B.B. King, War, Van Halen, and Dizzy Gillespie. Right here is where many of the most famous surf shops created their best fiberglass art.

It was also right along here where the 1986 OP Pro Surfing Championships blew up into a full-tilt, police-car-burning riot. It was ugly. And it was pretty much the grinding linchpin that "inspired" the HBPD to cultivate what they apparently still see as a proud reputation.

There seems to be a kind of official and civically endorsed LEO attitude here that leads to things like the local merchants' annual Fourth of July t-shirts, which depict their friendly beat-cops in situations that don't always reflect the "Serving With Honor" axiom painted on the city's patrol cars.

The 1999 shirt was an especially biting classic. It featured Eric Cartman—the annoying and abrasive fat kid from *South Park*—dressed up in HBPD riot gear, with a truncheon in one hand and a stick of dynamite in the other. "Welcome to Huntington Beach...Respect my authority!" is on the back, with Cartman in the foreground of an actual shot of HBPD officers in their riot gear. (One officer is carrying a medieval mace; probably—but not necessarily—a photographic alteration.)

There are a lot of fairly solid reasons that it's stupid to ride through Huntington Beach.

Yep, there are a lot of fairly solid reasons why the prevailing wisdom among bikers is that "it's a stupid move to ride a Harley through Huntington Beach"— *or* its neighbors, Newport Beach and Laguna Beach. I believe all three cities have now adopted similar official mottos: "A decibel meter for every exhaust pipe."

On December 18, 2005, The *Los Angeles Times* published a 2,200-word article, headlined: "Making Bikers Pipe Down." It was the long, highly detailed saga of sixty-year-old Laguna Beach police officer Tom Wall; a cop to whom the California citable noise limit of ninety-five decibels is the ultimate matrix.

"My job is to sell the [excessive noise] citation and make a point. I try to use as much of what I call posture to get their attention and let them know I'm serious," Wall says in the article. "Once we've reached that understanding, that I'm in charge, that this is my traffic stop and that this is how we're going to do it..."

But it was an early and quiet Sunday morning full of SoCal sun, surf, sand, and a nearly deserted street a few miles north of Wall's little fiefdom. I had lowered my guard. I had been seduced by the scene. Hell, Buzz and Tod from *Route 66* had been here. Right here. This was paradise. Pacific Coast Highway is the coast-groove link that makes California *California,* for God's sake. What could go wrong?

A motor officer on his Japanese motorbike was passing me northbound. (The HBPD has ridden Japanese bikes for as long as I can remember—my guess is, they still do. But I don't know for sure because this Sunday morning would prove to be my last visit to their city.)

The officer looked at me.

Like I said, there weren't many other vehicles on the road at this time in the a.m.; it was a serene time that seemed to slide right out of the lyrics to Kris Kristofferson's "Sunday Morning Coming Down."

Except that I wasn't hungover or wearing "my cleanest dirty shirt." My head was as clear as a Weems & Plath brass bell; I was freshly showered; and I was quick to become annoyed when I saw the black-trimmed white Kawasaki make a U-turn to get in behind me.

I've had this feeling many times before.

I know what it means and I know what can happen.

Another tune crossed my mind: Warren Zevon's musical plea, *"Send lawyers, guns, and money…the shit has hit the fan."*

It could have been worse. The citation I wound up with was a laundry list that included a "non–DOT-approved helmet" and "no turn signals" on my sleek and nifty custom FXR. But it was essentially just a fix-it ticket, nothing more.

I had no thoughts of taking it to court. I was just going to replace the turn signals, pay the helmeted piper, cut my aggravation losses, and stay the hell out of Huntington Beach. But when I reached my ultimate destination of Cook's Corner (a genuinely friendly old-school biker roadhouse, trying to survive urban creep out in Modjeska Canyon) I ran into a few other people who had risked the Huntington Beach minefield this sunny Sunday morning; and it turns out they had ridden by the cop and me as we were "discussing" things. They introduced me to other folks who had stories to share; stories indicating that maybe the t-shirt with Cartman in the HBPD get-up, swinging the billy club and explosives, wasn't that far off the mark.

I have the power to have all the powers I want.

—Eric Cartman;
South Park

So I decided to do the noble thing. The little man was about to fight the oppressive system! Helmet laws have always been nebulous as far as the steaming heap of legal details go; so I figured that just maybe I could step up, Davy Crockett–style, and "right some wrongs"!

My day in court started out just as perfect in its own way as that Sunday morning had, so many weeks before. We all know that if the cop doesn't show up for a court date, your case is dismissed. My LEO friend didn't seem to be there. But neither was my name being called to come up and have my case scrapped.

Nearing four o'clock, it became apparent that my case would be the very last one. It was seriously damned apparent, because I was the only one left in the courtroom other than the judge, the bailiff, and the court reporter.

At ten minutes to four my man shows up.

He was in full uniform, had an armful of notebooks, and wore the thin smile of the "boss" in *Cool Hand Luke*. The timing of all of this was not coincidental. This little drama had been scripted long ago—and no doubt reenacted many times.

I had been set up like a rich drunk rube in a border town. It turned out that the cop was the *host* of a local TV cable access show—about motorcycle safety! As he began spreading out his charts, graphs, and diagrams on the table, I felt my "noble" goose broiling on the spit.

Throughout the proceedings, the officer's droning on about the "protective padding thickness in DOT-approved versus non–DOT-approved motorcycle helmets" sounded like the "waa-waa" noise of the adults speaking in the *Peanuts* cartoons. But all I kept hearing in *my* mind was that part in Arlo Guthrie's "Alice's Restaurant," where Officer Obie plays out his dramatic courtroom scene, attempting to get Arlo convicted after throwing him in jail for the heinous crime of littering. Obie brought out "twenty-seven eight-by-ten color glossy photographs with circles and arrows and a paragraph on the back" along with "pictures of the getaway, the northwest corner, the southwest corner" and "aerial photography."

This cop *was* Officer Obie. He and the judge were winking at each other more than owls in a sandstorm.

The whole game cost me some money, but the entertainment and education was worth it. Although, as mentioned, I haven't been back to Huntington Beach on a motorcycle (or in or on anything else, for that matter) since.

The entertainment and education was worth it...I think.

Two years later I spent some similar—but much more grim—quality time with Las Vegas Metro and their Gang Unit at the 2005 Laughlin River Run. This little meet-and-greet made my experience in Surf City look like the small potatoes that it actually (in a legal-ramification sense) was. These Metro boys (and girls) were dead serious. They were no Officer Obies; they were a lot more like *The Shield's* Vic Mackey.

The details of the Laughlin River Run (my 2005 experience, as well as a full account of the 2002 shootings) are recounted later in this book. But it truly *was* a case of "fool me twice." I was an idiot to go into post-2002 Laughlin with a patch on my back—for *any* reason.

It won't happen again.

And the fact that my *only* crime was flying those colors made that trip something I could never "look back on and laugh about." It had no entertainment value at all. It wasn't educational, either, because those lessons had already been learned. Many times over.

Law enforcement's paranoia and outright hysteria that blew out

of the barrel of the 2002 Laughlin shootings was seen as justified in some circles. Then again, so was the attempted "profiling" that came out of 9/11; of course, *that* caused the civil libertarians to scream like jackals in a spike-trap. For some reason, those *same* civil libertarians haven't expressed the *same* loud "compassion and concern" at the profiling that has been part of life on a motorcycle for decades.

The truth is that over the years there *have* been many of those "meetings" that Officer Katz downplays in his opening quote here.

The sins of certain fathers, as well as RICO becoming the law of the land, dug a hole big enough for all of us on two wheels to fall into.

The question of *why* there is such obvious profiling is often asked. Being a large, loud target comes to mind. And those two four-letter words that keep coming back to haunt and titillate: Fear and Envy.

Both could be answers.

There are other answers as well.

One may be the occasional "incident" that spills uncomfortable stickiness into a motorcycle event. It's like an airplane crash, though: the one-in-a-million gory slam into the mountain gets the headlines; the zillions of ho-hum, safe, here-to-there flights that don't scream down in flames seldom get much attention.

Most motorcycle events don't involve flames, guns, or bad medicine. *Most*. But then again, they are motorcycle events. They are not cardigan-sweatered conventions of people united to preserve the fine art of collecting cuckoo clocks or building intricate cedar birdhouses.

And while you can probably find examples of even the well-dressed meek getting out of hand—maybe even busting up each other's birdhouses—*that* simply doesn't carry the heavy press clout that even a drop of mayhem in leather and chrome does.

In 1948, many of the same clubs that had been in Hollister the previous year met in the inland California town of Riverside. Riverside actually hosted two bike events in the wake of Hollister: one on Labor Day '47, the other on Independence Day '48. It was the 1948 gathering that once again provided hot headlines: "Riverside Again Raided by Gang" and "Cyclists Take Over Town."

Although eyewitnesses and even a public letter from Riverside Undersheriff Roger Abbott cited more media hype and exaggeration, the image was indelibly tattooed.

A bit of calm followed Riverside, however. The 1950s were reasonably quiet.

What came after was not.

A powerhouse of red and white strength and image was being built in Oakland. A new California Attorney General would try to tear it down.

In 1963, the so-called "Porterville Raid" picked up the theme of bikers taking over towns. This time, instead of the Boozefighters being center stage, the media—and the law—now focused on the Hells Angels. Reports had about three hundred Angels and members of other "outlaw" motorcycle clubs "taking over" the town of Porterville—*again,* in California—fifty-three miles north of Bakersfield, at the mouth of the Sequoia forest.

A year later, the "Monterey Rape Case" shot up the media's hit parade. During that year's Labor Day get-together, four Angels were charged with (and several others accused of) raping two underage girls who allegedly wandered into Nick's Bar, where club members had gathered.

The national press coverage of the Monterey incident now added "gang rape" alongside "taking over towns" to the public's perception of common biker pastimes.

Law enforcement's attitudes were intensifying as well.

Although *all charges* against the Angels stemming from the Monterey incident were dropped within a month of the arrests, the case provided the potent catalyst that drove then–newly elected California Attorney General Thomas Lynch to launch his 1965 landmark investigation. The result was a dossier known as The Lynch Report.

The antagonism between cops and bikers just got formalized in white paper.

The aptly named "Lynch" Report was less than twenty pages long; a short but potent chronicle of alleged crimes and dirty little secrets of the Hells Angels. It was designed to lay bare all the lurid details that Lynch claimed were part of everyday life in the club.

Fear and envy…

Both *Time* magazine and *Newsweek* virtually plagiarized the report with articles extremely similar in subject matter. The style of writing was even alike.

And the media was *still* hungry.

Later that year—eighteen years after Hollister—it was "déjà vu all over again":

> *Come to the riot. See Weirs Beach burn*
>
> —Article headline;
> *LIFE* magazine, July 2, 1965

This was the 44th Annual New England Tour and Rally, held in the Laconia / Weirs Beach area of New Hampshire (or, according to the chronology of today's official Bike Week organizers, the 42nd running of the event known simply as "Laconia").

And yes, there was a "riot."

And yes, it was blamed on the Hells Angels.

> [Police Chief Harold Knowlton] *blamed the riot on a contingent of California's notorious Hell's [sic] Angels cycling club. "We knew they were around and that they had taken over a town out west, but they weren't going to do it here,"* *he said. His words were all but drowned out by the insolent roaring of engines as the last of the cyclists kicked their bikes to life and went zapping out of town.*
>
> —Michael Mok;
> *LIFE* magazine, July 2, 1965

That issue of *LIFE* was still very much alive and in store racks when the Hells Angels decided to make their 4th of July run to Bass Lake, California, just outside Yosemite and 3,110 miles from Weirs Beach. Whether the "California contingent" of troublemakers used the two weeks between the end of the Laconia event and the beginning of the Bass Lake run to leisurely head west, cutting a path of evil and destruction as they traveled, has never really been addressed.

But the Bass Lake run that year has.

Hunter Thompson devoted a huge portion of *Hell's Angels* to it, focusing on the interaction between Sonny Barger and the sheriff of Bass Lake. Their initial encounter at the start of the weekend had all the drama of two determined heads of state at a summit meeting; each with his finger on his version of The Button.

According to Thompson:

> *...the local sheriff, a giant of a man named Tiny Baxter, had decided to keep* [the Angels] *out of this area by means of a second roadblock about a half mile from the center of downtown. It was Baxter's decision and he backed it with his three-man force and a half dozen local forest rangers.*
>
> *By the time I got there the outlaws were stopped along both sides of the highway, and Barger was striding forth to meet Baxter...*

The media saw it differently:

> *Ultimately only about 150 riders, including girls and members of other outlaw clubs, got through, only to be met in Bass Lake by 100 heavily armed officers with dogs and all the latest electronic-tracking equipment...*

> —William Murray;
> *Saturday Evening Post*, November 20, 1965

In his book, Thompson himself became a monster focal point as he (and his car) landed dead center in the heart of the "beer procurement" element of the story; an element the entire weekend revolved around.

Murray, however, dismissed it (and Thompson—a man about to become an iconic American writer) fairly lightly:

> *...stores were reluctant to sell* [the Angels] *anything. (Their beer supply was finally secured through the efforts of a blockade-running free-lance writer collecting material for a book.)*

There was no riot at Bass Lake, but that didn't slow down the notoriety. Both major San Francisco newspapers of the day published pieces that essentially said, "nothing happened" (articles about planes not crashing were absent, however).

Interviewed at the Yuma Prison Run in 2008, a well-informed and well-connected old-timer had something to say about those particular days—and beyond:

> *It all hit so fast after the Monterey case, the Laconia mess, and then the weekend up at Bass Lake. Sure there was the* Easy Rider *movie and Altamont around '69 and all of that shit; but as far as cops and legal shit goes, the two years that really stand out to me are 1987 and 2002. In '87 you had Sonny Barger's conviction on a "bombing conspiracy." He wound up going to prison here in Arizona for nearly five years.*
>
> *In that same year you had all that weird shit going on with the feds trying to frame George Christie, the "P" of the Ventura Red & White. That was a crazy case, man. First he runs in that "torch relay" for the '84 Olympics in L.A., and then the charity that was supposed to get the money he raised didn't get it. He gets on TV and tries to get the thing straightened*

out, and—bang!—he apparently steps on the toes of Eunice Shriver, the sister of that pig Ted Kennedy, and the rest of the Kennedy bunch. She was the head of this Special Olympics thing that George raised the bucks for, but she wasn't sending the dough where George requested in the beginning for it to go. All of a sudden he gets swallowed up in a federal charge of "solicitation for murder" of some inmate…again, at a prison here in Arizona. Lots of strange shit goes on in this damn desert!

Anyway, it was one of those "fact is stranger than fiction" things…hell, you had this guy named Mike Mulhern who was a snitch and a supposed founder of the Mexican Mafia. How do you become the founder of the Mexican Mafia with a name like "Mulhern"? Sounds like he should be running an Irish pub or something! Anyway, he was allegedly the hit man, but his testimony and "believability" wasn't exactly what the prosecutor had hoped for, and Christie was acquitted.

People just can't seem to get enough of dive-bombing at the Angels, and there always seems to be a snitch around trying to be somebody.

Then there was the Laughlin River Run in 2002, of course—the biggest thing since Hollister in '47 as far as the repercussions that it caused. I was right there at Harrah's when the shooting started. There have been a million cop theories as to what and who started it, but I expect the real story is known only by the few who should know and no one else. I was up in my room there when I heard the "pop's." They were muffled-sounding from the room and all, but there's no mistaking that sound. There was pretty much a collective "Oh shit!" from a lot of us!

Then they started on loudspeakers or bullhorns or some shit telling us to stay in our rooms and all. We were stuck in those rooms for hours. They had cops stationed around the halls who would yell if you opened your door. Finally, some food *was sent around by someone—fruit and stuff, mostly. We were watching the TV news and we were getting cell calls from our friends outside. We couldn't get out, and they couldn't get back in. This went on for—what—a day or so? It sucked.*

We heard that there were two Angels killed and one Mongol, and that they found another Angel dead out in Ludlow. They had tons of surveillance video of the shootings. They made their arrests, but I don't think they ever came up with who shot the Angel out in Ludlow. Word has it that he was riding alone; when they found him, he'd been shot execution-style and was lying on the ground off the side of the road. His bike was still there with his driver's license on the seat, they said, but I really don't know for sure.

After Laughlin, the runs were cancelled like falling dominoes...the Ventura Beach Ride...Palm Springs...Four Corners...although they claimed the Four Corners cancellation had to do with the Indians and the fairgrounds up there or some shit, but Laughlin had to have been on their minds— it was on everyone else's. It still is. All these years later.

—"Sweet Lou," looking back

The major "power clubs" don't allow law enforcement officers to become members.

Period.

A potential member's prospect period often includes a background check to make sure he is who he says he is. It's a good idea to have told the truth.

Other clubs have various thoughts on the matter.

The clubs that *do* allow cops tend to use three main arguments to *attempt* to strengthen their case.

One is: "If you're not doing anything wrong, what's the problem with having cops around?"

A second is: "If you allow cops in, then at least you know who they are."

The counterpunches to these first two optimistic schools of thought are: (a) having *known* cops in the club doesn't stop an infiltrator *on a mission* from being there too, and (b) an infiltrator's idea of "not doing anything wrong" might be very different from the club's.

An infiltrator, by definition, is self-righteous and adrenaline-amped. He's like the hyper-energetic first-time manager of a hamburger joint: a brand new community college degree in one hand, a clipboard in the other, and a mind-set that sees "conquering the world" as a quickly attainable goal on his "to do" list.

With drive and zeal like that, an infiltrator can discover anything he or she wants to—in *any* social strata: politics, religion, motorcyclists, or Campfire Girls.

And they do.

If you go out to the front lawn and spend enough time digging, it's a safe bet you'll eventually find some slimy worms. Sure, you can bring in a shovel full and dump them on your kitchen table—or the middle of your bed if you want; but why not just leave them be, buried deep beneath the greenery, the fresh air, and the good times?

And it's always a matter of degree: just how ugly *is* what you just spent so much time and effort digging for? And were its "activities" down below really all *that* bad anyway?

> *Marijuana is the flame, heroin is the fuse, LSD is the bomb. So don't you try to equate liquor to marijuana, mister, not with me. You may be able to sell that jazz to another pothead, but not to somebody who holds some sick kid's head while he vomits and wretches on a curbstone at four o'clock in the morning. And when his legs get enough starch into them so*

*he can stand up and empty his pockets, you can bet he'll have
a stick or two of marijuana. And you can double your money
he'll turn up a sugar cube or a cap or two. So don't you con
me with your mind-expansion slop. I deal with kids every day.
I try to clean up the mess that people like you make out of 'em.
I'm the expert here, you're not!*

—Sgt. Joe Friday (Jack Webb),
talking to a Timothy Leary–like character;
Dragnet, 1968

Spies and infiltrators are nothing new. Governments and their espionage wings are good at it. It's been S.O.P. in some circles forever.

It was simply a natural progression for the cops to try and fight the "gangs" from the *inside*, too. Maybe Hunter Thompson gave them the idea, but informants like the infamous Anthony Tait took it to the extreme. His name is not one you want to mention in the presence of any members of the HAMC. Another snitch, Serge Quesnel, has been given a new identity and tattoo removal procedures. He may even be the guy bagging your groceries down at the market, nervously fingering the broccoli stalks while he wonders if he'll ever run into any of his old "brothers."

And it's a good bet there have been a number of less-mentioned infiltration attempts that encountered a few bumps along the way. A good many reports—and books—probably didn't *quite* get written.

The *third* argument for letting cops into a club is the hope that it might take some of the police heat off the organization; you know, the "professional courtesy" slant on things.

That may not exactly work.

Straight-laced cops are not *that* much more enamored of their biker "brothers" than they are of bikers *without* the badge.

> *Actually, before the Choir Boys* [Law Enforcement MC] *even started, my partner* [Scott Shonts, co-founder of the club] *and I bought Harley-Davidsons. We were quickly confronted by middle management within the department, who expressed to us that owning a Harley is conduct "unbecoming a police officer."*
>
> —Jay Ellsworth,
> Co-founder, Choir Boys MC;
> Interviewed in *American Biker,* the film

That has left cops who are also bikers (a true oxymoron to many) in an awkward position. To make things more "comfortable," clubs like the Blue Knights—"for law enforcement officers only"—began to form as early as 1974. The club has since expanded to 28 countries, at last count.

Another highly recognizable LEMC (Law Enforcement Motorcycle Club), the Wild Pigs MC, came out of San Jose, California, in 1987.

In 1991, the Choir Boys was formed and rapidly became one of the more high-profile LEMCs. According to their own figures, they have approximately 500 members in Southern California alone, with many chapters throughout other states.

And there are more. Some have a membership exclusive to law enforcement officers; others, like the Law Dogs MC, also allow firefighters and other emergency personnel.

Sure, there's an enigma here—amongst "bikers with badges" and those without. You have two super-divergent factions—with often-violent confrontations—who have two super-charged commonalities: the motorcycle and (at least variations on) the lifestyle that goes with it.

And while the shared essence of the American Biker carries a lot of weight, it's sometimes just not possible to look directly into the eyes a polar opposite and call him "brother."

What we think, we become.

—Buddha

Fair enough.

Maybe that's why some people think *only* about getting their bikes out in the wind—while others keep thinking about digging up those worms.

And a lot of those "worm diggers" actually wield their secret shovels quite efficiently, making things a bit rough for those they eventually impale on their hooks. What's really scary, though, is the ignorance that often guides them in their trolling.

Two things I always remember—that I always equate with cops—are both blasts from the past: The Firesign Theatre's Deputy Dan, and the movie *Reefer Madness*. I loved the Firesign Theatre for years—still do; I laugh my ass off at those old albums. I'm sorry, but the "Deputy Dan has no friends" bit is one of the funniest things ever recorded. And every time you think of Deputy Dan, you think of Jack Webb's Joe Friday. Except Webb was serious.

So was *Reefer Madness*.

The common ground here is that obvious disconnect with reality; the reality we bikers live in, while so many on the outside—cops, in particular—don't have a clue. It's like a parallel universe.

Deputy Dan, Sgt. Friday, and *Reefer Madness* were basically cartoons—caricatures. But not long ago I picked up a different kind of book on eBay. It was actually more of a workbook, used in a 1990s training class to educate law enforcement officers about "outlaw motorcycle gangs."

The credibility of the thing was shot, right off the bat, when Page 1 listed Hollister as happening in '46, not '47. A small error, yes, but an important one. Their entire version of Hollister was goofy and disjointed, like it was being told by *Reefer Madness's* twitching jazz piano player. And the rest of workbook got even worse.

Was I *somewhat* amused by this? Not really.

Out on the streets, "goofy" turns to serious apprehension when you see these young, young faces behind badges these days. These "officers" haven't lived enough life to begin to understand it yet—let alone understand *ours*. All they know is what they're being taught; taught with enlightenments like *this* from that workbook (note again, that this "wisdom" is presented just as it was written, unedited in any way):

> With upwards to 900 dangerous motorcycle gangs in existence, it's difficult to list all the various acts required for new members to perform during initiations. Each gang has its own requirements which run from the low key college type stunts to the most outrageous, disgusting and shocking acts one could think of. Rituals range from stopping a woman in public and demanding she take off her underpants and hand them to you, to laying on the ground face down while fellow bikers urinate, defecate, and vomit on your original colors. Some clubs may just pour grease and oil all over you, while others may require you to submit to the sexual pleasures of the club mascot which in most cases is a dog... The above mentioned rituals for the most part are still performed by the majority of motorcycle gangs today.

Wow.
And this is from the '90s!

I've worn a patch for quite some time now and—hard as this may be to believe—I've *never* been boned by a basset hound or sodomized by a shih tzu. But next time I get pulled over by some wet-behind-the-ears kid with a badge, I expect he'll be checking me for fleas or to see if I'm expecting a litter before he calls his Gang Unit.

Believe it or not, I've never been boned by a basset hound or sodomized by a shih tzu.

No wonder "Deputy Dan has no friends."

Chapter 6

The "G" Word

RICO & Out-and-Out Seizure

Roaring into town on their motorcycles,
they are both a menace and a myth.
They have been called everything from barbarians
to "the last American heroes."
They are against everything but each other.
And they glory in the title of Hell's [sic] Angels.

—William Murray;
The Saturday Evening Post, November 20, 1965

Murray composed his archival piece sitting in a Fontana, California, bar. Yet he wrote that he felt like he "had blundered into some sort of obscene children's party."

Menace.

Myth.

Barbarians.

Heroes.

Obscene children's party.

Words mean things. And usually they're framed with a certain vocal inflection or written context designed to sway the listener or reader toward a specific opinion.

And *usually* that's no big deal. We all do it. We all value our own opinions.

But sometimes it *is* a big deal. People who refer to motorcycle organizations almost always use either the term "club" or the term "gang," generally depending on whether the speaker or writer is approaching the subject from *inside* or from *outside* the lifestyle.

Law enforcement *always* refers to serious motorcycle clubs as OMGs (Outlaw Motorcycle Gangs).

Spike, the president of the Hessians MC, speaks for a good percentage of seasoned bikers—and virtually *all* club members—when he states unequivocally:

> *There are no motorcycle gangs;*
> *there are motorcycle clubs.*

He has a lot more "thoughts" on the subject, as well:

> *There is something alluring in our motorcycle culture for every bike-riding enthusiast; whether it's the freedom, the brotherhood, the excitement, or some other personal attraction to riding or the lifestyle.*
> *This is understandable.*
> *As a club-riding biker, what amazes me most is not the allure, but the negativity; the hostility and ignorance directed*

by others towards bikers. Bikers—especially "clubbers"—are singled-out, harassed, and misrepresented by government, by the media, and especially by law enforcement. We have become a persecuted minority group—misunderstood, unfairly judged, and discriminated against across the board.

Government and law enforcement waste huge amounts of time, energy, and the public's money trying to justify and execute a war on bikers. Their discrimination needs to be replaced by education—and the education passed along to the media—to paint a true, honest picture.

Then one day, I might be able to ride my beloved Harley without the constant traffic stops and harassment by law enforcement; enter any facility in biker attire; be accepted as an equal; and referred to as a "club member," instead of the misleading "gang member" with all its negative connotations.

Open your eyes and see the real bikers!
HFFH.

—"Spike,"
President, Hessians MC, MCOC

And sometimes words have *legal* ramifications.

The term "gang" is integral to the 1970 RICO Act (Racketeer Influenced and Corrupt Organizations Act, Title 18, United States Code, Sections 1961–1968): a law initially designed to eliminate the mafia, but that has been expanded and used time and time again to pursue and indict members of motorcycle clubs as well.

"Gangs" exist for mutual protection, normally out of fear.
The bikers that I know fear nothing.

—Martin Dixon;
Brooklyn Kings: New York City's Black Bikers

The RICO Act swims in a spaghetti soup of definitions. A "criminal street gang" is said to exist as soon as an "informal" group of three or more individuals commits "two or more gang crimes... in relation to the group"—if one of the crimes is a "crime of violence." By definition, a "crime of violence" can include simply defending oneself when attacked, or shooting the wrong species of fowl while hunting.

One of the most controversial statutes in the federal criminal code is that entitled "Racketeer-Influenced and Corrupt Organizations," known familiarly by its acronym, RICO. Passed in 1970 as title IX of the Organized Crime Control Act of 1970, RICO has attracted much attention because of its draconian penalties, including innovative forfeiture provisions; its broad draftsmanship, which has left it open to a wide range of applications, not all of which were foreseen or intended by the Congress that enacted it; and the sometimes dramatic prosecutions that have been brought in its name. RICO's complexity has attracted several efforts to unscramble the many issues of interpretation it poses.

—*Columbia Law Review*, May, 1987

The RICO statute also specifies that "membership in an enterprise that deals in crime is itself a crime, regardless of whether or not the individual is involved in actually committing an act of racketeering." This apparently is the driving force behind complaints from motorcycle club members that, once stopped by police—even for low-level traffic matters—they are asked to sign "information cards" that ultimately serve as legal documents identifying their entire club as a "gang."

On September 15, 1988, sixty federal, state, and local law enforcement authorities—including the FBI, the Internal Revenue Service, the U.S. Treasury Department's Bureau of Alcohol, Tobacco, and Firearms, the Milwaukee police, the Milwaukee County Sheriff's deputies, and the Wisconsin State Division of Criminal Investigation agents—raided the southside Milwaukee clubhouse of the Outlaws MC.

They shot and killed two German Shepherds penned in the back of the clubhouse, used a torch, shotguns, and a 9 mm pistol to break through the front door, seized everything they could get their hands on, and then went on to use the local newspapers to try to convince the public that the goods they'd confiscated had some criminal significance, even though they didn't arrest anyone.

Authorities openly admit that the law-enforcement agencies had been presenting evidence to the Milwaukee grand jury over a period of several months in an effort to get the club indicted under the Racketeering Influenced and Corrupt Organizations (RICO) Act.

Unfortunately, the RICO Act allows indiscriminate blanket prosecution of group members rather than targeting individual crimes…[if] prosecution is successful in proving organized criminal activity anywhere within the club, all Outlaws could be jailed for being members of the club…

Looking at it another way, the RICO Act could even be applied to the U.S. Congress. If a number of congressional members' offices were covertly searched…and evidence of some kind of illegal organized behavior—such as drug dealing, prostitution, or weapons trading—were discovered, Congress could be considered as an organized crime family, and every congressman and congresswoman could be arrested under the RICO Act.

—*Easyriders* magazine, January, 1989

Many years later, in 2007 and again in 2010, the song had remained the same:

DAYTONA BEACH—Police forced their way into the Outlaws Motorcycle Club on Wednesday morning and federal agents broke down the door to the home of the club's boss, rousting him and his wife out of bed.

Johnie Trail, 48, who identified himself as the clubhouse boss, said authorities came looking for guns and drugs at the North Beach Street headquarters.

...Raids were also carried out at Trail's Ormond Beach residence and two other Outlaws clubhouses in Jacksonville and Citrus County.

Police used concussion bombs to get inside the clubhouse and in their wake, a window with the club's insignia was shattered and the front door broken.

...Federal agents lugged boxes from the headquarters at 615 N. Beach St. They mostly contained personal photographs of members, computers, CDs, cameras, camera cards, notes and clubhouse T-shirts emblazoned with the words "Snitches are a lying breed," according to a list left behind by FBI officials.

"They took my wedding pictures and the wedding pictures of other guys that got married here," Trail said Wednesday, motioning to the clubhouse. "They knocked down my door at home and my wife and I were asleep. They scared her and the dogs."

...The grand jury indictment in Detroit is on various charges, including assault and drug distribution. Eleven leaders and high-ranking members of the gang were arrested after a five-year investigation.

...Though the tough-guy reputation of the Outlaws is what many people go by, some members said Wednesday they're just regular people with families who like to ride their motorcycles, hang out and drink beer.

...other neighbors along North Beach Street agreed, saying club members shoo crack dealers and prostitutes away from the area.

"They watch our place and we've never had a break-in," said Gary Patrick, who owns Florida Restaurant Supply just south of the clubhouse. "If they see anyone hanging around that they don't think works here, they'll say something."

Faye Mayo, who owns Flamingo Homemade Ice Cream, says she deals with club members regularly....Mayo recalled the night she was accosted by two vagrants outside her restaurant and two Outlaws members came to her rescue.

"From that night on, they would always watch for me while I walked to my car after work."

—Lyda Longa;
Daytona Beach News-Journal, August 16, 2007

Federal agents raided the south side Milwaukee clubhouse of the Outlaws motorcycle gang Tuesday and arrested its purported national leader—part of a seven-state roundup that included a shootout in Maine where a gang leader was killed.

..."Today's arrest of the national president and leadership of the American Outlaws Association mark another aggressive attempt by the Department of Justice to dismantle what the indictment alleges to be a gang whose entire environment

revolves around violence," said Neil MacBride, U.S. attorney for the eastern district of Virginia...

"If you think a guy who is running a moving company can run the Outlaws from thousands of miles away, I would beg to differ," Burke said after the hearing. "He is a working stiff."

...Several neighbors said they have never had problems with the club. Members notify neighbors when they are organizing large motorcycle rides and make sure their vehicles don't block nearby driveways, residents said.

—JSOnline, *Milwaukee Wisconsin Journal Sentinel,* June 15, 2010

In 1979, nearly a decade before the 1988 RICO raid on the Outlaws MC, the Oakland chapter of the Hells Angels Motorcycle Club and the homes of many of its members were the target of a similar incursion storm. The trial that resulted—*The United States of America v. Ralph* [Sonny] *Barger, Jr, et al.*—cost somewhere between four and seven million dollars (that's *1979-value* dollars) in legal fees, and involved eighteen defendants; eighteen attorneys; a thirteen-month stay in the San Francisco County jail for Sonny and the other defendants; and a jury that acquitted Barger of RICO violations and remained hung on other various counts.

In a statement to the press—also reprinted in Sonny's autobiography, *Hell's Angel*—defense attorney Kent Russell summed up the long proceedings:

"No Angels have been found guilty of being racketeers. The Hells Angels Motorcycle Club has been vindicated. The government failed to prove the club itself is an illegal enterprise. Conspiracy is easy to prove and the government failed to do it after two years of investigation, millions of dollars, and buying witnesses that we proved lied on the stand."

Perhaps the main reason the trial resulted in a favorable verdict for club members was that they all stuck together as defendants; no deals or plea bargains were made as in previous RICO prosecutions.

The whole thing is a slimy, legality-fueled cat-and-mouse game, aimed at the "strength in numbers" biker mentality. The combined efforts of the media and law enforcement have made motorcycle collectives the most intriguing—and hunted—fraternal organizations on the planet.

And while authorities often mediate urban "street gang" wars, they express "concern" about motorcycle clubs *peacefully* co-existing. Strangely enough, *that's* a problem for them:

> *The major OMGs have recently formed confederations. In the late summer of 1998, members of the Hells Angels, Outlaws, Pagans, and Bandidos secretly met to work out details of how they could "stop killing each other" and focus on law enforcement. The OMGs believed law enforcement had success investigating them over the last 10 years because they committed overt acts against one another. Consequently, they agreed to stop the infighting and turn their attention to law enforcement tactics such as traffic stops, field interviews, and any operation that they can term harassment. OMG members use the threat of lawsuits to deflect law enforcement attention away from the daily activities of the gangs.*
>
> *According to Lieutenant Terrence P. Kinneen, President of the International Outlaw Motorcycle Gang Investigators Association, threats against and confrontations with law enforcement by OMG members appear to be increasing.*

—From a 2000 report,
National Alliance of Gang Investigators Associations

Of course, that was two years before the Laughlin shootings—shootings that (as mentioned) were apparently orchestrated by law enforcement, as reported by undercover mercenary Alex Caine in his book *Befriend and Betray*.

And Caine should know. He was *there*.

Six years after *that*, a court ruling came down that could change the face (and patches) of motorcycle clubs forever.

Early Tuesday morning, October 21, 2008, federal and local agents began issuing federal arrest warrants for 110 members of the Mongols Motorcycle Club, in six states: California, Nevada, Oregon, Colorado, Washington, and Ohio.

The warrants—reportedly obtained based on evidence collected by four members who became paid government informants—were for violations that included murder, attempted murder, drug trafficking, assault, procuring, money laundering, and firearms violations. Law enforcement netted sixty-one arrests.

But the *big* fish in the haul was yet to come.

At least from an LEO standpoint.

Shortly after the busts, U.S. District Court Judge Florence-Marie Cooper issued a ruling prohibiting members of the Mongols, their families, or their associates from wearing, licensing, selling, or distributing the club's logo. The judge and prosecuting attorneys used a trademark claim to "seize" the logo and the name, under government forfeiture rules; much like the seizure of other property belonging to criminals (drug dealer's cars, for example).

U.S. Attorney Thomas O'Brien stated: "This trademark is subject to forfeiture. If the court grants our request...then if any law enforcement officer sees a Mongol wearing his patch, he will be authorized to stop that gang member and literally take the jacket right off his back."

This logic could be frighteningly extended to—and have ramifications for—*all* motorcycle clubs.

In late August of 2009, a second wave of convoluted legal sewage swept over Judge Cooper; she thankfully responded by choking up a reversal of her decision.

In late 2009, the Mongols were finally allowed to appear in public wearing their colors once again.

But the stench still lingers.

Who will those on the "other side of the fences" try to ban, censor, eliminate, dismantle, and drive underground next?

Chapter 7

Vietnam

Reestablishing the Legacy;
Running for the Wall; (the Other) Fonda;
Wine, Women, and Motorcycles

There were doors all round the hall, but they were all locked;
and when Alice had been all the way down one side
and up the other, trying every door,
she walked sadly down the middle,
wondering how she was ever to get out again.

—Lewis Carroll,
Alice's Adventures in Wonderland

The USS Vestal was a repair ship tethered to the USS Arizona at dawn on December 7, 1941. Paul Nelson was a young sailor stationed aboard the Vestal, when the morning went wrong and wild, and the world was changed forever. So, of course, was he.

When the bombs and blood hit hard, Nelson's skipper quickly ordered the tether cables cut and the Vestal beached. Paul and some of his 466 shipmates survived; at least physically.

The country ultimately survived, too. And it stuck together. From Rosie the Riveter to patriotic big band songs to Loony Tunes depictions of Hitler, it was all about unity. Even Hollywood was on America's side, *then*—with the likes of Bing Crosby, Gary Cooper, and Spencer Tracy unashamedly waving the flag on theater screens.

Paul Nelson was lucky enough to return home to Wisconsin after the war; to the daughter he'd yet to meet, and to father a son and two more daughters. The youngest daughter would eventually leave the insulated quiet of the rural countryside and marry a Vietnam-era biker who'd ridden all along the crazed California coast during the '60s and '70s.

The lives of men like Paul Nelson and his daughter follow a stingingly emotional timeline. This is America—a country that has cultivated the most precious wealth of all: Freedom. Freedom is the ultimately intoxicating treasure; a treasure coveted and jealously disdained by the greedy and weak of the world.

Throughout the relatively short (but always commanding) history of America, a bit of a chronological roll of the dice has determined just when and where this freedom has been defended—and by whom. This has especially affected the vulnerable fates of the young. And those dice came up with very different numbers as they rolled from WWII to Vietnam. On a gaming table, coming up with a three versus a ten has great impact as those dice bounce between big bets and dreams. Nearly a half-million of those "dreams" were snuffed out by WWII; during Vietnam, 58,169. But the prevailing public attitudes toward these two sacrifices were as different as a glitzy casino in the heart of the Strip and a low-rent dive downtown.

The nation and the veterans who clawed their way out of the "conflict" in Southeast Asia were different from those of the FDR–Truman–D-Day generation. Things were especially different in California.

They always are.

The fuses for most things volatile tend to ignite there. Especially in the evolution of the American Biker.

Phase One shot out of Hollister, when war—and its effect—naturally linked men and mad motorcycles.

Phase Two set up shop in Oakland and 'Berdoo, when thoughts toughened, and men and motorcycle clubs became much more organized and focused.

Then came Phase Three.

War and its effect turned very strange as JFK, LBJ, and Richard Milhous Nixon introduced America and its military to a small country called Vietnam. The Vietnam War years turned into an intense epoch, which rivaled WWII in how this lifestyle once again closed psychological wounds; how bikes and brotherhood helped soak up the haunting mental bleeding.

Solid and serious motorcycle clubs like the Vagos, the Mongols, the Warlocks, the Hessians, the Viet Nam Vets, and many others blasted out of that era, becoming as established as their counterparts had twenty years earlier.

But the national unity that bonded the United States after Paul Nelson and his WWII naval brothers watched their Pacific paradise burst into a Kamikaze hell was never a component of the war in Vietnam.

Confusion, dissension, and political pratfalls hardly inspire unity.

Before the 1964 election in which Lyndon Johnson crushed the hard-edged Barry Goldwater, Johnson made the vehement comment that he didn't want "to send American boys nine or ten thousand miles away from home to do what Asian boys ought to be doing for themselves." And during his "partial term"—served due to JFK's assassination—when the Joint Chiefs of Staff pressured Johnson to do "all that was necessary" to prevent the Communist National Liberation Front from controlling South Vietnam, he was "unwilling to take unpopular measures like sending troops to fight in a foreign war."

Until *after* the 1964 presidential election.

"Just let me get elected," Johnson told his military advisers in a now-infamous quote. "And then you can have your war."

The unfolding of WWII created a national coming together. It had tangible evils for all citizens to focus on: Hitler, Mussolini, Hirohito.

The Vietnam War progression, however, was gang-banged with explosive and polarizing prods. The era was penetrated by the youth Mecca of Haight-Ashbury and its perpetual drug haze; Cal Berkeley; Kent State; Chicago '68; the Chicago Seven; Jerry Rubin's mouth; Sonny Barger's letter to the president offering the services of his Hells Angels Motorcycle Club as a military force; and the Angels' heated stand-off with Berkeley war protesters on October 16, 1965.

"We didn't hit any women or kids," says Barger in *Hell's Angel*. "There were more than enough guys in love beads and madras shirts to push around. Some of the protesters scattered while others fought back. There was no heated discussion or emotional political arguments. Our fists and the end of our boots did our talking."

Popular songs during WWII featured lyrics like *"He's the boogie woogie bugle boy of Company B,"* *"Praise the Lord and pass the ammunition and we'll all stay free,"* and *"Off we go into the wild blue yonder, climbing high into the sun; Here they come zooming to meet our thunder, at 'em boys, give 'er the gun!"*

The soundtrack to the Vietnam War was a bit different.

"Well, come on mothers throughout the land, pack your boys off to Vietnam," suggested Country Joe McDonald in his 1965 "I-Feel-Like-I'm-Fixin'-to-Die Rag." *"Come on fathers, don't hesitate, send 'em off before it's too late. Be the first one on your block, to have your boy come home in a box."*

And Grace Slick and the Jefferson Airplane were soothing society's discontent and ills in 1967 with the lyrical prescription: *"One pill makes you larger, and one pill makes you small...and you've just had some kind of mushroom, and your mind is moving slow, go ask Alice, I think she'll know…feed your head…"*

It's social-swarming times like these—when the most influential politicians in the world are flipping bent mental coins to make their decision; the most vocal of the nation's youth are drugged up and ripped to their pacifistic little tits; and more than fifty-eight thousand of our nation's bravest kids are walking the plank—that the solid unchanging roar and reach of a motorcycle cyclone seems pretty goddamn therapeutic.

Holy Jesus, those were strange days.

In 1969, I was just nineteen, my girlfriend was barely eighteen, and our son was a baby too. At first, these kinds of "ill-planned" factors merited a "draft deferment" for the male involved.

But that didn't last.

My impending fate was the subject of constant discussion—along with every other overheated aspect of the war. Among my peers in the music business, I was in the minority: I told anyone who'd listen that I didn't care if I had "to go" or not—but if I did, I damn sure wanted them to teach me how to fly a big-ass plane and drop big-ass bombs on those bastards doing all the damage "over there." I wasn't *real* excited about slogging around a wet jungle, but I had no a problem with the idea of wielding a big weapon and blowing the hell out of anyone I considered an enemy.

I knew the other longhairs disagreed. I knew they didn't care for my carefully crafted (and always tactfully expressed) point of view. But they never said anything; at least not to my face. Fear was pervasive in those days, on many different levels.

When December 1, 1969, finally rolled around, Congressman Alexander Pirnie (R-NY) of the House Armed Services Committee pulled the initial ball out of a big glass container, kicking off the first draft lottery since 1942. September 14th "won"—or *lost*, depending on your point of view.

My "number" (my birthdate) came up 321st out of the 366 possible. My family, at least, breathed a collective sigh of relief.

I was raised in California but had cousins in upstate New York. They *all* went into the military. They *all* went to Vietnam. Amidst the logistical shuffle of service life, one of my cousins wound up on a short leave in Southern California. He looked me up.

This was in 1968, before the draft lottery. Those deferments were fading away, and at that time I still could only guess what my future might be.

My cousin had already been to 'Nam and was going back.

Now, granted, there have always been steep cultural differences between "Easterners" and "Westerners"; but the war and the '60s made this meeting with my cousin feel especially alien. It was like Alice talking to the hookah-smoking caterpillar:

> *"Who are you?" said the Caterpillar.*
> *This was not an encouraging opening for a conversation.*
> *Alice replied, rather shyly,*
> *"I—I hardly know, sir, just at present—*
> *at least I know who I WAS when I got up this morning,*
> *but I think I must have been changed several times since then."*
>
> —Lewis Carroll;
> *Alice's Adventures in Wonderland*

There was no real talk of the war or the military or politics between my semi-distant cousin and me. All he wanted to do was go to the famous Sunset Strip.

I knew it well, of course. Working in the record industry and playing in a band, I practically lived there; so many of us did. We all knew Hollywood—"the Whisky" (the Whisky-A-Go-Go), the Hullabaloo (later changed to The Aquarius Theatre), Gazzarri's, Ciro's, the Troubadour, and the Roxy (a few years later). You'd see the "L.A. bands" in all those places—The Doors, The Byrds, Love, The Seeds, Spirit.

It was a weeknight but that never mattered much; The Strip was crowded as usual. There were three of us, so I couldn't take the old Panhead; we parked my race-ready '61 Ford Galaxie on a side street near Pandora's Box. We walked along Sunset then made our way north to Hollywood Boulevard.

I remember my cousin not talking much—just looking, feeling, absorbing it.

True, Hollywood didn't quite have the clout of the "Haight" up in 'Frisco; but in some ways it was weirder. Mainly because you had that lunatic juxtaposition of the pretentious glitz of the city itself with those stumbling around it in a brain-blasting intoxicant-fog. At least the Haight-Ashbury district and its inhabitants were all pretty much on the same level, "fashion-wise."

We listened to a few bands at a few clubs and then wandered into one of the many "head shops" along Hollywood Boulevard. There were lots of them, occupying cheap storefronts sandwiched between once-elegant, giant art-deco movie theatres built in the long-ago glamour-past—joints like Grauman's Chinese Theatre, The Egyptian, and The Pantages.

The Beatles' "White Album" had just been released, and everyone was playing it nonstop (that "everyone" included Charles Milles Manson, who interpreted the hidden meaning of "Helter Skelter" as predicting an impending worldwide race war; apparently giving him a bloody license to fly on the gory nights of August 9th and 10th of the following year).

My cousin, my friend, and I entered the store.

"Why Don't We Do It in the Road?" was cranked up as high as that day's state-of-the-art equipment would allow. Zillion-candlepower strobe lights beat a non-stop pulse outside the main vein of the "black light tunnel," where posters of Jimi and Janis and the Lizard King glowed in chemical neon.

Just another "day in the life" within the Hollywood howl.

My cousin became fascinated with something in the glass case counter. These cases always had buttons with sayings and pictures on them: "protest buttons" with peace signs and political slogans; rock 'n' roll buttons of The Who or Frank Zappa. Others, too; graphic weirdness by the ton. My cousin asked to see a button that was a picture of just an eye.

He looked at it for a long time.

By now, the White Album was on side three and "Birthday" was rattling the windows. He asked the guy behind the counter how many of these buttons he had. The guy found a box and poured out about thirty of them. My cousin bought them all.

In actuality, this wasn't all that odd. Excesses in the '60s were quite the norm—in some circles anyway. Drugs, sex, food, alcohol, marathon music playing, marathon philosophizing, bongo pounding, sleep, sleeplessness, volume, road trips, renounced ownership of anything material, huge collections of completely worthless junk, dour drama, street theatre, clown behavior—just about anything could be carried to the extreme. And—in *those* circles—it was just "groovy" and accepted.

But as my cousin methodically pinned each and every one of those eyes to the front of his military coat, I became very uneasy.

I never did see the things he ultimately witnessed in Vietnam. And I never saw what he saw in—or *with*—those eyes he bought in that sleazy shop. Maybe he didn't either. Maybe he was just *trying* to see something that he just couldn't ever seem to focus on.

We left the shop and headed back to the car. I realized that everyone walking toward us was being stared at by a total of thirty-six eyes: two longhairs, and a regulation cut with a torso of little round glares. In the background, Lennon's voice could still faintly be heard from the head shop, softening the "Revolution."

When we got back to the Ford, another constant of life in the '60s (again, at least in *some* circles) lit up the night.

As I put my key into the driver's side lock, I was blinded by the hot beams of the put-up-your-hands spotlights of a sheriff's squad car, parked—and apparently patiently waiting—in the shadows of a driveway, perpendicular to where I had parked my Galaxie. Two more black-and-whites screeched up quickly from behind and an all-too-familiar dance began.

My freak buddy and I were just standard fodder for these cops; but my cousin was a puzzle to them. Especially with his chestful of eyes staring at them from beneath the anomaly of a decent haircut.

They tore the Ford apart. The rear seats were pulled up and thrown in the street. The rugs and everything in the trunk followed. The front seat was of course bolted to the floorboard, but the upholstery was easily sliced and diced.

Two years later, when David Crosby sang *"It increases my paranoia, like looking at my mirror and seeing a police car,"* he *knew* what he was talking about. It sure went with this particular territory at *this* particular time.

The cops were looking for drugs, of course; they always were. And we fit the profile. The irony was that through all the '60s and throughout my involvement in the music scene, I *never* took drugs. I *did* drink like a fish—even while underage—but no chemicals.

That night I wasn't even drinking much. I'd sensed that I needed to be on my game with my "stranger in a strange land" cousin, so I'd kept things light. It turned out to be a good move because the cops had nothing to hold us on. They eventually just drove away, leaving us in the early morning darkness with the guts of my ride scattered across the residential area adjacent to Crescent Heights and Sunset.

My cousin was real quiet all the way back to the beach. He seemed to take the cop thing in stride, just as we did (as we had *learned* to do). Hell, after what my cousin had been through, their little ninja act in hopes of confiscating a sandwich bag full of herbal contraband was just a game. In real life, these cops spent a lot of time shooting their guns at paper targets in clean, well-equipped ranges; all buffered up with those slick orange glasses and ear protectors. My cousin was spending *his* time in a sticky jungle halfway around the globe killing *actual* people—while entire towns like Berkeley and a nation of college campuses bitched about it.

Maybe he needed all those damn eyes just to try to keep "all of this" in perspective.

I remember the next time I hit the Strip. It was just a few days later. By then I figured my cousin was probably back in the jungle. I was alone; on the old Pan. I went into the Whisky. Spirit was onstage playing "Fresh Garbage." I rubbed my eyes and watched through the smoke and colored lights as they launched into "1984." I looked around at the chicks; there were always a lot of them. I watched other longhairs around me sharing their dope. I looked into the eyes of the smiling waitress as she handed me another Seven and Seven—without ever asking for an ID that would allow me to drink *legally*. I looked back at the stage as Spirit began "Dark Eyed Woman."

I could only imagine what my cousin was seeing at that same moment.

War and its effect: both are anything but passive. Both require an outlet. But this time the outlet was laced with anger. The WWII boys were heroes when they came home; the Vietnam boys were not.

When this new generation turned to the freedom, the power, and the escape of big motorcycles, the purpose was more intense than so many years before; it went beyond fun and forgetting. But that wartime link—that edgy common denominator—was there. It was a booster shot for the biker culture and a reestablishment of the legacy of the American Biker.

> *When we came home, the only people who welcomed us*
> *or said "Good job!" or anything was the biker community.*
> *Everybody else didn't even want to fuckin' acknowledge us.*
> *Bikers were the only people who said,*
> *"Hey, great, nothing wrong with you. Come with us!"*

—"Popeye,"
Pacific Coast Regional President and Longtime Member,
Viet Nam Vets Motorcycle Club

Meeting Popeye was emotional. Just about everything that deals with *that time* is. It was all such a disjointed puzzle; a confused mess with jagged pieces that didn't fit then, and don't fit now.

"My dad was a full-bird colonel," said Popeye, "and he never asked me a fuckin' thing about what I ever did in Vietnam. Not one word. 'Cause he was convinced as much as anybody else—the Korean vets and the World War II vets were all convinced—that we were nothing but a bunch of rapists, druggies, and murderers. It was ridiculous.

"At one point after I was back, my wife and I went to a VFW hall. I went up to the bar to get us a drink and the bartender told me that they only served vets at the bar. I explained that I had just gotten back from Vietnam.

"'Like I said,' the bartender repeated, 'We only serve vets here.'

"I have a bracelet upstairs. It says on it, 'Time is on our side.' I had one; one of my closest friends had one. We covered each other over there—all the time. We made that promise. We came home; he went through thirty days of withdrawals. Well, he came over about seven or eight months after we were home and he says, 'I can't even get a job in a car wash. Nobody wants me. Nobody will even talk to me about a job. I put down that I'm a vet and they won't do shit!' He says to me, 'I'm goin' back! I'm good at what I do and I get respect for what I do! I'm goin' back!'

"I tried to find him down through the years after that, but I could never seem to track him down. In 1988, I was in my gym, and a guy came in and threw the book about The Wall monument on my desk. The book with all the names of those who died. So I thought, well okay, I'll look through it. I found his fuckin' name on The Wall.

"Another guy I knew came back, and after about a year he calls me on the phone and says, 'I'm going down to the VA…I'm turning myself in…I'm fuckin' nuts. There's something wrong with me. I'm going crazy.'

"He was in the VA for almost a year and then he calls me and says, 'Guess what I've got? I'm not nuts; I got fuckin' worms! My shots went bad and I've got worms all through me!'

"He was in the hospital under quarantine for a long time. He just went through hell. His shots broke down before he got home.

"Before he went to the VA, he got real, real thin. I'll tell you what, though; when I signed up for the service I weighed 215 pounds. I was already power-lifting. But they told me I was 'obese.'

"I said, 'Well, does that mean you don't want me?!'

"'Oh, no,' they said. 'We'll straighten *you* out!'

"When I came home from Vietnam eight months and four days later, I weighed 143 pounds! I had no idea I'd lost that much weight until I came home and started trying to put on my clothes!"

The WWII boys regrouped quickly. It took the Vietnam vets a lot longer. But again, the component of big motorcycles helped the healing process.

"Brother Frenchie came up with the idea for the Viet Nam Vets MC," says Popeye, "and he drew the patch on a napkin—that's how we started. The idea began in '80, but '85 is the official anniversary date.

"We have a 3-piece patch. Not because we consider ourselves 'outlaws'; but because when we came home everyone else considered us 'outlaws.' 'Outlaw' is the title that's been put on us; we consider ourselves the *elite* military motorcycle club.

"What the patch stands for is this: It's red and black; they're our colors. The red is for the blood that we shed; the black is for the mourning. The shape of the land you see is Vietnam. The green in it is the way it was when we came; the brown is what we destroyed. The eagle stands for the freedom that we fought for, and the eagle's holding the bomb that we *didn't* drop. And the U.S.A., of course, stands for the country we fought for.

"Our Legacy Vets wear the same thing, except their patch has *their* name and a *world* map because they're open to allied armed forces throughout the world."

Captain Ron (left) is a longtime member of the VNVMC.

Clubs have sprung up supporing all branches of the armed forces.

Obviously, the pool of potential VNVMC members who are legitimate *Vietnam vets* is finite; and—let's face reality—so is their lifespan. The original club was planned obsolescence in a way—having made such a bold "blaze of glory" statement of a singular brotherhood. The Legacy Vets help ensure that the heritage and overall spirit of the VNVMC will be carried on.

The passage of time has other effects, too.

"We don't do the things we used to do. We can't. Our own brotherhoods will make damn sure that 'If you wear my patch and you do something wrong, *I'll* take you out.'

"It's the RICO act...the whole thing...you've got to be aware of that. Sure, I might have some brothers who don't do *everything* according to the law. Who the hell does? We *all* break the law. And you're a fuckin' hypocrite if you say you don't."

I felt a sick irony as we discussed the *law*. "Back then," it was against the law to dodge the draft, to slink over the Canadian border, to doctor up your tell-all urine at the draft board medical clinic. Many did. Not Popeye and his brothers. But *that* outlaw behavior was legally forgiven and officially forgotten when Jimmy Carter signed the "amnesty law"—Executive Order 11967—on January 21, 1977, the day after his presidential inauguration.

Evidently, the term "outlaw" is fluid—depending on who or what is doing the defining. Or the absolving.

As Popeye and I discussed this, a bit more dank irony crept in. The newspapers, the radio and TV media, and the official ATF website were all reporting a story on another Vietnam-era club.

"Operation 22 Green" had hit:

ATF, California Sheriffs Arrest Members of Vagos Outlaw Motorcycle Gang

'Operation 22 Green' Nets 25 Bikers Across the Southland; 85 Warrants Executed

SAN BERNARDINO, Calif.—Special Agent in Charge John A. Torres of the Los Angeles Field Division, Bureau of Alcohol, Tobacco, Firearms and Explosives (ATF), and Sheriffs Lee Baca of Los Angeles County, Gary Penrod of San Bernardino County, Bob Doyle of Riverside County and Michael Carona of Orange County announced that more than 700 federal and local law enforcement officers fanned out across California's Southland early today to execute 63 federal search warrants and 22 arrest warrants for members and associates of the Vagos Outlaw Motorcycle Gang.

The three-year investigation was centered in Los Angeles and worked collectively by the Sheriff's Departments of San Bernardino, Riverside, Orange and Los Angeles.

"The Vagos are a ruthless criminal biker gang that virtually held our communities hostage," said ATF's Torres. "My office remains steadfast in our commitment to reduce violent crime and protect the public, and this joint investigation, coupled with today's arrests, has lessened the grip of fear and intimidation that the Vagos placed on our neighborhoods."

Today's arrest warrants netted 25 Vagos members and associates for various state charges and federal firearms and narcotics violations. All of the arrests were executed without incident....As a result of the 63 federal search warrants executed, the following items were seized: 95 illegal firearms, illegal drugs, $6,000 in U.S. currency, two stolen motorcycles and Vagos Colors (riding vests) indicating gang affiliation.

—From an ATF Press Release, 2006

It was interesting to both Popeye and me that after a *three-year* investigation, involving *four* county law enforcement agencies and one federal bureau, *this* was the climax. *Sixty-three* federal search warrants produced a grand total of six thousand bucks (what's that: ninety-five dollars per person?) and a handful of other allegedly incriminating stuff (including the club members' cuts!).

It seemed to us that virtually any local police agency could roll up to any corner in or around the area—maybe downtown Los Angeles, downtown Santa Ana, or the Westminster and Garden Grove vicinities where Asian street gangs roam (now officially designated "Little Saigon," complete with freeway exit signs)—and collar twenty-five arrests; find under a hundred weapons and a couple of ripped-off wheels; and get six grand in cash out of the baggy-pants pockets of the first two or three serious drug dealers they chased down the nearest alley.

Then again, a *lot* of things seem like they should be fairly simple and straightforward.

I'm tired.
I'm tired of feeling rejected by the American people.
I'm tired of waking up in the middle of the night
worrying about the war.

—Lyndon Baines Johnson

Dr. Victor Westphall probably had a lot of sleepless nights too.

The first physical memorial to the Vietnam vets was constructed near Angel's Fire, New Mexico, and dedicated on May 22, 1971. It was spawned from the love that Dr. Westphall had for his son, Victor David Westphall III, who was killed in Vietnam on May 22, 1968.

Dr. Westphall (now deceased) was far ahead of his time. Other memorials and tributes followed; but not for awhile.

"At that time such a project was not popular," said Westphall. "Even so, we led the nation in memorializing all Vietnam veterans; the living, the dead, and the maimed in body and spirit. We could not have known that within two decades, a chastened and belatedly grateful nation would extensively follow our lead…Now, perhaps no one knows how many [Vietnam veterans memorials] are scattered across our broad land.

"We had no idea of changing the mores of a nation. All we wanted to do was assure that our son, and all his buddies, were properly recognized."

Years later, came a seriously "proper recognition."

On March 16, 1982, ground was broken in Washington, D.C., to build "The Wall." Officially known as the Vietnam Veterans Memorial, this wall is a black granite five-hundred-foot-long valley of tears.

The memorial was dedicated on November 13, 1982, and it only took a few years for another heavy link between the American Biker and the fiery heart of this country's war veterans to meld: the Run For The Wall.

The Run For The Wall was begun in 1989 by two Vietnam vets, James Gregory and Bill Ewans. And according to its participants, it isn't really a "run"; it's a "mission."

The "mission" begins each May in Ontario, California, and reaches The Wall in D.C. in time to celebrate Memorial Day at the nation's capital. The Run For The Wall is an adventure that wraps the ultimate freedom machine in a sacred shroud of tempestuous emotions; a combination not experienced on or in any other motorcycle event.

It takes a strong soul and a willingness to cry to ride this particular path.

Just when I was afraid my country had been folded, pressed,
and stuffed into the reality TV handbasket to hell,
and the only cultural significance America had left to offer
the world was the mindless, puerile antics
of Paris Hilton and Britney Spears;
I took a ten-day trip across America with Run For The Wall.

—Randall Wilson,
Producer, *The Long Ride Home: Run For The Wall*

In 2005, Randall Wilson and his Guerrilla Docs film crew chronicled every face, every mile, and every tear of the Run For The Wall. When asked to review his resulting epic, *The Long Ride Home: Run For The Wall,* I was honored and forever impacted by this film's journey.

My review—and the film—speak for themselves:

The Long Ride Home: Run For The Wall

Reviewed by Bill Hayes

In 1989 the annual Run For The Wall began. This near-religious pilgrimage finally established—in the strongest and most visible way—the powerful link between bikers and the veterans of the Vietnam War...The Run For The Wall is easily the most emotional gathering of bikes, bikers and the American spirit that there is.

"It's almost overwhelming. There's so much going on.
It's an emotional roller coaster...up and down.
You can't call it fun. It's a mission. It's an experience.
But I can't really say you'd call it fun.
On overpasses, there would be six, seven, eight—
sometimes twenty—thousand people waving,
and they've got flags waving. It really makes you feel good.
It makes you feel like finally we've been welcomed home."

—*A rider and Vietnam veteran,
on the Run For The Wall*

Run For The Wall gives Vietnam vets a second chance to be welcomed home.

"There is so much going on" is a wide understatement. This run isn't just about getting an enormous pack of bikes from

Ontario, California, to The Wall at the Vietnam Veterans Memorial in Washington, D.C. No. It's about the innermost soul of a very special breed of people; it's about a country and a time that was unlike any other in our history. And there is definitely "so much going on" as that particular socio-psychological door is opened.

The film…pulls those of you who have not participated in the run right into the journey that you are watching… The emotions and force in this documentary reduce "real" big-time network ["reality"] *productions like* Survivor *and* The Amazing Race *into the same limp league as Big Bird singing the alphabet to drooling toddlers.*

The documentary certainly presents the monumental "travelogue" aspect of a mammoth run like this but that is not the film's true focus or purpose. This is ultimately about the veterans. This is about what they felt then and what they feel now. If you didn't live

through the Vietnam era, prepare yourself for a history lesson that has all the subtlety of an ice pick to the jugular.

If you are a product of the late '60s / early '70s, get ready to step over a surreal threshold into the past; one that will truly sear your senses…

"Before the shoot," says Wilson, "I prepared my cameras, my tape, my crew, and stocked our SUV with the obligatory pallet of bottled water from Costco and everything else we felt we needed…but what I was not prepared for was how the run would affect my life.

"Travel across our great country with veterans, their families and friends, and you'll see America like you've never seen it before. These patriotic, selfless, compassionate and dedicated people give you a renewed faith in mankind; a renewed faith in—jingoistic as it may sound—America. Men and women who have sacrificed and given everything for a country that—in the case of Vietnam—essentially turned its back on those who gave all…I thank you, every man, woman and child featured in this production for allowing me to share your journey. Thank you for your service. You are not forgotten."

—Bill Hayes;
Thunder Press, 2007

The Run For The Wall really combines two events. The cross-country run ends in D.C. for what is known as Rolling Thunder; a gathering of bikers from all over the country (and the world, actually), celebrating Memorial Day in America's capital city. This gathering grasps the concept of what a "memorial" truly is: *all* the memorials, from those of the presidents who led to those of the soldiers who died. It's a time when no one takes anything for granted. It's a time when life, death, and freedom shine with their truest meanings.

Rolling Thunder grasps the concept of what a "memorial" truly is.

It was of May 2007. I had been to D.C. many times, but in the twenty years of the event's existence I had never been to Rolling Thunder.

It was time.

In so many ways, the trip epitomized the essence of the American Biker.

I experienced many "firsts" and that was perfect. Spontaneous and new sensory input *should* be the norm when you're in our nation's capital during the sacred, solemn time of Memorial Day; surrounded by more motorcycles and bikers than I have ever seen in one place at a single time (I kept trying to get an "official" estimate, but no one seemed to want to commit. The *Washington Post* simply referred to "thousands of motorcycles," "the largest ride yet," and a "record turnout").

One "first" I experienced was relatively mundane. Time constraints forced me to "fly and ride," so for the first time ever, I rented a bike. No problem. It was worth the effort and the slight price gouge ($170 a day). There was *no* way this event could have been enjoyed and experienced in its deserved glory from the caged constraints of a rental car.

No.

(However, at the end of the weekend I amused myself with the thought that for what I spent to rent the cool blue Heritage, I could have bought a used import outright somewhere in D.C. and abandoned the thing just before I flew home—a 1985 Gold Wing with 45,000 miles was going on eBay for *half* what I laid out for use of the Heritage. But the thought was strictly an amusement; never close to a reality.)

The other firsts I experienced were far more important and poignant.

Since my last trip to D.C., the World War II Memorial had been erected (dedicated in 2004) as had the Korean War Veterans Memorial (dedicated in 1995). These are stark—very stark—monuments.

Memorial Day is essentially about war; its toll and its impact on our freedom. Officially, Memorial Day (originally called Decoration Day) is "a day of remembrance for those who have died in our nation's service." This remembrance was first observed on May 30, 1868, when flowers were placed on the graves of Union and Confederate soldiers at Arlington National Cemetery.

Here on May 27, 2007, flowers were still being put on graves in Arlington; the impact of war is still being felt; and this nation is thankfully still free.

The Vietnam Veterans Memorial is without doubt the most attended and observed monument during Rolling Thunder; but *my* goal was to experience personal firsts by paying tribute to the WWII and Korean War remembrances as well.

Over four hundred thousand Americans died as a result of World War II. Millions more have enjoyed liberty because of what they did. The WWII monument, with its round courtyard-like design, which features tributes to each state, pulls you in as though enveloping you in the gentle palm of a giant hand; but a solid, unyielding hand. Engraved on the walls are the war-driven words of wisdom by the leaders who were there, from FDR's famous "day of infamy" quote to General Eisenhower's encouragement to the troops that "the eyes of the world are upon you."

To go from the WWII Memorial to the Vietnam Memorial is a strong double-shot—especially to those of us from the "baby boom" generation. Our parents lived through the worldwide horror of WWII; we lived through the national horror that was Vietnam.

In the middle was the Korean "conflict."

Perhaps more than any other monument, the Korean War memorial conveys the pure abject grind of war. It consists of 19 statues of soldiers in the battlefield: 14 Army men, 3 Marines, 1 Navy Corpsman, and 1 Air Force man. They are also an ethnic cross-section of America, with 12 Caucasians, 3 African-Americans, 2 Hispanics, 1 Asian, and 1 Native American.

But the most compelling feature of the soldiers is that each is roughly 7'3" tall. You are truly in the land of giants: giants in stature and giants in what individuals like these have done to preserve our freedom. At that size, you can see their faces so clearly. You can read their expressions—their eyes. You can feel what they felt. You can cry their tears.

Of course, just as history produces heroes, it also conjures up villains.

—Still a common biker vest patch

I'll tell you, we vets have long memories. We'll never forget all the shit that stupid bitch Jane Fonda did and said while we were over in 'Nam. That's why we still wear these patches.

Then there's that other stupid bitch, Cindy Sheehan. She shows up here in D.C. awhile back or someplace with this t-shirt on that says: 2,245—How many more? *I'll tell you how many more, bitch: How many more is how ever many more it takes to keep the freedom that we all have. That's how many!*

The real heroes will keep dying for freedom just as long as there are bastards out there that want to take it from us... and judging by the state of the world, there ain't going to be any lack of those bastards anytime soon!

—"Ohio Bob";
Interviewed at Rolling Thunder, 2007

Sunday is the main day of Rolling Thunder: parade day. All the "villains" are either under their rocks or in the shadows; out of sight and (mostly) out of mind.

It's a day that shines with a love for every man and woman who made the ultimate sacrifice so that days like this—days of military appreciation—are enjoyed voluntarily; in freedom, not forced upon a frightened populace by some maniacal uniformed dictator.

It was a day of unbridled patriotism—when petty politics stepped aside.

It was a day of unbridled pride.

It was also a day, when the festivities were over, that it felt especially good to climb on that bike. To feel the rumble—the rolling thunder—that so perfectly represents the liberty that the *true* giants of our society have preserved for us.

But the respect for being one of society's giants came very late for the veterans of Vietnam.

Many *never* got to realize that feeling.

For many, any semblance of "normal life" was shredded by memories and thoughts and a blistered lost youth that they somehow survived. The addition of true "rolling thunder" was often what made that survival possible.

Gene Long—Vietnam vet, American Biker, and club member—explains all that pretty damn well:

Wine, Women, and Motorcycles

by Gene Long

> One of my first days riding my brand new Simplex Service Cycle to junior high, a kid named Barry Powell came up and told me he had a Cushman Eagle. He couldn't drive it to school yet, but his dad let him ride it on weekends. We started riding the thing together the very next weekend, in 1958.

Today, over fifty years later, we still ride together. We finished school together, joined the Air Force together, got back together when I came home from Vietnam, and became roommates after each of us got our first divorces. We immediately went out and bought Yamaha street/dirt bikes and began to race. Cross country, scrambles, motor cross— they were our bread and butter. It was fun and exciting.

But first I am going to talk about coming home from Vietnam in 1966, and deal with that.

I thought long and hard about how to tell this story after I came home from overseas. Before I went, I married my high school sweetheart (really she was Barry's old girlfriend and they'd broken up). We married on December 22, 1962. I faked my driver's license and her mother was with her to give her permission. We went to Weatherford, Texas, for the license and then got married in a small missionary Baptist church while I was home on leave for Christmas. My best man was Airman Eugene Mays. I have tried for years to find him, but never with any luck. My wife's name was Beverly Sue Mills. Susie Mills—she was and still is a beautiful angel.

In January of 1964, Tammy René was born, and just before I left for Southeast Asia, Richard Eugene was born in September of 1965.

Susie sent me the Dear John letter while I was off serving my country. Saddest part, the guy she hooked up with was a "Conscientious Objector" and wouldn't go to war for "religious reasons." But he could fuck the wife of a guy who was over there. Makes no sense. I would rather have died than be stuck with the thought in my mind of being a pussy for the rest of my life. He did everything in life to be macho, but deep down, you know he knows—and his whole family knows—"pussy."

Deep down, you know he knows: "pussy."

I basically came home to nothing. No wife, no job, no car, no money.

Somehow, though, in no time at all I had a motorcycle. The first one was an old '62 Harley and I immediately used it to leave town. Where, in 1966, would a "biker" go? I went straight west. Arriving in the "City of the Angels" was a quick-life experience. I met bikers. I had my bike stolen. I was crawling over fences to steal meat from restaurants. I stole a Harley from the same group of guys who stole my Harley and headed home.

I made it back to Fort Worth, took the bike apart, sold the pieces, and went and bought me a new Honda 305 Scrambler with an electric starter. I got a job at Bell Helicopter. Barry came home from Colorado. Things looked good.

After about a year, I quit work, started hanging out with the biker crowd, lost my apartment, and basically went to shit.

The biker lifestyle in 1967 was bleak at best (on the surface), but the parties were fun, the booze great, and the girls even better. I raced my 305 and won. I got drunk and climbed Benbrook Dam with a girl on the back. Coming down was a whole other deal. She panicked and fell off. I slid and went sideways a lot, but made it to the bottom.

Funny, the things you remember. I still remember that girl mostly for her nipples. They were staged like a rocket. First round, then brown in a tapered area, then the nipple tapered at the end.

I slept most of the time behind her couch. She and her roommate had a two-bedroom house on the south side of Fort Worth. I would sleep on the floor in the living room, behind the couch, because her mom and sometimes her dad would fight and then come over and stay. I would listen to them talk on the couch, sometimes for hours. Imagine if you will, a war-crazed drunk vet/biker lying a few feet away from you, listening to all your thoughts. All night. Thank God I didn't snore.

When no one was around it was great. Sometimes, though, I'd coast down the hill on my bike, with the motor off, slip under the house because they were there, and sleep on a piece of canvas with my leather jacket as my pillow and blanket. Such was life; but considering where I had been in the war, it was great. At least no one was trying to kill me. (Although if they had known I was around, most likely the parents would have wanted to.)

Time just marched on. I got a job at General Dynamics as an inspector. I bought a Yamaha when Barry bought one, and we started racing. I married a blond beauty named Sharon. We were married five years. I was a shit; she deserved better. We divorced. We had no children.

I was still riding and bought a Honda four-cylinder 550 to cruise on. It would fly.

I up and moved to Tulsa. Glen Barnhill and I took turns riding the bike and driving the car as we traveled there on one day's notice.

Drinking, sex, fun, work, bikes, babes, you can make your own story here. But you don't need to make up a story because it all happened. Susie, Sharon, Marylyn, Kris, Cindy, Paula…

They are all gone.

Here I am in my old age, and you know my heart really pines for those gals. Wherever you all are, I miss you and loved you.

But the pattern was set long ago.

Wine, women, but not song—the last word in that old saying became "motorcycles."

And that, my friend, has always been the key word.

—Gene Long,
Vietnam veteran and American Biker

Chapter 8

"Wild, Roaring Sexrides"

The Media's Biker-Orgy

What had more influence on which:
the film on motorcycling or motorcycling on film?
I think there was a symbiotic relationship;
they fed off of each other.
Screenwriters constantly delved into newspaper headlines
for plot twists and for characters, but at the same time,
motorcyclists looked at these movies and said,
"Hey, I can look just like that guy on the screen."

—Mike Seate,
Author, *Jesse James: The Man and His Machines;*
Interviewed in *American Biker,* the film

The big leagues of the biker culture has always had a lot of strong leaders. True, as Seate notes, a lot of motorcyclists looked at the biker flicks and said, "Hey, I can look just like that guy on the screen."

Certainly. There are wannabes in any group. But the key here is that the *initial* biker image—while definitely, and progressively, enhanced by the media—was as real as it gets.

The World War II heroes who traded their bombers, jeeps, tanks, and squadrons for powerful motorcycles and powerful brotherhoods weren't the product of a screenwriter's greasy fantasy. Neither were the men who came after, stealing the social spotlight from the limp angst of beatniks, dingy coffee houses, and whiny political folk music. Men like Wino Willie Forkner, Otto Friedli, Sonny Barger, Tobie Gene Levingston, and George Christie didn't need movies, books, or television to tell them who *they* were.

But who they were—*are*—and the American Biker essence that they share is the fast blood in the media-infested water that has incited many an entertainment feeding frenzy. A frenzy in which you're either the one with the teeth; the one who becomes lunch; or the one who simply observes from the protection of the cage.

The Lifestyle on the Big Screen

…chains, cycles and broads!

—Tagline;
A biker movie poster from the '60s

Movies have always offered the tastiest media bait. And—as already established—*Easy Rider* was one of the most whettingly seductive.

The "true story" of the origin of *Easy Rider* comes right out of the perfect setting: San Francisco's Tenderloin District. It spans across the Golden Gate Bridge, and reaches into the upscale world of Mill Valley and the home of a prominent media star.

In one of my street-corner raps with author Miles Davis (*Motorcycle Yoga: Meditative Rides through India*), Miles asked if I was aware of the "real truth" behind Fonda and Hopper's flick. With all due respect, just the phrasing of that question sent my initial thoughts drifting toward the aluminum foil–hat crowd—the ones who have the hidden "truth" about everything: the alien saucer crash victims from Roswell being kept alive and studied daily in cryogenic cubicles beneath SAC Command in Colorado; Dick Cheney's other-world connections with dead Popes; the cabal of Masons and white supremacists controlling our weather; and all the other important stuff that isn't allowed to be known by us "common folk."

But then I noticed how serious Miles was.

Miles has solid street credibility in the motorcycle world. He's ridden the kind of distances in the kind of exotic places that would make most of us who consider ourselves hardbutts whine and cringe like puppies who haven't even learned yet how to pee on a newspaper in the hall.

So I listened.

The story centers around characters who may not be aliens or dead Popes, but they ain't common folk either:

Fonda and Hopper, of course.

Peter Coyote.

Bill Fritsch.

Coyote is the author of *Sleeping Where I Fall*, probably the definitive narrative of the excessive highs and lows of the 1960s. He was one of the famous "Diggers" of Haight-Ashbury. His Renaissance man persona includes actor, author, and biker.

Fritsch, a.k.a. "Sweet William" and "Tumbleweed," was a Hells Angel. He still refers to Sonny as "Chief." He was on the Altamont stage when the deal went down and the blood spilled. He was shot in Fresno while selling cocaine during a house party organized to raise money for the African Student Movement, leaving him with permanent paralysis of one side of his body and a bullet still lodged in his brain.

One thing I have always experienced when meeting someone who was, at one time, a genuine badass is that (thankfully) I cannot envision this person as anything but the badass they once were. That title is earned and it can never be taken away. That goes for war heroes who grow frail and aged and are relegated to "homes." It goes for long-forgotten comedians, musicians, and entertainers who made us laugh, made us dance, and made us cry but are now holed up in lonely dark rooms, looking forward only to shitty cheese sandwiches; watery cheap "juice"; generic we-don't-want-to-be-bothered-with-you drugs; and someone with a warm spot in their heart to occasionally change their diapers.

I knew Bill Fritsch was a badass. He had to be. I didn't care that he now lived in a small room in an area of "The City" that wasn't necessarily the best. I cared about who he had been and who he essentially still was.

An identity is forever.

I cared about how, when Miles and I opened the door to Fritsch's room, the first thing I saw was an old, high-mileage Sonny Barger t-shirt hanging on the wall.

I cared about the history that this badass carved out before half the synapses in his body were blown away.

The paralysis and the squalor may have been a high price to pay for the life he led, but a lot of people pay high prices and *never* really live—never become anybody or anything. Sweet William Fritsch was somebody and something in a time and place that truly defines the meaning of "you had to be there to understand."

We took Sweet William to a relatively pricey street-chic Columbus Street Italian restaurant. The three of us talked, ate, and drank beer. With a bit of prodding, we got Fritsch to revisit that era and relive the "*Easy Rider* germination controversy," as he called it.

One of the binding social elements of the '60s was one borrowed from bikers; it's still the overarching principle that unites all bikers—especially club members. That principle is brotherhood.

The general social brotherhood shared back then by the hippies, the freaks, the musicians, the drug benders, and the street people was, of course, far looser than the serious commitment of motorcycle club members; still, they shared common ground in that "I never met a stranger" type of attitude. In a clubhouse, you may see a brother from another chapter who you've never actually met face to face; but if he's wearing the same patch as you, you're part of the same family. There is never that "ice breaking" period. The ice was broken when you both committed to that patch; no matter if it happened years and miles apart. Amongst the long-haired sub-level of the '60s, the icebreaker was the drugs, the music, and the spit-disdain for anything authoritative or structured by "normal" society.

There were also the ever-present fantasy flights, in which—backed by the hiss of everyone in the room sucking on smoke—they would all share their grandiose plans for changing the world back into the peaceful Eden it once was; when everyone was happy, naked, and living on pure Mother Earth–grown berries, long before even those sick vicious apemen in *2001* discovered the evils of weapons and domination. Usually these sessions also included the loudly played daily soundtrack of the long version of Iron Butterfly's "In-A-Gadda-Da-Vida," The Doors' "The End," and the long, long, *long* version of the Chambers Brothers' "Time Has Come Today" (complete with the somewhat uncomfortable grunts and sighs at the tune's struggling end).

With that kind of "family life" in place, it's no wonder Peter Coyote's group of counterculture think-tankers, the Diggers, began to hobnob with the Hollywood stars—a self-appreciative society that always seems to gravitate toward the latest twist on being "in," "now," and creatively outrageous.

Another part of that hip gravitation was the counter-culture's paradoxical embracing of the Hells Angels. The reasons were many. Things like a taste for notoriety; anti-establishment behavior; the "occasional" drug imbibing; and an appreciation for wild abandon were all a part of that awkward common ground.

So it wasn't particularly strange that when a group of capitalistic music producers tried to stage a fundraising event in Los Angeles centered around the Diggers' name and aura, Coyote and Sweet William, along with a couple of others, drove to L.A. Their purpose was to object to the Diggers' name being used to raise something as pedestrian and dirt-worldly as money.

After they had nobly scuttled the event, the group was invited to stay at the house of Benny Shapiro, the manager of sitar god Ravi Shankar. While there, they were visited by Peter Fonda, Brandon De Wilde, and Dennis Hopper. In this environment of artistic energy and ultimate '60s hipness, they brainstormed ideas for how this entire stratospheric social "scene" could be morphed into film (into The Film, as it were).

"You know what I'd do?" Sweet William said, cloaked in the aura of his Hells Angels colors. "I'd make a movie about me and a buddy just riding around. Just going around the country doing what we do, seeing what we see…you know, showing the people what things are like."

There was the answer. *There* was the essence that became *Easy Rider*.

But the project wasn't to become a partnership of *all* the original players—at least not all who shared in the ideas, thoughts, and feelings that night that led to the landmark film.

According to Coyote, the evil specter of money again popped up. This time, though, it evidently wasn't so pedestrian and dirt-worldly.

Several months after the get-together at Shapiro's, *Easy Rider* was apparently rolling beyond just the dream stage. It was going to happen. Fonda and Hopper contacted Coyote to gather his San Francisco Mime

Troupe together to write, direct, and perform in a segment of the film that featured such a band of entertainers.

Coyote tried to negotiate some "remuneration" for his troupe. He was offered just twenty dollars a week for himself; a "place on Fonda's couch"; and nothing for his group. The movie was being done on a very low budget, Coyote was told, and it was more of a social statement than a commercial venture. Therefore, money wasn't— or *shouldn't,* they said—be a driving force.

Coyote declined.

When *Easy Rider* hit the theaters, it indeed featured a street performer scene. Coyote's troupe had called themselves "guerrilla theater." The troupe in the *film* presented signs proclaiming themselves "Gorilla Theater," which Coyote interpreted as an insult. It's also another pretty good example of the most idealistic time in American history suffering a nut-kicking by human nature and greed-fueled reality.

As Sweet William recounted these details, it was apparent that— by this time—it didn't really bother him much; he gave a bent one-shouldered shrug when I asked him if he held any grudges about having his idea "borrowed."

After being brothers with The Chief; being onstage when Meredith Hunter's blood stained that Altamont field; being a white target for a Black militant's bullet; and being relegated to a small tenement room full of memories—maybe it really didn't matter that he never got credit for coming up with the seed for a classic film; a revered existential journey into the guts of an entire generation.

He just kept eating, and we ordered more beer.

Maybe the paper credit for the fantasy didn't matter so much to Sweet William because this man had actually lived it.

> *Art and entertainment influence different individuals in varying ways, depending upon their characters, intelligence, upbringing, and social situation. For a relatively few predisposed youths, the modus operandi of a crime depicted in a film might inspire them to incorporate those details into a violent act. For a far greater number, the same violent work will be relaxing, cathartic, or simply entertaining.*

—From BRIEF AMICI CURIAE OF THIRTY-THREE MEDIA SCHOLARS in INTERACTIVE DIGITAL SOFTWARE ASS'N, et al. v. ST. LOUIS COUNTY, et al., No. 02-3010, United States Court of Appeals for the Eighth Circuit

"Relaxing, cathartic, or simply entertaining."

Or just completely bogus.

I had been out on the bike all day. Riding. Enjoying the sunshine and the peace. I came home to find a DVD in the mail; a DVD that I was to review for one of the magazines I write for.

Fine.

I've done many reviews. The subject of the review—be it a DVD, CD, or book—is red meat thrown into the cage of judgment. Sometimes it's tasty; sometimes it's not. Sometimes it's seasoned with a creative spice that gives it into an entirely different flavor from anything in its genre.

Sometimes that's not a good thing.

I learned long ago that the biker culture—and everything closely associated with it—lives on extremes; probably more so than any other sharp slice of life. The media is no exception.

Extremes.

Names like Brando, Lee Marvin, Fonda, Hopper, and Nicholson rolled through the credits of *The Wild One* and *Easy Rider*. On the other hand, 1957's *The Motorcycle Gang* headlined the late Carl Switzer ("Alfalfa" from *The Little Rascals*).

*It's amazing how many [biker movies] had
"kill, rape, burn, pillage, hell, angel,"
or something like that in the title of the movie.
It's no wonder there's a negative stereotype of American Bikers
after all these "B" movies that were so bad.
They weren't even "B," they were probably "Z" movies.*

—Senator Ben Nighthorse Campbell

Next to my computer I have a '60s movie theater poster from a "quadruple feature" that screams out:

*4 SUPER-CYCLE SHOCKERS!!
In one hell-raising show!*

The sub-screams warn:

*What they want, they take! Get out of their way if you can!
…chains, cycles and broads!*

Okay, sure, that was the '60s, but things haven't really changed much in a half-century. The swing in the quality of biker media has always been huge, and unfortunately there's more down-thrust than up, especially among the flicks.

If you can't stand the heat, get out of the theater!

181

I looked at the cover of this *newly released* movie as I removed the packaging.

Then I looked back at the old poster.

"Things haven't changed much…"

This modern, high-tech, high-res, big-wheel DVD jacket cover was from the same shock template as the faded poster. The only real difference was that some of the hype included new-age lingo:

Outlaw Riders against the Asian Mafia!
Deadly Bio Chemicals!
Corporate Greed and Corruption!
A Loving Father desperately trying to save
his kidnapped Teen daughter!
A Curvy Temptress playing each and every one
traps him into A Mad Race against Time!

I ripped off the shrink-wrap, opened the case, and discovered *two* DVDs. Oh, I see, one was the "theatrical release," while the other was the "director's cut"—weighing in at a hefty two-hour running time.

I had a bad feeling.

But I needed to do my job.

The film, as far as its intrinsic plotline went, was hyper-complex. It had lots going on.

Lots.

Naturally, there was the motorcycle "gang." There was an evil woman. And the Asian Mafia. And a secret vial of crawling flesh-peeling bacteria—or something like that—that was about to be unleashed on unsuspecting innocents. There were rave parties and strobe lights and really loud, really bad rock 'n' roll that served to distract people from discovering the secret headquarters of the corporate CEO greed-monster. And there were guys in full-face helmets doing front wheelstands on sport bikes in the dark. A frightened kidnapped daughter was thrown in to add human-interest sympathy and cliff-hanging fear.

Ultimately, I'm pretty sure that none but the most astute would ever guess which plotline was intended to be the focal point. But that didn't really matter; *I* knew what the main plotline was.

Intentional or not, the focus of this cinematic stew—for me— was these two guys who were more or less the "stars." They weren't bikers—but they *really wanted to be*. This was the *truly* frightening part of this movie. And—in so many circles—so horribly real.

These two guys looked like young stockbroker types, or at the very least, mid-level executives in a mid-level company making mid-level bucks. I found myself fixated on the fact that they were— by their own admission—trying to "buy their way into the biker lifestyle" (nearly verbatim dialogue from the movie—at least in the "director's cut," if memory serves me). They did this by getting high-dollar bikes and hanging out in a cartoonish biker bar, where they stood out like weasels in a fish bowl.

"Hey, check *these* guys out," says a "gang" tough named "Blade," when our clean-cut heroes stroll into the apparently-off-limits-to-anyone-except-*real*-bikers saloon. "Somebody just walked into the wrong damn bar. Let's rough 'em up a little. Give 'em a little scare."

"You know, I'm not so sure this was such a great idea," says one of our boys, looking around warily.

"Hey, relax…trust me," says his buddy. "This is what you said you wanted, remember? Hangin' out in bars with tough bikers and their chicks…the dark side…on the edge."

I kept watching.

The strobes kept on strobing to The Beat; Asian men with sinister-looking briefcases kept sneering; those helmeted-guys on sport bikes kept doing backwards wheelies; the corporate guys kept snickering; and the kidnapped girl kept crying.

While I couldn't find much cinematic value to talk about, my review keyed off my initial premise of these guys trying to "buy their way into the lifestyle." (This is perhaps the core element of the bitching that many old-timers in this lifestyle hurl at the newbies, RUBs, and weekend warriors with the virginal, low-mileage bikes.)

Amid the evil spies and the biological dread and the crying kidnap victim and the guns and all the rest, the real terror for me was seeing these guys be so upfront and matter of fact about what they were trying to do. It brought the same discomfort as viewing your first zero-conscience, remorseless slasher movie.

The idea of becoming a "bull in a 'Chinese' shop" (as Archie Bunker always said) and slamming headfirst into a culture you know nothing about is a short fuse to disaster. It would be like me trying to, say, be a golfer—something I have no clue about. My not taking a little time to learn the social ropes and protocol would be more than ugly; it would have the same sad result as putting a parakeet in a microwave. Maybe I'd have enough money to "buy my way onto the course" and get a decent set of clubs and stuff, but I guarantee I'd make an ass of myself, piss off a lot of people, and probably break things in the process.

I mentioned in my review that the filmmakers were very much like the two stars of their show. They didn't have a clue. They had the money to produce this product, but they didn't have the slightest insight into the world they centered their attention on.

While the premise of two buds buying their way into the lifestyle may have been valid, the depiction of the leather-lined arena they wanted to score a seat in was right out of the Eric Von Zipper mold. But even the goofy "Von Zippered" surfer movies that made people wonder if every tanned, toes-on-the-nose, board-carrying beach freak was in some way a salt-water clone of Gidget, Moon Doggie, Frankie, or Annette died a merciful early death. They didn't come close to lasting through six decades.

But this stuff—these *"Super-Cycle Shockers"*—have.

An ironic side-note: In writing *this* book, I found myself re-ordering—spending *actual* money on—this same DVD (seeing as I had "misplaced" my original copy). Opening the shrink-wrap this time, I was stunned to see on the back cover, a "positive" reviewer quote. Even more stunning: It was from *me*!

"The 21st century phase of the evolution of the biker flick!" it read. I admit it. I *did* write that. And unfortunately, what I wrote is true. Things haven't changed much...

Far removed from the motion picture community's crazy—sometimes outright berserk—portrayal of the biker lifestyle, is a documentary film that unintentionally but hauntingly captured a *real* aspect of biker culture.

Gimme Shelter was the Maysles Brothers' "reel" chronicle of the Rolling Stones' 1969 concert tour. However, its jagged focus exploded far beyond its intended coverage when it wound up being eyewitness to the bedrock end of the '60s time-twist "love generation"—a time when bright-white denials of reality accompanied equally blinding slides into fantasy. It's a time many of us still look back on with feelings that range from simple head-shaking to palsied nausea. The events at Altamont demonstrated that life simply *can't* twirl around in a psychedelic spin-cycle of suspended reality forever.

On December 6, 1969, somewhere around 300,000 people packed themselves into the rolling hills just east of Livermore for a one-day music festival at the Altamont Speedway. This expansive spread just outside the hive of the San Francisco Bay was the "grooviest" setting possible for what was billed as the "Western Woodstock."

The musical line-up was a "flower power" all-star team: the Jefferson Airplane; Crosby, Stills and Nash; Santana; the Flying Burrito Brothers; the Grateful Dead; and the Rolling Stones.

The Dead never *did* go onstage, but according to the band's lyricist Robert Hunter, their song "New Speedway Boogie" was later written about the event.

Gimme Shelter captured what happened too.

It was the ultimate face-off between the delusional "Age of Aquarius" and the heavy hammer of reality that was, is, and always will be the biker's driving wheel.

Oakland's KTVU news described the incident:

"As the Stones rocked on stage, a member of the notorious Hells Angels motorcycle gang, hired by the band to provide security, attacked, stabbed and killed [eighteen-year-old Meredith] Hunter."

Alan Passaro was the club member accused—and then acquitted—of the stabbing. A jury found he had acted in self-defense because Hunter had pointed a gun at the stage.

For more than thirty years following, prosecutors tried to prove that a second Hells Angel was involved in the stabbing as well.

Finally, in mid-2005, authorities in Alameda County closed the case for good when even the most modern investigative technology could not come up with another suspect. Enhanced and slow-mo'ed film footage *did* show, however, Hunter brandishing the handgun just before Passaro leapt from the stage and stabbed him.

In a 1998 interview for the History Channel's *In Search of...* series, Sonny Barger explained some simple realities about the Altamont incident:

> *"This Black guy, who—if you see the film and everything, you can see the guy is wired to the gills— he's running around. He's looking for trouble. He got on the stage; he got pushed off the stage. He didn't like it. He came out with a gun and he fired the gun and he shot a member* [of the Hells Angels] *in the arm. When he shot the guy in the arm, people started stabbing him. The guy killed himself by pulling a gun and shooting it into a crowd.*

"And, to me, that's just part of everyday life in the Hells Angels. Somebody shoots you and you stab him."

And to *me,* it's that kind of fundamental, to-the-point truth that separates the American Biker from people who find it necessary to continually search for—and eventually drown in—tangential complexities of their own doing. The kind of tangential complexities that were so pervasive in the '60s; the kind of tangential complexities that must especially haunt the likes of '60s peace-and-love paradoxes like Manson-ites Susan Atkins, Patricia Krenwinkel, and Charles "Tex" Watson every time their parole is once again denied.

Gimme Shelter may not have featured "chains, cycles and broads" or "Outlaw Riders against the Asian Mafia." But it did feature something unique: The Truth.

The Lifestyle, The Musical...?

Another true biker story, *Mask*—the tearjerking saga of young "Rocky" Dennis (sufferer of the rare, deformative disease, lionitis)

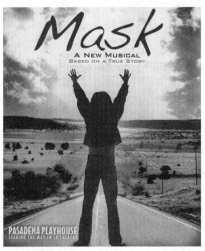

whose dream is to travel to Sturgis—made its way onto the silver screen (starring Cher!) and then, even more surprisingly, onto the legitimate stage as a musical.

I was privileged enough to attend this show's premier at the Pasadena Playhouse. I have to admit, as strange as the production may sound on paper, I actually found it pretty damned entertaining and well-done.

Who knows, maybe this'll start a trend—Bikers on Broadway!

The Lifestyle in Print

Wild, roaring sexrides…

—A description of the biker lifestyle;
Biker Orgy magazine

Magazines provided the first true media mobilization on the motorcycling community. The expanding culture had been featured in early newspaper reports, of course. But it was the double-whammy of *LIFE's* and *Harper's* Hollister-feedback that pretty much made America—and the world—aware that some way, somehow the *connection* among motorcyclists was very different and intense compared to other "socially active" groups.

It was a connection with *power*.

A couple of decades and plenty of frightening media water under the bridge later, the first issue of *Easyriders* magazine hit the stands in June of 1971. The slick and classy Paisano Publishing empire was established. *Easyriders* and its sister publications—*BIKER, In the Wind,* and others—became bellwethers of the genre.

But not everything printed about the biker lifestyle was "slick and classy."

There were things like *Biker Orgy*: "Wild roaring sexrides by the Devils Angels on wheels. "

And *The Real Story Behind the Hell's* [*sic*] *Angels and Other "Outlaw" Motorcycle Groups*: a magazine proudly offering "an intimate photo story of their every act—from smoking pot to love making—their women—their bikes—their drunken orgies—their kids."

And they weren't alone. Like the movies, there was no lack of genuine dog feces in the publishing industry. Plenty of rags set themselves up as vessels of biker truth. Many—both good and bad—preceded *Easyriders* and its family.

Not everything printed about the biker lifestyle was "slick and classy."

One of the "good" ones was *Colors:* a magazine considered by many to be "innovative, pioneering, and validly legendary"; those three adjectives also apply to John "Rogue" Herlihy, one of *Colors'* founding contributors. Rogue's words and photographs would later help elevate *Easyriders* to its position as king of the biker-mag hill.

Author and artist Tom Brinkman's history of *Colors* not only defines what the magazine was and stood for, but it also exposes the fear and stand-offish apprehension that has always surrounded *true* media depiction of *actual* motorcycle club activities:

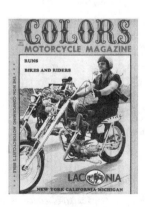

Colors Magazine

by Tom Brinkman

Colors *is a very hard-to-find, short-lived mag, which predated* Easyriders' *summer 1971 debut. It was founded and edited by Phil Castle, a biker who ran a fuel oil delivery company in New Jersey while trying to make the mag a success.*

Colors *was primarily focused on the East Coast bike*  *clubs and events, as that was its home turf, so to speak. But the money ran out before the mag caught on, and by the end of 1971 it had folded, after only five or more issues. It also suffered from poor distribution, as some newsstands, hypocritically, wouldn't carry it, and the first issue was banned in a few states....*

Colors *was a hands-on production, by those* [who had a] *love of their motorcycles and non-conformist lifestyles. It went against the odds, and flew in the face of a hostile reception by some newsstands and motorcycle shops.*

One of the original contributors [was] *John Herlihy*  *a.k.a. Rogue...a one-time Air Force gunner and photographer...He is on the cover of the second issue (Fall 1970) on his bike "Crazy Horse," which was featured inside....*

Colors *was pivotal in that the focus was on the outlaw clubs. All the biker mags that had come before were more focused on technical specs, articles on customizing, etc. It was the mag closest to the outlaw segment of the biker population at the time....*

Colors *was maverick, different from the rest, and it paved the way for the more club-friendly cycle mags to come.*

—Tom Brinkman,
Author, *Bad Mags: The Flip Side of Popular Culture*
As Seen Through Magazines and Tabloids

But those "club-friendly" cycle mags that *Colors* "paved the way for," always seemed to suffer from that same apprehension. And fear. Today, no mainstream magazines actually focus on motorcycle clubs—and few even acknowledge their existence.

In 1966, the heaviest print about the biker world was between hard covers. Hunter S. Thompson's *Hell's Angels: The Strange and Terrible Saga of the Outlaw Motorcycle Gangs* was published, and it became the bellwether of *its* genre: "biker books."

While potentially infinite in meaty flavor—these books have become highly imbalanced, leaning away from simple tasty tales, and instead toward overspiced, stomach-souring exposés. These "tell-all's" are usually by former club members who are either disgruntled or have found some sort of divine redemption that compels them to publicly denounce the rampant "heathenism" of the lifestyle. This dramatic airing of dirty leather—for various bounties or moments of fame—has been hung out by a wide assortment of rats, snitches, and turncoats.

And then there are the true "Infiltration Books": the unending stream of titles by undercover cops, feds, and their informants who make careers of "befriending and betraying"—as openly admitted by mercenary-infiltrator-author Alex Caine—in order to condemn, convict, cripple, and collapse the major motorcycle clubs and their memberships.

Thompson, at least, never seemed to represent himself as anything other than what he was: a journalist who wanted a story. But the inside/out genre that his *Hell's Angels* set into motion raised the "vicarious-living" bar pretty high. There's an obvious hunger for this kind of stuff—and no end of truth-tainted writers / operatives who are eager to supply it.

Of course, some are *talent*-tainted too:

> *Take a look around at your fellow bikers. Look them in the eyes. Do they have "sunken eyes" or eyes "narrowed to slits" or eyes like "pellets"? Do they have eyes that are "skittish"? Do they have eyes "like chips, veined and scratchy as if dried too long in the sun"?*
> *Take another look around.*
> *Check the overall expression of the nearest biker to you; does he look "like a spider, his smile tight and forced, his gaze menacing and accusatory"?*
> *If not, maybe you're not with real bikers! At least not the kind of allegedly genuine bikers that populate the pages of* Running with the Devil *by Kerrie Droban.*
>
> —From my review of *Running with the Devil;*
> www.bikersinnercircle.com

Running with the Devil is one of several books (and easily the most "eye-crossingly" bad) that recount the allegedly "true" story of the ATF's infiltration of the Arizona Hells Angels in the early 2000s. A lot of literary mileage has been squeezed out of that particular operation.

But despite these books' variations in quality—and truth—virtually each and every one of them shares one highly telling component. Down through the years and down through the books—somewhere along the course of the undercover sting, or "operation"—a time comes when the "hero," the top cop in disguise, has second thoughts about his allegiances. Almost without exception—in nearly *all* of these "missions" and, consequently, in nearly *all* of these books—the lamenting, introspective, second-guessing agent compares the life he has as a law enforcement officer with the bonds he has cultivated within the biker brotherhood. A time comes when he wrestles so brutally with just what really *is* important in this life and just who *is* the real *him* (or *her* in some cases).

I have to admit that I absolutely love and look forward to these epiphanies. It's why I read these books. And yes, I'm always disappointed that none of these guys actually ever goes over to the "dark side" and tosses their badge into one of the graves they may have dug along the way. But it tickles me to no end to see them squirm so uncomfortably in their identity.

Something else tickles me as well. Through all of the infiltrations, exploitations, lies, and heaviness of so much biker literature, an element of humor is also needed—and not many writers touch upon it.

J.J. Solari does.

J.J.'s stuff has appeared in *Easyriders* magazine for years. Like a grown-up version of *Child's Play's* "Chucky," Solari can take some wicked bites out of you, even as he doubles you over in hysterics.

As a kid, J.J. was one of TV's original Mouseketeers ("Jay-Jay"). Contemplating this evolution is like looking at a flesh-hungry leopard knowing it was once simply a "kitten."

J.J. has some interesting thoughts on the essence of biker literature—and by extension, the essence of the American Biker. Given J.J.'s rules-don't-apply e e cummings–style of writing, it's necessary to absorb Solari's thoughts raw—just as they flowed through his smile-and-slice mind. And pen:

Bikers in Literature

by J.J. Solari

> By "bikers in literature" what we're talkin' here is Biker Fiction, not "bikers in the news." We're talkin' about Creative Writing By Bikers or About Bikers, not "creative writing by zombie journalists about bikers." And for the record, there ain't what I would call a lot of it: creative writing by bikers or about bikers, that is. And what there actually is of it—creative

writing by bikers or about bikers—is kind of…not very good. Kind of like the situation with "biker movies." Which would be…not very good.

What there is of "biker literature" is not something that would make you go, "Yeah: I would like to be livin' like that." Because nobody would want to be livin' like that. Which would basically be livin' in a world of dopey drama; bad dialogue; extremely predictable situations; wife-beater-t-shirt-style "macho-ness"; endless "gents" with rodent-related qualities, either of gaze or disposition or hygiene; relentless references to liquor and the "tossing-back" of this and the "taking swigs" of that; "pieces" stuck into boots—which, when the diminutive weapons are "brought into play," perform feats of target-score-level accuracy and killing power on a par with elk hunting; and virtually no aesthetic-level writing about the fucking road itself.

On the other hand, maybe I just don't read enough "biking stuff." But of all the "biking stuff" I do read, goin'-on by people who write about "biking stuff," it's usually "I went here, and then I went there, and then we came back through here, and then at ten in the morning we got off our bikes here, and walked over to there, and then came back and got back on over here, and then we rode to over there, but then it rained, so we stayed here instead of there, and then this thing broke, so we limped into this town here, and that guy there fixed this thing here."

Jesus Holy-Rolling Fucking Christ. And that's just the reportage. When "bikers" start writing biker fiction, it gets a whole lot worse:

Red knew that Wildman Tim was lookin'
for him. Tim took no guff and took no prisoners.
Red knew that whatever he said to Tim would

have to be believable. Otherwise Tim would get at the truth "Tim's way." Red knew that Tim knew all about him and Brenda. Tim considered Brenda his personal chattel. You fuck Brenda and you fuck Trouble. Well, Red fucked Brenda. And now Trouble was comin'.

Wildman Tim was suddenly in the room. "You fucked Brenda and that means you fucked Trouble! Brenda is my bitch!!"

Red threw a knife. It caught Tim in the belly and went in deep. Tim pulled it out and tossed it aside and laughed. *So,* Red thought, the stories about Tim were true—he laughed at death.

And so on and so forth.

And that's bad enough. But as many of you know, bikers are not only mad-dog mean and Timex tough, they are also wild and crazy happy fun-lovers, always ready for hijinks and mischief and shenanigans. So when this *attribute of "biker nature" is put into fictional print, it usually looks like this:*

Eddie got rip roarin' drunk! He got up off the log and stumbled right into the campfire!! Holy shit!! He started yelpin'!! Oh man!! Augie pulled him out and tossed him to the ground. He was smolderin'!! So we all pissed on him!!! Oh fuck!! It was wild!!

Nobody wants to read this. It's not funny. And just because the writer insists that it actually is *funny, he is wrong. It is not funny.*

195

However, this *would be funny:*

Eddie got rip roarin' drunk. He got up off the log and stumbled right into the campfire.

Bob said to Bill, "No way he's gonna be able to get outta that mess on his own."

The fire began to heat its way through Eddie's drunkenness and he began to register small signs of increasing sobriety.

"That fucking screaming is really starting to fuck up my buzz," Moe said to Bill, angrily. "If you don't pull him outta there, I'm going to."

Bill looked at Moe exasperated. "You know that Eddie's an informant. He just doesn't know that we know. He's savin' us all a lotta trouble with his clumsiness."

"Fuck you," Moe said. "He's starting to stink. His skin-fat is starting to cook."

"I like it," Bob said, lighting a smoke. "It's like, I dunno, the smell of that barbeque at the fair."

"Yeah, well," Moe said, spitting on the ground, "they weren't barbequin' drunken lifer oil-covered meth-heads at the fair. They were cookin' ranch-raised beef."

Eddie now looked like one of those ignited Fourth of July snakes after it's uncoiled into a tube of ash.

"Well," Bill said languidly, "you can pull him outta there if you want, but then we're gonna have to bury *two* things. If you just leave him right there, on the other hand, we'll only have to bury the fire pit."

Moe thought about this for a very long time.

Eddie's femur blew apart from the boiling internal water vapor in the marrow, making a report like a .22 magnum pistol. Small sparks fluttered into existence and disappeared in unison with the bang.

Eventually Moe said, "I guess that makes sense. Guess I just got a little peeved." He walked over to Bill. "Tell me straight: you think I need anger management courses?"

Bill looked at Moe for a long time and then said, "I think you just need to get into the habit of listening to the other man's point of view before you decide to get mad. Listen first: *then* decide."

Moe reached down and shook Bill's hand, and they both nodded at each other.

Moe then went back to his own log, stepping through the campfire rather than going around it, and then sat down and scraped some of Eddie now-in-tar-form off his boots.

While this is not a real scene from a real story, it's kind of an example. It's a way of showing that bikers, while maybe not this amusing (well, I think this is amusing), are a bit on the "unruffled" side. Three men having a calm discussion about life and proper behavior while a fourth man is burning to death in the campfire right next to them is an exaggerated, for-entertainment-purposes-only, example of the "biker perspective."

Now, if you've ever read anything of Solari's (which you now have)—you'll find that his stuff is much more than a "laff riot." There's a serious side to his "biker perspective"; one that he's only too happy to explicate. It's a perspective that hops into the fun and stuns you; like an Easter egg hunt turned haywire by a fuzzy pink bunny with a Taser.

In real-life terms, what helps develop the creation of this so-called "biker perspective"?

Well, for one thing, when you decide to "live the life," it does not take too fucking long on a Harley to realize that everyone in a car is trying to kill you, because (a) they know they can get away with it in a court of law and (b) they know they will come away from the accident unscathed, while you will likely die—"So fuck it, I'm turning left in front of this two-wheeled hobo."

And it doesn't take too fucking long to realize that every cop in uniform is trying to get you into a penitentiary and bring your life to an end and destroy your whole family, like a Muslim with a bomb who has a similar hatred for Christians; and he will intrude his braindead presence into your life every time he sees you to see if you have violated one of America's ten trillion laws. And if you haven't, he will say you have.

People, you see, are cowardly pieces of shit and see in bikers everything they decided not *to be because it would have taken some effort and some honesty.*

So once you get this realization, after being a biker for awhile—that basically you have absolutely no non-biker allies—you can do one of two things: go berserk on society with a .30 mm cannon, or bury your hate and disgust in an Everest-sized cocoon of understatement.

This is *the essence of the biker sense of humor: deadpan, morbid, gallows-shaded, graveyard, black, bleak*

Witnessing J.J. Solari's transformation from Mouseketeer "Jay-Jay" to biker writer-activist is like being Tasered by a fuzzy pink bunny on Easter.

understatements of the obviously horrible. Kind of like the old joke of having mixed emotions when seeing your wife (mother-in-law, boss, wife, hated neighbor, wife, guy you owe ten thousand dollars to, wife, lawyer, wife) go over a cliff in a new Maserati.

And, as Sam Kinison said over and over, it never ends.

On top of all the aforementioned frustrations of biker life, there's always room for more *screaming exasperation, because there's also the inherent danger of motorcycle-riding itself, which is never taken for granted for even one second by the wise, long-lived biker who actually values his life. A life protected by the government road builders by only a line of paint on the ground, creating an annual human-road-kill body count that the government considers absolutely not worth even glancing at; and if they do, the deaths are the vehicle builders' fault or the operator's fault. It's everyone's fault except the entity that forbids anyone to make roads but itself.*

And then, of course, there's the hailstones in the face. And the underreported fact that a fucking Harley weighs a goddamn fucking ton, and if it ain't moving forward, it's lookin' for a way to pull you to the ground with it because they fucking fall over!

So, whatdafuck!

It all adds up to either developing a "style" to save your sanity—and maybe the community's lives; or becoming a commuter with a briefcase and a strained smile.

For my own personal part in not adding to the horror file of biker fiction, I have tried to sculpt that "style" into comedy fiction yarns that depict the American Biker as someone who never ever ever loses. Ever. It's true: I romanticize bikers. Why not? Romance is fun. And in my universe, fun comes first.

To me, anyone who writes about bikers at all—in fact, or in fiction—and manages to make it boring: he ain't writin' about bikers. Because bikers are a lot of things; but boring sure ain't one of 'em.

Bikers deserve a bit of effort on their behalf when they are hauled into the artistic—get this—milieu. Bikers in art deserve more than just "Red got pissed!!" or "Jamie's tits looked hot tonight!!" or "Big Jim was my bro, goddamnit!!" or "I felt the gnarled cold hand of death on my [throat, heart, soul, spine, will, strength]."

Even Eddie the Rat died in the campfire with imagery and fun for others, if not for himself.

Bikers deserve something better than your very worst effort. Even the worst fictional bikers don't deserve: "Big Jim was my bro, goddamnit!!"

—J.J. Solari,
Author, *When Bikers Meet Humans*

The Soundtrack to the Lifestyle

Here I come a-ridin' on the road again,
ridin' down the highway with all my goodtime friends.

—Charlie Brechtel;
"Where I Live"

Music also fits into "biker media." It's always a centerpiece of runs, events, clubhouse parties, or fireplace relaxation after the bike has been parked.

It's vital.

It's right up there with good booze at the end of a long ride, in terms of setting—and prolonging—the mood.

As the biker lifestyle evolved, so did its music. But the real stuff was all de facto—just like every other part of this brotherhood. The tunes that bikers like are simply the tunes that bikers like. Taste can't be forced; especially upon an intensely independent spirit like the American Biker.

Force-feeding *has* been attempted, however—most obviously in the movie soundtracks. Most of the music laid down by producers of the ancient '60s swill had the same inspirational quality as the Velveeta-cheesy tunes that pumped the primitive porn of the era. (Pioneer fuzzmaster Davie Allen was a major exception, if for no other reason than his complete originality.)

It wasn't until *Easy Rider* that someone finally "got it." Featuring cuts by artists like Hendrix, Steppenwolf, The Byrds, and Charlie Daniels, the movie's soundtrack (released in August of '69) demonstrated how cerebral "biker music" could be.

The true American Biker soundtrack melds music and thoughts and emotions with the road.

And like the road, the music isn't one-dimensional.

201

Like the road, biker music isn't one-dimensional.
(From left: Blues Legend Deacon Jones, Bill Hayes, Charlie Brechtel)

The blues, Southern rock, outlaw country, and straight-ahead no-B.S. rock 'n' roll are all part of the roar; the musical equivalent of being in the wind on a long fast highway.

Michael Stein is the Editor-in-Chief of *Easyriders* Europe, and one of the world's most passionate aficionados of U.S.A.-bred biker music.

"Music preferred by bikers," says Michael, "is simply done in an honest, almost handmade way. The bands favored by bikers are those who don't always hanker for technical progress. As brutish as the V-twins are, the perfection of modern computer beats aren't needed for the biker's rock 'n' roll. What counts are other things—the important things. 'If I have to explain, you wouldn't understand' is a well-known saying in connection with Harley-Davidson motorcycles. If you transfer it to music, perhaps nothing has to be explained. Just listen. Listen to The Allman Brothers Band, Lynyrd Skynyrd, The Outlaws, Charlie Daniels, Charlie Brechtel, Big Mike Griffin. Just listen…"

(As discussed in Chapter 13, organizers of the Harley 100th should have heeded Stein's advice. Of course, if you have to explain…)

The Lifestyle on the Small Screen

It's about biker gangs. And it's on FX.
That's pretty much all you need to know.

—A network description of their series *Sons of Anarchy*

Though the Set [of club patches] *is from a fictional MC,*
there may be other outlaw MC members
who may feel it is disrespectful, please think twice and
WEAR THIS ITEM AT YOUR OWN RISK!

—Disclaimer on an eBay auction
selling a complete set of *Sons of Anarchy* colors

That's pretty good advice.

Parading around in "fake" colors amid the *real* biker world would be like dressing up in a bright orange pantomime horse outfit and doing a barnyard dance to "She'll Be Comin' 'Round the Mountain," in an attempt to fit in with a herd of wild mustangs

Potential bad judgment and commercial exploitation aside, the September 2008 debut of FX's *Sons of Anarchy* was genuinely groundbreaking.

Movies, magazines, books, and music have all dedicated *huge* slices of creativity and marketing toward the biker lifestyle for a very long time.

Television has not.

And *Sons of Anarchy* was the first series to be actually—*ostensibly*, at least—about life within a motorcycle *club*.

Of course, a typical day (condensed to a TV hour or so) in the life of the brothers of SOAMC (and their women) consists of things like international arms dealing, blowing things up, drugs, murder, bribery, near-necrophilia, some good- and not-so-good-natured assault, the always-enchanting image of Katey Sagal engaged in oral sex, plus a lot of other stuff.

It certainly isn't Michael Parks on his Sporty, discovering his inner-self and the country in 1969's *Then Came Bronson*. It sure isn't the Fonz on *his* Sporty (or Triumph) reliving those innocent *Happy Days*. No. If nothing else, *Sons of Anarchy* is indeed 100 percent focused on a pure biker *lifestyle*, unencumbered by ethereal symbolism or happy-go-lucky nostalgia.

And for good or ill, it stands as the lone "dramatic" pioneer.

"But wait—there's more!"

Reality TV had *already* discovered that our lifestyle could sell as many serious commercials as crying fat people and marooned schoolteachers.

The cable networks' documentaries and bike-building shows brought national (and worldwide) exposure—and a sort of greasy glamour—to our culture.

And that *really* changed things.

A lot.

The Movies:
A Short Encyclopedia

In 1996, a writer named Clint Armentor put together a perfect chronicle of the worst (and a few of the best) biker movies up until that time. First published in Easyriders *magazine, his article—and the statements it makes—definitely deserves a second look:*

Scooter Cinema – The Best and Worst Biker Flicks

by Clint Armentor

The Motorcycle Gang (1957): Low-budget, sputtering *Wild One* rip-off. Corny bikers with smoked salmon breath wear goofy-looking helmets and do Three Stooges–type pratfalls offa their Triumphs.

Motor Psycho (1965): A cast of shapely, shrieking women with extremely large honeydews are terrorized by a "gang" of three delinquent clowns riding little Honduh 90cc trail bikes. Thanks for the mammaries.

The Wild Angels (1966): Peter Fonda leads the "Angels" as the hyperactive Heavenly Blues, while bug-eyed psycho Bruce Dern stirs up a buncha shit that gets all the "gang" in trouble with "The Man."

The Wild Wheels (1966): Idiotic *Beach Blanket Bimbo* romp, with the evil bikers vs. dung buggy dipshits. The bikers burp, stink, and grimace while dune buggy warrior Casey Kasem looks constipated.

205

Hells Angels On Wheels (1967): Jack Nicholson as a hassled gas station attendant named "Poet." Sonny Barger cameo appearance. The Hells Angels MC sued the producers for defamation of character.

The Glory Stompers (1967): The "stompers" are clean shaven, wear clean underwear, and use deodorant. Their nemesis is the filth-encrusted "Black Souls" club, led by a freaked-out Dennis Hopper. Club enforcer Bob Tessier swings a mean tire iron and runs over some dude's face.

You know it's bad when the Hells Angels choose YOUR movie to sue for defamation of character.

The Born Losers (1967): The first silly Jack, er, ah, I mean Billy Jerk movie. The biker "gang" leader wears a pimp's hat and Cher's sunglasses. Features senseless violence and a coupla gang bangs.

The Rebel Rousers (1967): aka *The Rebel Warriors.* A wild-eyed Bruce Dern officiates a biker wedding ceremony, reading from a greasy Harley shop manual to join a scruffy Jack Nicholson and some kidnapped chick in everlasting stupidity.

The Devil's Angels (1967): These bros are in dire need of a road map. They're looking for Butch Cassidy's "Hole-In-The-Wall" hideout, where they can "be free and love each other." "Rosemary's Boo-Boo" star, John Cassavettes, plays the Den Mother.

The Savage Seven (1968): Bikers vs. Indians. *Dances With Wolves* it ain't. Penny Marshall of "Laverne & Squirrly" fame plays a kosher Injun. Gather the choppers up in a circle there, Mongo!

Angels From Hell (1968): Sadistic violence, mamas, hippies, the fuzz, a G-rated orgy, bad acid trips, warm beer…oh wow, man.

The Black Angel (1968): aka *Black Bikers From Hell.* The lead character, Chainer, carries a 10-pound chain on his belt. The exciting (yawn) bike chase sequences will inspire you to sell your VCR. Check out the mid-'60s choppers. The cops are so poor in this film that they can't afford patches for their uniforms or insignia for their squad car.

She Devils On Wheels (1968): All-female gang putters around on their menstrual cycles and prays to Gloria Swineham that the wind doesn't mess up their beehive hair-dos.

Girl On A Motorcycle (1968, British): aka *Naked Under Leather.* Mick Jagger's ex-ol' lady Marianne Faithful is a femme fatale who rides a '68 Electra Glide. Yep, she gets nekkid. The shapely Miss Faithful's stunt double looks suspiciously like a dude.

Run Angel, Run (1969): Muscular bad-ass biker William Smith (no, not that beanpole bozo from "The Fresh Stench Of Belched Air") snitched on his club members and is pictured on the cover of "Like" magazine. His bros are out for blood, and Angel runs. Twangy Tammy Wynette theme song.

The Angry Breed (1969): Stars *Hawaii 5-O's* James "Danno" McArthur as a powercrazed, neo-Nazi who wears an S.S. uniform and rides a little Honda. Some pretty girls in bikinis, breasts that almost get fondled, an LSD freak-out scene—along with illegal biker debauchery. Book 'em, Danno.

Hells Belles (1969): Biker gang movie veterans Adam Rourke and Jeremy Slate square off for the final showdown. A moto-cross racin' cowboy wins a new custom Triumph race bike, which promptly gets ripped off. So now the cowpoke hasta saddle up and track these thievin' varmints down. It's frontier justice and gas tanks that never run empty.

Bigfoot (1969): Even the great character actor, John Carradine, can't save this drowning turkey. Freshly scrubbed college kids ride through the woods on stock ring-ding Yamaha-ha 250s and encounter a rubber-faced creature that looks like Geraldo Rivera.

C.C. & Company (1970): aka *Chrome Hearts*. Starring Broadway Joe Namath, Ann Margaret, and William Smith. Big budget, blooper-filled biker exploitation gang-banger. Good opening scene. Great theme song.

Angels Die Hard (1970): Even in death, bikers can still get it up. More Neanderthal gang shit, a stupid plot, moronic dialogue, and dumb ending.

Black Angels (1970): According to author Mike Seate, "This was sort of a cross between *Superfly* and *Hells Angels On Wheels*; it offended everyone equally."

The Losers (1970): Biker commando raiding party takes on Vietnam rescue mission 15 years before the *Rambo* flicks and his superhuman exploits. Obviously based upon the 1966 letter that Sonny Barger sent to Lyndon Johnson, volunteering the Hells Angels MC for military service in Vietnam.

The Naked Angels (1970): Swaggering, guffawing biker gang members with poor oral hygiene spit big mucoid "luggies" in each other's beers… and they drink up! They ride, rumble, and ream the mamas.

Angel Unchained (1970): Features Tyne Daly from TV's obnoxious bulldyke cop show "Skagney & Gaycey" as a somewhat flabby flower child. Chain-swinging macho bikers team up with flower-sniffing vegetarian hippies to battle troublesome rednecks. "All we are saaaay-ing…is give peace a chance."

Chrome & Hot Leather (1971): Genghis Khan–type barbarian bikers on Harley choppers get hunted down like dogs by vengeful Vietnam vet and his buddies who ride lightweight Japanese dirt bikes.

The Hard Ride (1971): No, it's not a porno flick. The real star of this movie is "Baby," a super radical and classy 1936 Knucklehead chopper. The plot, well, things kinda go downhill from there.

Werewolves On Wheels (1971): This movie is much better than the hokey-sounding title implies. The "Devil's Advocate" MC encounters an eerie Satanic cult hideaway, and the devil worshipers want to set up ol' Lucifer on a blind date with a hot biker babe!

The Peace Killers (1971): The Age of Aquarius, peace, love beads, flowers, incense, peppermints, naked hippie chicks, evil bikers, violent torture, and death. Bummer, man.

Psychomania (1971, British): Limey Triumph riders kiss frogs and commit suicide so they can return as "Living Dead" biker zombies. 'Bout half-way through, you'll wish this movie would croak like the damned frogs.

Savage Abduction (1971): Bikers with a lower I.Q. than Gomer Pyle, kidnapping, bondage, flabby cleavage, clenching female buttocks, face slapping and generally less than half of the raunchy perversion and raw human sewage that you'd find watching "Sicki Lake" or that air-headed nitwit "Sally-Messy Daffy-as-hell."

On Any Sunday (1971, documentary): Highly recommended. No Hollywood bikesploitation bullshit in this one. An interesting, serious, funny, and fast-paced look at various types of motorcycle sports. Steve McQueen rides the trails with champion racers Malcomb Smith and Mert Lawwill.

Evel Knievel (1971): Before the hot air filled stuntman became an Officially-licensed Harley Hero, and before he beat the crap outta his business partner with a baseball bat, the daredevil Knievel was portrayed by George Hamilton. Not too bad.

The Jesus Trip (1971): This is what happens when you give cameras and film to a buncha incompetent lamebrains. The writer and director of this ignorant disaster seems to be just as confused as the befuddled actors, who ride around in a fog of stupidity in search of a plot.

Satan's Sadists (1971): Bikers kill and torture 'cause they ain't got nuthin' else better to do. Hollywood biker's "things to do today" list: 1) Tune-up Harley, 2) Buy beer, 3) Kill five innocent people.

Angels, Hard As They Come (1972): It's bikers vs. bikers in a desert hippie commune. Biker Scott Glenn tries to find *The Right Stuff*, but whiny hippie Gary Busey tries not to fall down and hit his head. "Oh, that'll be the day, when you make me cry-yi…"

Electra-Glide In Blue (1973): Robert Blake stars as a misfit motorcycle cop who wants to trade in his leather jacket and helmet for a detective's suit and Stetson hat. An above-average motorcycle movie. Recommended.

HEX (1973): aka *The Shrieking*. A very unusual tale, set in the rapidly disappearing Western frontier in 1919. Just after World War I, wandering bikers on vintage machines encounter two very beautiful but dangerous witches. Nice, authentic antique bikes from the Bud Ekins collection.

Freedom R.I.P. (1976): aka *The Northville Cemetery Massacre* or *Harley's Angels*. Stars a real biker club, the Scorpions MC from Detroit. Music score by ex-Monkee Michael Nesmith. One of the better, more realistic gang films.

Hog Wild (1981, Canadian): Somewhat silly, though fast paced. The biker gang leader does a cornball take-off on Marlon Brando's *Wild One* mush-mouthed mumbling. This gets old real fast, but the movie is a fairly well done biker action / comedy.

Return Of The Rebels (1981, made for TV): Don Murray reunites his old bike club, "The Eagle Rock Rebels," to fight some snot-nosed Generation Brand-X teen punks who are terrorizing resort owner Barbara Eden. Sure, these old bikers are as clean as a *Leave It To Beaver* episode, but don'tcha get a bit tired of the usual TV and movie biker format of rape, pillage, torture and kill?

The Loveless (1981): A really offbeat story about a small group of bikers riding to Daytona Beach in either 1959 or maybe 1960. The delinquent scooter jockeys flagrantly display a Beavis & Butthead mentality intermingled with the constantly horny, macho, crotch thrusting sexual prowess of Joey Buttafuoco.

Hells Angels Forever (1983, documentary): Ten years in the making, this well-done film was actually put together by members of the Hells Angels MC. Good counterpunch to the endless parade of Hollywood biker gang movies that attempted to exploit the club's name.

Hellriders (1985): A thoughtful, though braindead biker, wearing a rebel helmet, pulls out his dangler while standing on the roof of Tina Louise's car, and gives her dusty windshield a urine wash of recycled beer suds. Thus, the tone is set for this moronic movie. Adam "Batman" West tried to revive his stumbling career in this third-rate groaner.

Masters of Menace (1990): *Animal House* on Harleys. Mucho funny.

Cycle Sluts in Zombie Town (1991): aka *Chopper Chicks in Zombie Town*. An angry, snarling lesbo leads her panty-raiding dykes-on-bikes group of pathetic gang-ettes into a small desert mining town polluted with shuffling zombies that walk like Michael Jackson after a night out with the boys. This movie ain't no "Thriller"; it needs a proper burial.

The Blue Desert (1991): A quirky murder mystery, romance story involving a love triangle between a lone biker, his new girlfriend, and the cop who wants to possess exclusive "drilling rights" in this lusty melodrama.

Stone Cold (1991): Pro football washout Brian Bozworth began and ended his movie career with this rabid, anti-biker truckload of stereotype bullshit. Most likely, the biggest budget biker movie ever. Too bad the asshole writer and producers had to go the "let's kill all the bikers" route. A more appropriate title would have been "Stoned Clod."

Harley-Davidson and the Marlboro Man (1991): This is more like it. Yet another big-budget biker movie for 1991, but the bikers are the good guys. Kind of a *Butch Cassidy and the Sundance Kid* remake with Harleys. Mickey Rourke rides a really unique-looking Evo.

Born To Ride (1991): 1939 Kentucky, three years before America enters WWII, U.S. Army cavalryman retire their horses and begin training aboard Harley WLA flatheads. A secret undercover mission in Nazi-occupied territory sets up the plot for bikin' action.

Roadside Prophets (1992): A very cerebral type of biker road movie. Two mismatched bikers hit the open road in a long quest to lay to rest the ashes of a dead bro. No funeral urns for this bro, as the ashes are righteously stashed in a Harley's fatbob gas tank! An interesting and unusual biker movie.

Beyond the Law (1992): Charlie Sheen stars as an undercover narc who infiltrates yet another one of them evil biker gangs. During his instant coffee biker indoctrination, he magically transforms an old and rusty and dusty junk pile of Panhead motor parts and rigid frame into a sparkling, shiny new Evo Softail. Meanwhile, he romances Linda Fiorentino, gets into some fights and drug deals, and tries to decide whether he wants to be a cop or a biker.

Running Cool (1993): Not to be confused with *Cool Runnings*, which was also a 1993 movie, about a buncha Jamaican bobsled bozos. *Running Cool* is one of the better, more realistic, and well-written biker movies. Easy to find. Highly recommended.

BIKER MOVIES SHACK OF SHAME: THE GROANER BIN

The Pink Angels (1971): Without a doubt, the worst biker movie ever made. A limp-wristed group of transvestite bikers swish and sway their way across the Southwest in

"Without a doubt, the worst biker movie ever made."

military-styled BMWs with sidecars loaded with their "gay apparel."

Sweet Savior (1971): aka *The Love Thrill Murders*. A Charlie Mansion imitator on a stock Triumph. Maximum groaner.

Bury Me An Angel (1975): This movie is about as exciting as watching a sick cat puke up a furball in your driveway.

Chapter 9

The Lifestyle in High-Definition

Mainstream Mania—
from Star Power to Stuffed Toys

Years ago you wanted to kill us
Now you want to be one of us

—T-shirt commentary

A few dozen of us were riding up to the famous House of Blues in Hollywood; right in the heart of the Sunset Strip. The stage there has been rocked, shaken, and souled-out by the likes of Eric Clapton, John Lee Hooker, Etta James, Joe Cocker, James Brown, LL Cool J, and Deep Purple, along with hundreds more of the best singers, slingers, screamers, and players in the business.

Tonight was somewhat different.

Onstage were the Teutuls.

Orange County Choppers' Teutuls. *American Chopper's* Teutuls. Paul Sr. and Paul Jr.

The scene brought back some of those glitz vs. grit memories; like when the '60s' Bay Area hipsters (counter-culture heroes like Ken Kesey—author of *One Flew Over the Cuckoo's Nest*—and his "Merry Pranksters") began to overlap social circles with the Hells Angels.

But weird memories aside, this *was* a party and it *was* the House of Blues—so what the hell? Sit back and eat, drink, and enjoy the evening on someone else's dime.

That "someone else" was TLC—The Learning Channel—celebrating and publicizing the switchover of the Teutuls' mega-hit show to TLC, from its original home at Discovery Channel.

Along with my shaky flashbacks, it felt equally shaky to consider that this high-level, big-budget splash was representative of the fourth major era in the evolution of the American Biker: The Star-Power Years. An age of custom-cycle celebrity, powered by cable TV and satellite saturation. Our lifestyle in high-definition.

WWII gave us the birth and bobbers. The next decades gave us a toughened image and choppers. The Vietnam years dramatically reinforced the reasons for this entire brotherhood. Now *this* era's tech-pushed customs and twenty-first-century TV blitz has made the lifestyle—or at least *portions* of it—big business.

Real big business.

Generally, big business is synonymous with the mainstream—and mainstream *generally* means accepted.

Generally.

That's what makes Phase Four a time to observe with wonder, humor, and a certain degree of terror.

After all these years of rebellion, envy, fear, and exploitation; could the American Biker possibly even *remotely* roll into "mainstream acceptance"?

The entertainment draw of the biker lifestyle has been there since the beginning. It always will be. But this isn't just a modern extension of what the media (and their movies and their books and their other outlets) did in the past.

This is so much more.

In a way it's like toying with giant gorillas: sitting down at the baby grand with Mighty Joe Young, or going to the theater with King Kong. Some beasts may *seem* like they'll adapt well to domestication, but whether they'll ever really curl up in your lap and purr is another story.

One reason this era has seen such an enormous new public recognition of the American Biker is that the opportunities for entertainment-gratification are so much more available in this quick-modern multimedia world.

And the American Biker never fails to gratify—or entertain. The excitement and the adventures are constant and infinite. The appeal is a drug.

And now the technology is there to serve it up 24/7. Right in your own living room.

As new-century publicity kicked in, custom motorcycles became recognized as works of art by an ever-growing audience. With the emotional magnetism of the lifestyle surrounding the "art," artistic and savvy custom bike builders became superstars.

Of course, artists have been creating with metal and paint since this all started. But what the new century also provided is much more to work with than what rolled off the factory assembly lines.

Monster V-twins—specialized Harley-like engines, from companies like RevTech, S&S, and Berry Wardlaw's Accurate Engineering—came together to implant brand new hearts into the now-bionic anatomy of the custom motorcycle. High-tech aftermarket billet, powder-coated, NASA-tolerance *everything* replaced the old shuffling "parts is parts" foundation.

Still, not everyone can carve The Pietà out of a block of marble, and not everyone can piece together a custom chopper—even with the *best* of parts. But *some* can. And people who see that kind of talent like to experience it, worship it.

Names like Arlen Ness and Ron Simms were already well-known in *our* circles—but America and pretty much the entire universe was about to meet the new kids in a "monster" way.

Keith Ball—former *Easyriders* Editor-in-Chief, Sturgis Hall of Famer, and head of Bikernet.com—describes the genesis of Phase Four of the American Biker evolution. And the talented, insightful guy who rolled with it:

Motorcycle Mania and Hugh King:
The Man Who Rode Custom Bikes onto Television
by Keith Randall Ball

What hit the American motorcycle industry like straight pipes and tire-sizzling burnouts at four o'clock in the morning? Television, in the form of Motorcycle Mania 1 *and* 2.

The introduction of chopper-building skills and rebel attitude, unleashed in broadband to citizens all over the country, rocked the biker world. Then chopper heaven in the form of biker build-offs struck for Round Two.

Who was responsible for this tsunami-boon to our lifestyle? It was Hugh King, the producer / director / writer and Editor-at-Large of Original Productions.

Hugh felt the crisp freedom and wild wanton wickedness of the chopper industry in 1947, as a Milwaukee youngster with his nose pressed against his living room window. An older neighborhood wildman, Billy Brody, screamed down the street on a bobbed '46 Indian Chief. He tore across Hugh's folks' lawn and slid to a stop on the front porch, ignoring the driveway and garage alongside the house.

That scene, on a common, generally serene oak-shrouded street, was emblazoned in Hugh's expanding creative mind for years to come. In fact, he added a wild black-and-white scene of a biker burning into a bar to his documentary résumé, while living off grants and making social-action films.

In 1989, Hugh hauled ass to California and scrambled for a position cutting Easyriders *Home Videos.*

Through the reams of vast, rough-shot motorcycle footage, he learned the Harley / biker industry, from event coverage to land speed record attempts. Hired by Original Productions, he produced reality shows.

Then one fateful day, while warm California rays graced his small Original Productions office, Tom Beers, his boss, wandered in.

"Discovery Channel called," Beers said. "They want a feature on the custom motorcycle industry. You've experienced the motorcycle world. It's your assignment."

Since the offices were located in Burbank, California, Hugh investigated valley shops and called motorcycle magazine editors. A mystery connection was made, and an old crooked finger pointed toward West Coast Choppers.

"And the rest is history," says Hugh. "Discovery didn't billboard the first Motorcycle Mania episode; they only mentioned it a half-hour before it aired. But by 'Act Four,' they knew we had hit a home run."

By Motorcycle Mania 2, Jesse James was a star.

"Viewers wanted to talk to him," Hugh says of the rapidly growing audience. "We filmed it for the average Joe and sensed immediately that people wanted to reach out and touch tools. There was a deep longing for the ability to make something out of nothing."

Jesse smacked a cord in young American viewers using a ball-peen hammer against a flat sheet of aluminum. Fans witnessed pure raw alloy shaped into sleek gas tanks.

"The footage of metal being annealed was graphically inspiring," Hugh says.

At that stage, King was the show's producer, director, writer, and editor (Tom Beers was the executive producer). Discovery was rocked and wanted more, so Hugh directed the first four Monster Garage segments and then kicked off the Build-Off series.

"We shot [Roger] Bourget versus Billy Lane and Discovery ordered three more," Hugh said. "It was another grand slam."

Life kicked into high gear for Hugh, and again Original Productions was approached by Discovery Channel to make Motorcycle Mania 3, subtitled "Jesse James Rides Again," starring Jesse James and featuring his buddy, Kid Rock.

Jesse had worked with wheelwright Fay Butler in Massachusetts to learn the intricacies of copper fabricating. Fay manipulates old yoders [sheet metal shaping implements] like an artist's brush, shaping copper. Yoders were used in WWII to fashion sheets of metal for fighter fuselages and wings. Jesse and Fay worked together to shape the Copper Chopper gas tank.

The Motorcycle Mania 3 *filming endeavor raised the bar for Hugh.*

"I had the opportunity to work with high-def film and top quality camera equipment," he says. "We got to use the highest standard automobile commercial equipment like a Shot Maker and Chapman cranes for dramatic rolling angles."

Hugh's life hit overdrive as he filmed the building of the Copper Chopper for Jesse and the American Bad Ass chopper for Kid Rock. Then they hit it to Mexico.

"Nothing went according to plan," Hugh said. "We changed the itinerary constantly. The people of Mexico were terrific as we shot from El Paso, Texas, and Juarez, Mexico— in 125 degrees—through 350 miles due south to Chihuahua."

Hugh filmed spectacular footage of the two riders passing smoldering sand dunes; sweeping vistas; and lumbering iguanas crossing the rugged roads toward Copper Canyon.

"We suspected trouble from Federales," *Hugh said, "but Jesse and the Kid befriended the law. They stood alongside the smoldering highway and blasted sand dunes with the cops' weapons."*

Having the time of their lives, they rode into Chihuahua, a growing city, and searched through the old market place. Riding west, they climbed six thousand feet to Copper Canyon—a canyon six times longer than the Grand Canyon—in the middle of the Sierra Madres. They slept in a small village on the lip of the gorge, in a town of sixty-five.

Jesse and the Kid accomplished their goal of escaping fame and fortune as they continued west toward the coast over torturous curved roads, through blinding lightning storms, and over a territory where the only vocation is hijacking.

"We slept in the camera van," Hugh said, "since there was no place to stay until we reached the white sand beach on the Sea of Cortez. It was a transcendental experience."

Hugh invested a year and a half into Motorcycle Mania 3
while directing biker build-offs with Billy Lane, Dave Perewitz,
Roger Bourget, Paul Yaffe, Indian Larry, Yank Young, Chica,
Eddie Trotta, Russ Mitchell, and Arlen and Cory Ness.

"Choppers have turned my life upside down," Hugh said.

Although the family man doesn't own a bike, he rides
constantly.

"I'll jump on anything the builders let me straddle,"
Hugh said, the motorcycle mania fever boiling in his gaze.

At sixty-five, Hugh ramped into an all-time high with
custom bikes. He's riding it for all it's worth—and the entire
industry benefits.

—K. Randall Ball

Motorcycle Mania; American Chopper; Monster Garage; the various
"build-off" shows; the "experimental" Speed Channel show, *Texas Hardtails*
("The somewhat true, totally unreal, life and twisted times of Rick
Fairless"); and many others have laid some big-ass smoking patches
of this lifestyle's rubber right into the center pixels of viewers' big-ass
plasma TVs, entering their homes with the same ease as *Dancing With
the Stars* and reruns of *Three's Company*. This ease-of-entry may not
exactly mean mainstream *acceptance* of bikers; but our presence sure as
hell has created a new jolt of recognition—and maybe even *respect*.

The motorcycle builders for reality productions are
followed around by cameras during their work and occasionally
in their private life, too. In terms of entertainment value, the
individual seasons are not inferior to conventional TV series.
Of a somewhat different kind is the "Great Biker Build-Off,"
also a very successful format on Discovery Channel. 2006 saw
the fifth season of this blockbuster. Two motorcycle builders
have a competition to create a machine in front of rolling

cameras. The audience decides on the winner at one of the great American Biker meetings. From the ranks of Build-Off participants, Billy Lane and Indian Larry, who had a fatal accident in 2004, gained a status that can definitely be compared to that of rock stars.

—Michael Stein;
Born to Be Wild: Harleys, Bikers & Music for Easy Riders

Back in the dark ages you had to really make an effort to see or savor "biker stuff." You had to go to movies or obtain a copy of *Colors*, *Big Bike*, or *Easyriders*; the latter two usually found on a liquor store magazine rack, not too far removed from embarrassing purchases like *Jugs* and *Gent*.

Today there's plenty of biker stuff just a safe and clean channel-surf away, or in a quick-grab at the local video store on the way home. People find it—and become hooked on it—sometimes by accident. It was *never* a viewing "accident" to leave the house, buy a ticket, and park or sit with strangers to satisfy a need by watching *Savages from Hell* or *Girls from Thunder Strip*.

Michael Stein was correct in comparing the new custom builders' status "to that of rock stars." And bikers certainly have more recognition now—at least in the sense of people realizing that we indeed exist outside of dark and violent shadows, and that many of us are even talented artists who can slide into mainstream entertainment venues and even become successful.

Even "scholars" have taken note:

> *Perhaps an additional period is unfolding in the outlaw motorcycle club subculture...Future research may reveal that certain members of the subculture seem to have attained something of an iconic status. American society may well regard members of the Hells Angels MC more as pulp*

fiction characters than as credible menaces to society. Indeed, the context in which many have come to know members of the subculture is that of cable television, with the History Channel, Discovery Channel, and The Learning Channel all cashing in on the appeal of outlaw biker documentaries, and with members of the Hells Angels MC appearing on television shows such as the Discovery Channel's popular series Monster Garage. *While certainly not all members of one-percent motorcycle clubs are talented mechanics and artisans, perhaps certain members of one-percent clubs are using these new media as venues to broadcast a more positive image of what it means to be an outlaw biker, or more specifically a one percenter. The image portrayed in cable television shows like* Monster Garage *is not that of a criminal element; indeed, the image is that of a craftsman. Whereas media coverage of the 1960s can be interpreted as casting an image of outlaw motorcycle clubs as destructive forces in society, certain outlets of modern mass media seem willing to broadcast an image that is very much that of creative individuals. And so the evolution of the outlaw motorcycle club subculture continues to unfold.*

—William L. Dulaney;
"A Brief History of 'Outlaw' Motorcycle Clubs,"
International Journal of Motorcycle Studies, November 2005

Yet *another* kind of recognition adds heat to this new-age commercial blast. And this one *isn't* new; it's been here since the beginning. It's the continuing recognition that this lifestyle is very, very special.

And now it's a recognition by an unbelievably vast, '58-Buick-sized audience.

Watching Jesse James and Kid Rock riding through the danger and the heat of Mexico, shooting and scooting along some serious badlands on some serious custom choppers, *says* something. Watching Indian Larry live—and die—for this way of life *says* something. Watching men and women put together a rolling, roaring work of art and then ride the thing a couple of thousand miles to Sturgis or Daytona *says* something. Watching the heartfelt, tear-filled construction of a bike that pays tribute to one of this lifestyle's or this country's heroes *says* something.

The entire way the American Biker lives says so much.

And it's pretty damn apparent that more and more people want to listen and to see. And maybe even to learn.

Maybe.

It kind of fractures me, you know, that there are bikes and bikers all over TV anymore. You got all the custom builders; you got all the shows on those history channels about the clubs and stuff. People love it. They watch the stuff like crazy. We're bigger than ever in the public eye. But does it translate into acceptance; into respect?

When things come up on their local ballots like the helmet law or new restrictions on our bikes, are people going to remember just how damn entertaining we are and vote in favor of the freedom they seem to admire so much in us? Or are they going to side with the mothering politicians who want our entire society sealed up inside a gun-free, smoke-free, smog-free, danger-free, noise-free, drink responsibly, Ziplocked, smiley-faced world?

When they're around club guys—3-piece patches—are they still going to sneak their cell phones into their pockets, getting ready to speed-dial 911 as soon as the trouble they just know is gonna come starts?

True story...I was out last weekend with the ol' lady. We took a ride, wound up stopping at this park, and decided to just take a walk. Well, it was a nice day, lots of families with lots of kids. We were walking by this one family, and the parents didn't exactly look like what most people would call bikers; but the kids were playing with these fuzzy stuffed dolls. I did a double-take. These weren't little rabbits or kittens or something; hell, they weren't even Tickle Me Elmos! No! They were stuffed versions of the Teutuls! Little furry Paul Sr. and Paul Jr.—and damned if Mikey wasn't there, too!

Now, I've seen the OCC t-shirts and hats and stuff all over the place. They sell it in just about every truck and travel stop I've been to from coast to coast; it's as normal as CB radios and road atlases. Jesse's iron-cross decals and shirts are everywhere, too.

And now Jesse has yet another TV series and was even on that stupid Donald Trump show! Plus, he's all over the supermarket tabloid rags with all that Sandra Bullock stuff.

And get this: I've even seen trading cards—you know, bubble gum cards as we used to call them—of custom bike builders. Jesus, when I was a kid you'd be out with your buddies haggling over things like trading one Manny Mota and one Carl Yastrzemski for one old Mickey Mantle. Now, I guess you probably hear: "Hey, how about

a Ron Simms for an Arlen Ness, straight up?" And these cards are actually pretty cool...mostly photos by Michael Lichter.

The custom builders and their shows have really put us on the map again, sure. But I guess the jury's still out as to what the bottom line will be in terms of acceptance and respect.

Whenever I do start thinking that this "new age" is leading to bigger and better days, something always happens to bring me back down to earth—to convince me that the more things change the more they stay the same.

The latest jolt came just the other night. My ol' lady somehow talked me into renting the movie Wild Hogs*—"just for kicks." Now, I had heard about this thing a few years back, but purposely didn't go to see it. I was pretty sure I knew what was coming…I mean, you don't have to actually fall off the roof to know it's gonna hurt.*

From the time we slid that DVD into the player, my mind was reeling. I kept thinking that while we were watching this, *somewhere on cable, someone else was watching reruns of* American Chopper *or* Gangland *or one of the other shows like that, just wishing they could be like* us.

Meantime, I'm watching just another piece of pure shit that portrays us exactly how we've always been portrayed.

The fucking biker "gang" was a bunch of creeps who pour beer and food on some poor suffering ethnic townspeople and steal motorcycles. We saw that kind of shit forty years ago. The "gang" takes over the town. We saw that kind of shit fifty years ago. The "gang" included at least one complete clown-imbecile. That's been done to death too.

Acceptance and respect? Not yet, I guess.

—A bit of philosophy from ".357";
Hollister, California, during the non-event of 2010

Maybe the *commercial* success of this lifestyle just translates into it all being Bigger. *More* people wanting to be us; *more* people looking at us; *more* people wanting to see what we do.

And a *much* bigger dose of fear and envy.

Is the American Biker a Character We Play or Is It Really Who We Are?

by Robert Patrick,
Actor and American Biker;
Hollywood, CA

From the time we're born, life becomes our journey—*how* we live becomes our road.

Who *is* the American Biker and what does he represent?

To those of us who ride, it's almost beyond comprehension to describe. How do you articulate a feeling, an essence, a level of living that can only be experienced?

Is the American Biker a character we play or is it really who we are? The cowboy from our youth, the romantic figure on his steed heading off for adventure, the lone solitary figure cutting a path through the night to some clandestine meeting with a brother?

To the American Biker, who we are is so often determined by *what* we ride, *who* we ride with, and *how* we ride. The motorcycle stops being a machine; it becomes a part of us.

We crisscross this God-given, great country. We go as far as we want and experience this land as deeply as we want.

Few have experiences like we have.

So often we are asked: "Where are you going?"

So often the answer is: "I'll know when I get there!"

Live free and ride!

Chapter 10

Blacks on Bikes

Buffalo Soldiers &
The Tale of the Racist T-Shirt

When you talk of the outlaw bikers
you automatically think of "them crazy white boys"
doing what a lot of folk wish they could do:
Live life like you want to, and fuck you and your rules.
Well, guess what?
There were some crazy Black bikers who felt the same way
and didn't give a fuck.
Thus was born The Black Outlaw Bikers!

—The Chosen Few MC,
Los Angeles, CA

Legal segregation isn't something of ancient history. Laws prohibiting interracial marriage; demanding separate schools, restaurants, and toilets for "colored" people; and other government-endorsed nooses around the neck of freedom permeated 1940s, '50s, and even '60s, America—eras in which a lot of us grew up.

231

Latter-day Jim Crow laws loop-holed Lincoln's Emancipation Proclamation, allowing bigoted business-as-usual to fill up the back of the bus for nearly a hundred years after slavery and the Civil War had officially ended. Not until the Civil Rights Act of 1964 and 1965's Voting Rights Act were the final murderous remains of *legally* sanctioned "separate but equal" segregation effectively buried.

Certain loops in the noose took even longer to unravel.

Up until November of *1994*, "White and colored persons shall not be taught in the same school" remained an official—albeit unenforced—part of West Virginia's State Constitution.

Regardless of actual hard laws on the books, human behavior *always* seems to exhibit a certain "birds of a feather" mentality. In the '60s and '70s, when government attempts to integrate schools through forced busing polarized the nation, the term "de facto" became a nightly news buzzword.

De facto: "Something generally accepted or agreed to without any formal decision in its favor."

Like so many parts of life that have evolved in America—from neighborhoods to social clubs to churches to circles of friends to everything in between—the biker culture was originally one of *de facto* segregation.

To a debatable extent it still is.

The motorcycle and the culture accompanying it cuts through so much in the way of differences; but it is not the *perfect* social tool.

As white American veterans made headlines in '47 and became recognized as pioneers of the biker culture, they *did* have counterparts in the shadows.

America had Black war heroes, Black motorcycle riders, *and* Black motorcycle clubs. And California was again the epicenter of it all.

I ain't got but one life to live.
I said I'd give it up for three things:
my family, number one...the Dragons, number one...
and for America.
If Uncle Sam asked me to die in the morning for him,
I'd die for America.
That's from my heart. I believe that.
And when I die, I want to die riding a Harley-Davidson.

—Tobie Gene Levingston,
President, East Bay Dragons MC;
Interviewed in *Glory Road*

In the mid- to late-1950s, the nattily dressed and precisely regimented all-Black riding clubs like the Star Riders, Berkeley Tigers, and Bay View Rockets gave way to real-deal Black MCs like James "Heavy" Evans' Rattlers in 1955 and Tobie Gene's own East Bay Dragons. The Dragons were originally a car club; transitioning to bikes in 1959 and closely sharing the fast streets of Oakland with Sonny Barger and the Hells Angels Motorcycle Club.

De facto.

Mutual respect? Perhaps. A sharing of the streets, and a common ground of bikes and the lifestyle? Yes. But that didn't translate into a *complete* color-blindness, with everyone diving into a single utopian rainbow pool. There wasn't exactly widespread interracial shuffling, and no one was proposing forced busing from one clubhouse to another.

But Blacks were definitely there. They were a part of this history and a part of this lifestyle.

They still are.

A biker rode up to us one day with a big cigar in his mouth—
one of those "cartoon" kind of cigars that looked like
it was gonna explode any minute.
He had that "long rider" look—
like he regularly rode from state to state.
When he got off his bike he looked at us and proclaimed:
"My Black is Legendary, My Black is Confident,
My Black is Triumphant!"

—"Buttnaked,"
International President, Retired, Pasadena 4 Horsemen MC

August 27, 1973, was long after the early Black riding clubs enjoyed their picnics, precision parades, and proper parties. It was long after the first deep Black MCs flew their proud patches right into the ethnic soul of the American Biker. The impact of all those two-wheeled Jackie Robinsons was strong.

It would get stronger.

During that 1973 summer, Harold O'Field, Percy Jones, Dallas Thibodeaux, Ulysses Wimbush, Wilbert Neal, Ernie Carson, Reggie Banks, Ed Smith, Terrell McKinney, Oscar Wright, George Washington, Gene Buckner, Curtiss Bates, and Roy Everage established the Zodiacs Motorcycle Club in Kansas City, Missouri.

The Zodiacs MC teamed up with the Vultures MC, the Crusaders MC, and various other Black motorcycle clubs a few years later to convene a "Bikers Roundup"—a small indoor event.

The resulting National Bikers Roundup—an annual rally kicked off later that same year—quickly evolved, overflowing to the outdoors and to a different state and venue each time (returning every ten years to KC, as a celebration of its roots).

The National Bikers Roundup (NBR) now stretches out for nearly a week, and it's *big*. Attended by forty to sixty thousand people whose ethnic make-up is predominately Black, the NBR provides yearly proof that the internal biker-need and the mental wind-rush that goes with it has few racial concerns.

And the event *does* receive some publicity and notoriety.

Some.

But where is the inclusion of Blacks in the high-profile motorcycle / biker media the rest of the year?

> *Black motorcyclists are probably the most invisible of all. They're not covered in the mainstream press...the mainstream magazines with high circulation...you'll never see a Black face. There have been no historical journals, either; most of it's just photographs you'll see from someone's uncle or grandfather...You don't see any books on the subject. Martin Dixon's* Brooklyn Kings *is the first photographic journal of Black motorcycling in this country that I've ever seen.*

—Mike Seate;
Interviewed in *American Biker,* the film

Seate was right: Aside from these insighful documentaries, Black motorcyclists are probably the most "invisible population" of all.

Brooklyn Kings: New York City's Black Bikers was released in 2000. Tobie Gene Levingston's *Soul On Bikes: The East Bay Dragons MC and the Black Biker Set* was published three years later.

Guerrilla Docs has given us the insightful film documentaries *Glory Road: The Legacy of the African American Motorcyclist* and *Wheels of Soul.*

And that's pretty much it.

Seate is obviously correct about the broad degree of "invisibility."

But *Brooklyn Kings* is a *very* visible visual trip into a formidable subculture within a subculture. It opens another of those heavy doors in the divine mansion of the American Biker to which there aren't many keys:

> *To enter this world is to leave all vestiges of your past behind. Far behind. Even if only for the hour or two you visit. There exists a Dodge City mentality that pervades many biker clubhouses; only the strong survive. Fuck the world—forever together. Police don't exist. Laws were made to be broken. No one is perfect. Brooklyn Logic again. "Get them before they get you...." "If you're not sure, do it and ask questions later...." "I'd rather be judged by twelve than carried by six...." I've heard them all. Among biker clubs, loyalty is paramount. No one rats out. All things are handled internally. "Justice may be blind, but we're not...."*
>
> —Martin Dixon;
> *Brooklyn Kings: New York City's Black Bikers*

There's not a *lot* of text in Dixon's book, however. A lot of text wasn't necessary. It's a photographic book; a book of images that speak fiercely for themselves. Its structure is very similar to Andrew Shaylor's *Hells Angels Motorcycle Club*—another book thin on words, fat on image. Both books rely on black-and-white photos (Dixon's exclusively, Shaylor's predominately so). Just as Ansel Adams "exposes" us to the raw majesty of *his* subjects without the peripheral distraction of something as inconsequential as color, Dixon and Shaylor do the same.

And that causes a bit of chromatic irony.

The use of black-and-white photos in both books makes the reader oblivious to, yes, black and white.

It's all about the faces.

It's all about The Image.

True, the faces in *Brooklyn Kings* are Black. The faces in *Hells Angels Motorcycle Club* are white (they are also primarily European, as Shaylor focused his work on British and other Euro HAMC chapter members). But they are universal in what they represent. Black, white, global, archival—even when photos are included of import bikes (as in *Brooklyn Kings*), or European bikers, the heritage and imprint of the American Biker holds a tight grip.

Cars do not discriminate when they run over your ass!

—"P. Wee,"
Defiant Ones MC;
Interviewed in *Glory Road*

But people do.

The following is an historical account of The Chosen Few Motorcycle Club, as laid down by the club itself. It's much more than a club history; it's a statement.

The History of the Chosen Few Motorcycle Club

The Chosen Few MC started around 1959 in Los Angeles, California. The founding members were: Lionel, Lil' Frank, Roger, Hawk, Slim, Shirly Bates, and Champ. These brothers all rode full-dress Harleys and chopped dressers.

The purpose of the club was to ride and enjoy the new Black biker set in Los Angeles and Oakland, California.

Two names were placed on the table as to what the club was going to be called. The Patriots of Iron & Steel was one, The Chosen Few the other. After choosing the latter, The Chosen Few MC was born.

The original patch was black and white. After awhile it was changed to red and white: an oval sea of "red blood" with white human crossed bones in the center and white letters saying "Chosen Few" arched across the top of the cross.

The 1960s was a hell of a time; with the civil rights movement; the Vietnam War; "flower power"; free love; sex, drugs and rock 'n' roll; and the crazy world of the outlaw bikers.

When you talk of the outlaw bikers you automatically think of "them crazy white boys" doing what a lot of folk wish they could do: Live life like you want to and fuck you and your rules. Well, guess what? There were some crazy Black bikers who felt the same way and didn't give a fuck.

Thus was born the Black Outlaw Bikers!

Clubs like the East Bay Dragons, Rattlers, Outlaw Vagabonds, Defiant Ones; and down south in Los Angeles, The Choppers, Soul Brothers, and, of course, The Chosen Few.

The first white boy to come to The Chosen Few was "White Boy Art." He came around 1960, followed by "White Boy Tom." Soon we started to attract other white outlaw riders who wanted to join us.

The Chosen Few became a multi-racial MC with chapters that were all Black, all white, half white/half Mexican, half Black/half white, all Mexican, and half Mexican and Indian, with a few Asians and one Iranian.

Our "Take None, Give None" 1%er diamond patch was given to us by "69 Jim" who was a five-foot-six radical Mexican. This patch has stood the test of time.

The club may have started out Black, but our white brothers took us head-on into the outlaw biker world. The white clubs knew about The Chosen Few. They knew it was a Black club. Then they saw the white bros flying the same patch as the Blacks.

The shit hit the fan.

A lot of the white clubs called our white brothers "nigger lovers" and said, "You belong to a nigger club." The white brothers didn't give a shit. They fought for their place in the outlaw biker world and flew The Chosen Few colors proudly. The white bros brought a true brotherhood to the club.

The Chosen Few was the first fully integrated outlaw MC.

It became well-known that "in black and white we really had might."

"It's not about the size of the few in the fight; it's about the size of the fight in the few."

"In black and white we really had might," say The Chosen Few.

"Buttnaked" is the retired president of another predominately Black long-lived MC, the Pasadena 4 Horsemen. His is another *statement;* another essential transcending of ethnicity. Another embracing of *the ride:*

Eyes to Ride

by "Buttnaked"

Not too many Black riders had Harley-Davidsons in the late '70s/early '80s. In fact, I knew only one Black rider who had a Harley at that time—and everyone knew him.

I just wanted to ride, so I saved up a little money and got myself a Kawasaki KZ1000. My mom took me to the dealership to purchase the bike. I knew how to ride, but had never ridden on the freeway. I had to get the bike home. With my mom and my little brother watching me from the car, I rode up on the freeway…and stopped. I couldn't move! Then a horn starting blowing at me! I got myself going, and at that point I knew that riding is what I wanted to do.

I would ride with a lot of different people, but one man in particular was a guy called "Spiderman." He stood only about five feet tall. He had a Kawasaki GP1100—the same bike that [movie star and famed martial artist] *Jim Kelly rode. We rode for some time together, and he taught me to take canyon roads at high speeds.*

I didn't see many Black riders until a friend took me out to a club in Pasadena; I met so many Black riders from so many different clubs. But one club stood out to me, because of the unity they had: the Pasadena 4 Horsemen MC.

I loved what their patch stood for.

Some club patches have no real symbolism. Some clubs have no bylaws; members just have a club to ride with. I was looking for a real purpose in riding, and a way to make a difference.

With the Pasadena 4 Horsemen I rode to the Roundups in Kansas, Texas, Arkansas, Colorado, Utah, and Fresno, California. Even with the extra burden in certain areas of being Black riders, we did all these rides on bikes—no trailers. We rode with anyone going the same direction. There was no difference to us with color.

"Buttnaked" has tried to change people's stereotypes about motorcycle clubs—especially Black ones.

When I was prospecting the club, my sponsor's name was "69"—a very tall brother. We talked about a lot of stuff and a lot of the changes made to the club.

Just the other day, "K-Nine" reminded me of a quote I told him years ago: "I have more miles backing up to a curb than most bikers have moving forward." I wanted to be part of a club that always moved forward as a unit.

I told one guy that when I came into the club, I thought it was only for Blacks. But then I got the breakdown of the patch: Red for bloodshed from fallen brothers and sisters. Black for no color boundaries. Yellow for California, "The Golden State." White for the purity of our spirit that will shine through, even after death. The two bikes in the patch represent both genders, and the chains represent bondage.

I look back at twenty-five years of riding with the Pasadena 4 Horsemen:

In December of 1990, I became President; I went on to be the longest-running President in Pasadena 4 Horsemen history.

I also became the club's International President.

When I assumed that office, I looked at K-Nine and "TZ"—two true riders who have the same "eyes to ride" that I have—and said, "I wish for all bikers to have a safe journey; but if you want to ride with me you have to be ready: you will have to be five miles ahead of me, because I'm already there— in a pack or solo."

I continued my desire to move the club forward by giving back to my community—by attending more charity events and producing our own.

I'm trying to change the stereotypes that people have about motorcycle clubs—especially Black ones.

Maybe someday when we ride up in a pack or solo, we won't get that look like trouble just rolled into town.

—Buttnaked,
International President, Retired, Pasadena 4 Horsemen MC

A century and a half ago, this country had horsemen of a different type. Emerging from the Civil War, the segregated Black military forces of the 9th and 10th Cavalry, along with the 24th and 25th Infantry Divisions of the United States Army, evolved into the proud and tough persona of the Buffalo Soldier: a persona that mirrors America's Black bikers in appearance, attitude, and the always-prevalent appreciation of freedom.

And in the will to stand up for what's right.

While the name "Buffalo Soldiers" has since been adopted by a well-known motorcycle club, the sure, walking-tall spirit of the original Buffalo Soldiers is essentially shared by *all* Black bikers.

Bob Marley immortalized the Old West's Buffalo Soldiers in one of his most passionate tunes. One that has a message and some thought-burning social commentary that just *might* finally be getting through.

At least in some circles.

At least to an extent.

Primarily, the most discrimination we find is not for color;
it's for the bike…the type of bike you ride.
The majority of bikers really don't care what color you are,
it's just what bike you ride.

—Buck Jenkins;
Interviewed in *Glory Road*

True.

But those circles that *have* expanded to where skin color is heavily eclipsed by whether or not you're riding an import have pretty much ended their widening there.

Most bikers today regard the *overall* brotherhood as something open for all to enjoy. Most are genuinely happy to share this lifestyle in a *broad* sense. But your odds of finding integrated clubs, groups, and gatherings with *truly* balanced mixed-memberships are slim to say the least.

You may see *some* whites in the mostly Black clubs and *some* Blacks in the mostly white clubs. *Some* whites attend mostly Black events and *some* Blacks attend mostly white events.

The reality is that we bikers do live in the same *de facto* world as everyone else—a world that seems to still be searching for another of Marley's passions: "Redemption."

At the annual Daytona Bike Week, the area along Second Avenue has long been considered "Black Daytona"—a *de facto* little corner of the rally that sprang up decades ago.

This area's growth in popularity and its impact as a major aspect of Bike Week may mark an evolution: when a "separation" like this becomes more of an enjoyable *tradition* than an accepted *necessity*.

> *I've talked with some of the old-time white bikers who have told me that the "Black Daytona"...reflects what Daytona had been like before the commercialization of the 1980s and '90s.*
>
> *It was a family gathering. You could take your kids there and not have to worry about them seeing naked coleslaw wrestling. There wasn't a lot of profanity. There wasn't a lot of violence. There wasn't a whole lot of drunkenness...They've combined in this little four-block area just a sense of family that a lot of the Black motorcycle clubs have.*
>
> *I think that—because they're a subculture within a subculture—people tend to be very, very close. If you ride into town and you're a Black motorcyclist, and you see another Black guy on a bike, usually he'll offer you a place to stay if you need it. And that's indicative of all motorcyclists, to an extent. But it's a lot closer-knit in the Black biker community; there's so much fewer of us.*

—Mike Seate;
Interviewed in *American Biker,* the film

One of those few is one of my closest friends.

Every time Steve called, I could only guess where he was. He'd call me from Sturgis, from New Jersey, from Daytona—from anywhere, everywhere.

He called one time with the usual "Guess where *I* am?"

And as usual, I didn't have a clue.

"I'm in Chicago. I rode out here to go to Buddy Guy's Legends blues club. There wasn't any place to park the bike, so I parked in a spot that was supposed to be Buddy's private parking place. I parked the bike there anyway. I figured he'd be happy to see that I rode all the way from California just to go to his club. But when he drove up, he wasn't happy at *all* about someone being in his parking space…not even a Black guy on a Harley!"

Steve Boyd: The toughest rider I've ever known.

Steve Boyd has been Black since birth, but he was definitely a biker long before that, while his soul waited its turn to take on some flesh. He's the perfect hardbutt. He's the toughest rider I've ever known, and a solid and loyal friend. He *lives* on that bike. He lives *for* that bike. He defines the term "biker" in the truest sense.

One time, Steve shows up in my driveway. As I come out the door, he's pulling something out of one of his saddlebags. He smiles and hands me a t-shirt that he got Sonny Barger to autograph for me. Steve got one for himself, too.

"I was pretty happy about meeting and talking with Sonny," Steve said. "I told him, 'There are only two people in this whole world that I ever really wanted to make a special attempt to meet: Jimi Hendrix and you. Hendrix is dead.' I held out my hand for him to shake, but he hugged me instead. A sincere hug. A brother's hug. It was good."

I received another t-shirt as a gift once. It was from an idiot.

Any of us who have ridden for any length of time have come across plenty of "wannabes"; the pose-and-pretend, all-talk-and-no-action bunch. The "I used to have a Harley…I'm going to get a Harley someday…I'd have a Harley if it wasn't for that money-grubbing bitch I'm married to" crowd. But being a wannabe doesn't necessarily make someone a *complete* idiot; there are plenty of other ways *that* particular title can be earned.

I was having a barbeque at my house; one where the occasional friend of a friend winds up with an invite. It seldom matters, because there's always more than enough beer and beef to go around. This one guy—this friend of a friend—had heard that I was indeed a "biker."

Fine.

He had brought a gift. And he was evidently anxious to "present" it because it didn't take him long. Upon arrival, he did the usual big-eyed perusal of the bikes. We heard the standard "I'm gonna get one someday" stuff. Then he said, "Hey, I brought you a t-shirt that I've had for a long time…figured *you'd* appreciate it!"

With a wide stupid smile, he went out to his car and brought back this black t-shirt. I unrolled it to read the axiom. There, surrounding an obviously pirated Harley bar-and-shield logo, were the words:

IT'S A WHITE THING, YOU <u>WILL</u> UNDERSTAND.

I thought about when Steve gave me the Barger shirt. Steve rode 365 miles to give me that shirt. It had dirt and scuffs on it from the saddlebags. It was real, and it represented real respect, love, and brotherhood. With the road dirt still on it, it went directly into a frame, where it hangs on my living room wall to this day.

This other little puke was here at *my* house trying to buy some feeble degree of respect by pandering to a side of me he knew nothing about.

I thought about this for a second.

The signed Barger shirt was pulled from a dirty saddlebag...

...the other shirt was from a dirtbag.

I considered several options for my reaction. I knew Steve was going to show up soon. I weighed the possibility of simply waiting; introducing Steve to my "guest" and showing him the shirt at the same time. Then just watching this pus-bag step on his tongue and shit his pants all at once.

But times have changed since the '60s; and so have I. The fuse isn't as short, but I know the explosion could be just as loud and destructive if I allowed it. I guess age—and wisdom—fosters discretion. It also fosters less legal hassles.

I simply pulled my "guest" aside.

"It's time for you to leave," I told him.

He was somewhat surprised; pretty damn slack-jawed, actually.

"Why?" he asked.

"It's just best," I said, looking again at the shirt. "*You WILL understand.*"

Chapter 11

She's Here Too

Ol' Ladies; "Ladies Love Outlaws"; "Property of…"; & The Ultimate Biker Babe

I am a honky-tonk angel
and a Southern Baptist deacon's daughter.
I can tell you down to the most precise second
how to make blackberry plum jelly,
turnip greens and fatback, or smooth corn moonshine,
and can rattle off the timing on a Chevy 350
or the paint code for Plum Crazy on a 1974 Charger.
I devour novels of every form and fashion, and men as well.
I ride Harley-Davidson, and only Harley-Davidson, motorcycles.

—Amy White;
Wicked Bitch

Logically, no one should ever be required to prove something that doesn't need to be proven. Unfortunately, *that* bit of common sense and truth doesn't always stop that thickheaded "prove it to me" mentality from surfacing.

For example, I'm pretty damn sure that Chuck Norris or Chuck Liddell never walk into a bar announcing that they "can whup any man in the place." They don't have to. But I'm equally sure that from time to time some idiot swings on them—figuring that he's better or tougher—and winds up getting his ass flattened. Some people just can't accept certain things. They literally have to have the truth *pounded* into them.

Even after that, some of them *still* can't accept it.

> *Conforming to polite society has never really held any appeal for me.*
> *I don't have much in common with most women*
> *and not all guys are willing to accept me as "one of the boys."*
> *Because of this, I've had to find my own place.*
> *It took me a while but I've decided*
> *I am the most comfortable just riding the yellow line.*
> *It gets me into trouble sometimes but it's always fun!*
>
> —Sandy Dell;
> *Riding the Yellow Line*

Evanston, Wyoming, is in the Bear River Valley, ruggedly caressed by the nearby arms of the Grand Tetons, Yellowstone, and Bighorn Canyon. It's also the place where my biker brother Steve came upon Yuriko as he rolled along I-80 on his way to Sturgis in 2006.

She was parked on the side of the road, her '79 Shovel melting down with electrical problems. I know—a lot of you are thinking: *Oh, an AMF-years Shovel having electrical problems? So what else is new?*

But this was no ordinary AMF Shovel. And Yuriko was no ordinary rider. Just twenty-seven years old, she had flown into L.A. from Japan.

Alone.

She'd had her bike shipped into the port of Long Beach, about twenty-two miles south of LAX. It was a kick-start-only, rigid-framed semi-rat that she had built herself.

She was in the midst of a solo ten-thousand-mile trip around the U.S. when the wiring decided to fry.

Yes, she was *solo*.

Alone.

Tandokude.

She was enjoying the "soul in the metal": the reward of having a *human* soul that is *biker*-specific, not gender-specific.

After Steve got her some help to revive the '79, they rode into Sturgis together. At the end of Bike Week, they parted ways. He went west on his Softail. She took off to the east on her rigid.

Alone.

Yuriko's 10,000-mile trip across the U.S.: Solo. Alone. Tandokude!

251

Women may not have won the right to vote throughout this country until 1920, but they were riding American motorcycles long before that. And I do mean *riding*.

Yuriko was alone as she cruised the states on that old Shovel, but she is not alone in her heritage.

> *All the fellows around here who have been bragging about*
> *their abilities as road riders are strangely quiet these days.*
> *And a woman has silenced them.*
> *She does not realize it herself—*
> *which makes it all the more enjoyable*
> *for some of us who have never made*
> *any pretensions of ability for riding rough roads.*
>
> —From an article about Della Crewe;
> A 1915 edition of a *Harley-Davidson Dealer* magazine

On June 24, 1915, Della Crewe set out on a solo run from Texas across America on her 1914 sidecar-equipped two-speed Harley-Davidson twin. Well, almost solo. She did bring her dog, "Trouble"—who lived up to his name a bit when the "authorities" stopped Della twice in Indiana, making her promise the dog would stay in her sidecar until she left the state, due to the Hoosier state's outbreak of hoof-in-mouth disease.

> [Della] *was just about to start on her trip*
> *when the skies opened up and washed out Texas roads*
> *and bridges for many miles in all directions.*
> *Her friends wanted her to ship her machine out of the flood district*
> *but Miss Crewe insisted that she was going to start right*
> *from Waco and "make every mile a Harley-Davidson mile."*
>
> —Ibid.

On that particular trip Della and Trouble rode 5,378 miles; going from Waco to Milwaukee to New York City, where she and the dog and the bike sailed for Jacksonville, Florida, with plans to ride into the South and then on into Cuba and South America.

That is *riding*.

A little over a month prior to Della's ride from Texas was when New Yorker Effie Hotchkiss and her mother got the wheels rolling on their little cross-country jaunt that would make them the first women to ride across America. Effie—with her mother in the sidecar of her three-speed Harley twin—spent two months on the road before the two were able to pour the jar of Atlantic Ocean water they had brought with them into the Pacific.

Saying "on the road" is a stretch, of course, because in 1915 there weren't that many actual *roads*. There were ditches, ruts, rocks, mud, and wilderness. White-tiled rest areas didn't exist, or gas stations every mile, or signs telling you where the next IHOP, Waffle House, or Denny's was. What *did* exist were women like Della and Effie and her mother: women who may not have been able to vote in every state in the union, but sure as hell could ride a motorcycle and grab this lifestyle by the 'nads and run with it.

> *Four guys from the suburbs hit the road...*
> *and the road hit back.*
> *A lot can happen on the road to nowhere.*
>
> —Promo tag;
> For the 2007 film, *Wild Hogs*

Maybe. But the idea of finding real "roads to nowhere"—both literally and figuratively—here in modern America is also a stretch.

They've become pretty damn rare within today's web of interstates, cell phones, call boxes, reasonably maintained asphalt, DUI checkpoints, and laser-fed police radar.

But there was no lack of wildness on the roads traveled and raced by Dorothy "Dot" Robinson, the woman generally recognized as the "First Lady of Motorcycling." The roads that she hit *definitely* "hit back."

Dot began racing in the '30s, competing in and winning some of the most grinding races of her day: crushing hundred-mile enduros and body-beaters, like the 1937 two-day "Jack Pine" enduro—a vicious test that Dot finished second in. Fewer than half of the entrants even finished at all. She won the thing three years later.

In 1940 Dot formed the Motor Maids—the first all-female motorcycle club in the U.S.—and she began to ride fifty thousand miles a year in a high-profile, high-flying promotion of female riders. During WWII, Dot became a motorcycle courier for a private defense contractor.

At the time of Dot's 1998 induction into the AMA Hall of Fame (at age eighty-six), she was credited with having conquered more than 1.5 million miles of "roads to nowhere," tough race courses, and her fair share of "ditches, ruts, rocks, mud, and wilderness."

Riding...

Dot's bike and accomplishments are commemorated in Milwaukee's Harley-Davidon Museum.

The road trip is filled with humorous moments
and often disaster.
For example, when they [actors Tim Allen, John Travolta,
Martin Lawrence, and William Macy]
cozily sleep close to each other, scantily dressed,
a policeman tells them this is lewd and lascivious behavior,
but it turns out that he is only teasing:
he is gay and actually jealous.

—From a Wikipedia synopsis of *Wild Hogs*

Yeah, that must have been really rough for those guys.
"Humorous"? Whoo-ee, a real knee-slapper! A "disaster"?
Travolta, et al. should have ridden with Bessie Stringfield...

"If you had black skin you couldn't get a place to stay" she said.
"I knew the Lord would take care of me and He did.
If I found black folks, I'd stay with them.
If not, I'd sleep at filling stations on my motorcycle."
She laid her jacket on the handlebars as a pillow
and rested her feet on the rear fender.

—Description of Bessie Stringfield,
Black Woman Motorcycling Pioneer in the '30s and '40s;
From the AMA Motorcycle Hall of Fame

Bessie was born in 1911 and began riding when she was sixteen
years old. She had twenty-seven Harleys in her lifetime (along with an
eventual total of six husbands) and actively rode for sixty-six years.
She was Black, she was a woman, and she rode big bikes solo.
She toured America's lower forty-eight states eight times.
Alone.
A rider.

Bessie Stringfield was honored in a Women in Motorcycling mural created by Paul Jamiol for the Grand Opening of the Motorcycle Heritage Museum in Westerville, Ohio. She is pictured with Jay Leno at the 1990 event.

"The *Enthusiast* Girl" was the name given to Vivian Bales. Vivian was on the cover of Harley-Davidson's *Enthusiast* magazine in 1929. In that year, Vivian took a seventy-eight-day, five-thousand-mile solo ride around the country; acting as sort of a "female rider ambassador," visiting H-D dealers and even meeting President Hoover.

Just before Vivian passed away (three weeks before her ninety-third birthday in 2001) she requested a motorcycle procession at her funeral. Her request was granted and the procession rolled, courtesy of Flint River H-D in Albany, Georgia.

A rider.

And there are more. Many more. Lots more. Women have been American Bikers essentially since there have been American bikes.

They've proven that they can ride.

They've proven just who they are.

Wendell Perry is the former Southern California Bureau Chief for the popular national biker publication, *Thunder Press*.

Wendell not only knows this lifestyle in and out; she *rides*:

I Ride

by Wendell Perry

In 1992, when Reg Kittrelle asked me to send in a little something about Southern California riding for a new Northern California motorcycle publication he was putting together called Thunder Press, *I was flattered to have been asked to write not* only *about women riders.*

My emotions vacillate between outrage and flattery when readers respond to something I've said, assuming I am a man; after all, my picture is at the top of my column. I have been told the picture doesn't do me justice; obviously not, if they can read the copy and then write in to complain about "that Wendell Perry guy." However, I'm gratified that they can read my thoughts and either agree or disagree with me as an equal, as another rider, no gender discount.

I started riding before there was a Ladies of Harley facet of the Harley Owners Group. Initially, I was offended at the idea of being segregated from the main group, but soon realized that the intent of LOH was to encourage women riders and passengers to participate. This has proven to be a very good thing, and has not driven a wedge between the men and women riders.

But my LOH participation has always been minimal, partly due to my increasing involvement over the years with Thunder Press, *and partly because the idea of riding with a bunch of women scares the living begeezes out of me.*

I learned to ride because I was a bad passenger. I liked the riding part. I just didn't like it on the back seat. So I had to get my own two wheels: a 250 Honda Rebel. I took the motorcycle safety course and got a lot of practice following my husband all over the San Diego County backcountry. I tagged along on my 650 Suzuki Savage in the back of the pack with my local ABATE chapter, which included a few accomplished women riders, riding alongside all the guys. I followed and watched and learned.

The first compliment I ever received from an older male rider was conveyed to my husband, as if I were somewhere else and not standing right there between them in front of my 1986 883 Sportster Hugger. He said that I was a good rider and that I could hold my line. He said that he'd ride next to me any day.

I could have cried. It really was tremendous.

I encountered my first "Property of" patches on the vests of women when I started venturing farther afield on my 1988 85th Anniversary Springer Softail. Taking in the Sturgis experience for the first time exposed me to riders from all corners of the U.S.A. and abroad; it was a real eye opener. That early in the game, a woman on her own big twin was a little unusual, and I felt the pressure to not make any mistakes and disgrace myself, my husband, and my gender. We weren't in Southern California anymore.

But I wasn't the only one who had to adjust to the different thinking of the longtime, old-time riders we encountered on our travels and as we became more well-known in our own local riding community. At an impromptu backyard barbeque/ party after a weekend ride, I was getting a little uncomfortable about one guy who made a point of looking right at me while he repeatedly told the story of his mother having to learn to pick up his father's Harley before his dad would let her learn to ride it. And, of course, the next step before even riding the bike, according to Mr. "Women shouldn't be riding, anyway," was to learn to kick it over. It was hard to tell if he was bragging or complaining as he told the tale of his mother's perseverance and eventual accomplishment; and I'll never really know because we had to leave the party pretty quickly after my husband made an offhand comment about the guy's mother being able to suck-start a Harley.

We have both found our limitations in dealing with the real old-school riders at times.

I read a letter several years ago in Thunder Press *from a woman who was upset about a bad experience in a motorcycle safety course. She complained about being yelled at by the instructors. She obviously hadn't been raised by a drill instructor and couldn't tell the difference between being yelled* at *and being yelled* to, *to get her to look in the right direction when executing the specialized exercises.*

I had no sympathy for her and have spoken of her letter frequently when talking to others about the dilemma of women motorcycle training / safety.

Over the years, however, I have come to realize that she may not have been alone in her feelings; I have increasingly encountered women with the desire to ride, but whose reticence and timidity have held them back. Their fear of messing up in front of men, or asking questions and possibly being ridiculed, has restricted their ability to get the experience and mileage that they really need.

On the flip side are the women I encounter who have let the "Hear Me Roar" myth drive them to some level of motorcycle megalomania, wherein they imagine themselves invincible superwomen. They brag and carry on about their wild road adventures as they ride that pendulum as far away from timid as it can possibly swing.

I know that riding a motorcycle is a challenging endeavor. It takes desire: a desire to learn, not just a desire to look cool. It takes skill; that can be learned with practice. And it takes lots of practice. Practice on the range in a class atmosphere is a good thing—but the practice that makes a rider is the practical kind, out on the road, laying down mile after mile of actual experience.

I had a distinct advantage of having my own riding companion to challenge me and help me through the tough spots. And I've never been afraid to ask questions if I think my safety or ability to ride better lies in the balance. That simply isn't the case for many women who have made the huge decision on their own to become a part of the motorcycling lifestyle.

I was finally convinced by the HOG Director at my local dealership that I could have some valuable information to share with the women riders in our group; I had a very good time participating in a training session organized by the Ladies of Harley officer and a couple of chapter Road Captains. The event was very successful, with over twenty women participants.

The agenda was pretty rudimentary, starting out with the basic identifying of important parts on the motorcycle—with the premise that detailing the bike can be a terrific opportunity to check things out and make sure that everything is there and tight, while you're making sure that it is clean and sparkles. Some great information was shared about the importance of *maintaining safe tire pressure, safe tire tread, and correct fluid levels. And, I was able to talk the LOH Officer through the steps of safely picking up her own motorcycle, after delivering a brief address on ways to avoid dropping it in the first place—although we all know it can happen to the best of us when we least expect it.*

After completing the classroom agenda, those who wanted to could participate in some confidence-building range exercises. As the patient male Road Captains were trying to explain the concept of counter-steering, or "push right to go right," I shared something that I would only have brought up with a bunch of women. I have noticed that when opening a can with a handheld can opener, sometimes on smaller cans, like tomato paste, if the opener is held in too upright a position as it is cranked around the can top, it will slip off the lip, making it necessary to clamp it on the edge and start again. If the blade of the opener can be leaned at an angle toward the middle of the lid, it will stay in the groove and go around the lid with no problem: thus demonstrating the "push down to go around" theory. The guys looked a little blank on that one, but the women all picked up on the significance, one even repeating as she nodded her head: "Push down to go around."

Women do think differently than men, but with patience and perseverance, we can accomplish the same result and all have a good time on the road. If I had one thing to say to women riders beyond any specific safety tip, it would be to quit the whining, and quit the bravado. Make every effort to get the training and the experience/practice you need, so that the next time someone asks, you can look them in the eye with confidence and say: "I ride."

—Wendell Perry,
Veteran Writer *and* Rider

While Wendell is on the West Coast, "Shadow" is on the other side of the country—a New Jersey girl. Their thoughts and feelings and accomplishments bridge America and its women riders just like Effie Hotchkiss did when she joined the Atlantic with the Pacific. Mixing that water was a symbol, of course—of something so tangible. Effie— a woman—had just used a motorcycle to pull the two coasts together; wrapping them neatly up like the ends of a soft towel around hot fresh biscuits. She served up something new; something to be savored— a full sensory blitz that wasn't caged in by gender or generation.

Shadow understands, too, what it is to be "uncaged":

On My Own Terms

by Shadow

The dreams were becoming more frequent. I'd wake up exhilarated, still feeling the wind whipping around me and the powerful motor throbbing underneath me. My first thought would be to jump out of bed and run out to the shed to take my bike out for another ride. Then, I'd slowly realize that my ex-boyfriend really didn't leave his old motorcycle in my back yard when he split. I'd sink back down into the mattress, somewhat deflated and not very eager to start the day.

Fast cars and hot bikes had been in my life since I was a teenager. Every weekend of those early '70s summers was spent going to Herb Harvey's Speedway in Lemon, Pennsylvania, where my then-boyfriend raced No. 24—his pink and white '56 Chevy—on the oval dirt track. And on days when there were no races, we'd rip around the back roads on his Honda 750 or tear through the mountains on his old, beat-up Harley enduro bike. Just by hanging around my boyfriend and his buddies, I learned some basics of car and bike maintenance. Well, I learned the lingo, anyway. Typical of that era, the only time I was allowed to touch a wrench was to pick it out of the toolbox and hand it over to whoever was fixing whatever was broken.

In those days, I was always the passenger. In the dinky little Pennsylvania town I came from, no girl even thought of piloting her own bike. It just wasn't done. Not 'til I moved to New York City in the early '80s did I see a woman riding her own motorcycle. What an inspiration!

And that's when the dreams started.

In the daytime, I worked at a high-powered corporate job in New York's financial district. There wasn't much time for leisure; no escape from the daily grind. I was focused on advancing my career and began making tons of money.

One day, I heard an old Van Morrison song that reminded me of another long-ago lover. Something deep inside drove me to find him, knowing that our next meeting would change my life. I made the trip back to my hometown, we met up, and he took me for a midnight ride around the lake on his Harley. It'd been years since I'd seen him and even more years since I'd been to that lake where I'd misspent some of my youth. The night was crisp and clear, and as the miles flew by, the years seemed to fall away. With every breeze, each variation in temperature, all my senses came alive. It was like pure electricity coursing through my veins.

My emotions ran wild. I felt great joy, and at the same time, a great sadness and longing for the past—for those wild, devil-may-care times when we thought the night would never end and we'd live forever. The wind carried my tears away so my old lover never even knew. And I realized I wasn't having any fun in my fast-paced New York City life.

I wasn't living life to the fullest—not even close.

Months after that night, I couldn't shake that memory of feeling so alive, nor could I find a way to repeat it.

The dreams got more intense.

It was time to live again. It was time to ride.

But this time, on my own terms, on my own time, and on my own bike.

The man I was dating was a straight-laced type of guy who didn't ride, and didn't even know any bikers. My best friend at work took me aside and said, "You know this is going to change your life, don'tcha? And that it'll probably mean the end of your relationship?" I looked her straight in the eye and announced: "Yep. I'm ready for whatever happens."

When I broke the news that I was going to take a riding course and buy a bike, my boyfriend didn't even flinch. "I know you'll be responsible," he said. "Besides, I don't expect you'll run off and join a motorcycle gang." He had no idea what a roller-coaster ride the future would bring.

But then, neither did I.

The relationship lasted about three months after I got my first bike. Oh, it had serious problems anyway, but my motorcycle carried me through a doorway to a whole new world. A shaky, scary world at first (I must have dropped my bike a half-dozen times in the first six months of riding), but exciting, and I was finally having some fun. I worked on improving my skills and pushing past my fears—there were many—and within a year, I joined a motorcycle club.

I'd moved out of the city by then, and I was looking for some riding partners in my new town and some camaraderie. The club had eight or ten other female members, but for the most part, they were wives or girlfriends of male members. These women were suspicious of me at first (I mean, what single woman joined a "co-ed" motorcycle club, unless to steal their husbands or boyfriends?), and the guys constantly tested me. But finally I was accepted as just another club member.

I became club secretary, and was eventually elected second vice-president. I took a lot of grief from old-timers in other clubs. In that area, women weren't even allowed *in most clubs, much less to become officers. The closest some women came to being part of these clubs was to fly "Property of" colors. Many of these women came up to me in secret and said, "I really admire what you're doing. I wish* I *could do that."*

Being part of a club was quite an education in many ways. I learned the rules of the road and the rules of respect. My bike took me one step closer to self-sufficiency—always an important credo in my life. In another year or so, I was ready for a real road trip. I'd become close friends with some members of a sober club, and I accompanied them on their annual trek to West Virginia, followed by a ride to Laconia, then to Daytona.

Finally I took the ultimate pilgrimage: the ride to Sturgis with my own club. That's when I learned the true meaning of brotherhood. The real bond with my club brothers began not in the clubhouse, not in a bar or at a biker party, but on the road. After having to bail each other out of various jams on that long ride, I knew we could depend on each other for anything.

Some nights on that trip we stayed with folks I had "met" on a motorcycle e-mail list. They opened up their homes to complete strangers with just a few hours' notice. Their hospitality and generosity was incredible, and I only hoped I could do the same when other bikers passed through town and needed a place to flop for the night.

Before the trip, some of my riding buddies (I'd developed quite a network by then) tried to dissuade me from riding to Sturgis. Most of the ride was boring, they said, and I'd be so tired that I wouldn't want to ride when I got there and I certainly *wouldn't want to ride back.*

Well, they were all wrong. I wasn't tired at all.

Once there, we rode all over the Badlands, into Wyoming, and through several Indian reservations and national parks. And there is nothing boring about the United States. This is a great and beautiful country, and I feel honored and privileged to live here, enjoying the freedoms that we experience. Each part of the country has its own allure, its own unique beauty. And I drank it all in. I inhaled it, felt it, smelled it, tasted it. I loved it all. Some mornings I'd wake up feeling tired or out of sorts. But as soon as I climbed onto my bike, started her up, and pulled away, everything was right with the world, and I was into the ride, into the journey.

Being on the road put a lot of things into perspective. That first ride to Sturgis was more than an endurance test; more than just another club run. Some months prior, I'd left my high-powered corporate job, because I couldn't stomach the soulless nature of the work. I was now dabbling in several vocations: I'd been doing some freelance writing, some work in a holistic center, some private investigation, and was even employed in a bike shop for a time. I needed this ride to sort things out; to figure out what I wanted to do next. I knew something monumental would happen on this journey, but I didn't know exactly what it would be.

When I finally got home, I had a new sense of clarity. The next morning, I called a realtor and put my house on the market. A few months later, I moved to a place that better suited my changing lifestyle. Doors and windows of opportunity flung themselves open, and I moved toward turning my passion into my vocation: writing, photographing, and editing for motorcycle magazines. I traveled more and learned to love riding solo—the farther, the better. The money isn't that great, but I'm finally living the life I've always wanted.

That said, it's not always carefree and easy for a bike-riding woman working in the motorcycle industry. There are those times when I'm involved in a motorcycle industry meeting or seminar, weighing in on the virtues of piston wirelox vs. circlips, or maybe projecting which production custom motorcycle manufacturer will go out of business next, and I'm thinking the guys around the table and I share a common bond—an equalizer. Then, after twenty minutes or so of deep discussion, one of the guys looks at me, smiles, and asks: "So, do you ride, honey?"

"Well, yeah!" I'll exclaim.

"No," he'll say, "I mean, do you really ride your own bike?"

At that point, it's obvious this guy hasn't listened to a word I've said. My response now is simply: "Yeah. Do you ride your *own*, too?"

Or the times I can't get someone at a bike shop to wait on me until after they've taken care of all the guys at the counter. Or when I ask a salesman a question and he directs his response to the guy I'm with, refusing to even look at me.

There are many guys (and even some women!) who believe females belong only on the pillion.

Then there are the questions from folks who see the lone rider at the gas pump filling up the tank: "Where are you going? What? Sturgis? Oh, my goodness! A girl—riding all by yourself?" Usually I just nod and smile weakly, not wanting to engage in further conversation with this person who doesn't believe a woman is capable of riding a motorcycle, much less traveling on her own. Sometimes these questions are followed by, "Aren't you scared riding alone? Isn't it dangerous?" I guess some people will never understand the inner strength and confidence borne of riding.

But these minor annoyances are far outweighed by the joy I feel when I'm on the road. The sheer physicality of riding wipes all that irritation away pretty quickly. And I'm living a life others can only dream of; so I consider myself fortunate indeed. As the years spin by, I find that I can take on greater challenges, in both my professional and my personal life, without fear holding me back. Riding has changed my life in ways I never thought possible.

Those dreams of seeking power and freedom? They've finally stopped—and I don't miss them at all.

—"Shadow,"
High-Powered Corporate Mogul–turned–American Biker

There *are* a lot of other women in this lifestyle besides the *riders*. Their personas range from something like Tammy Wynette in "Stand by Your Man" to pro-wrestler Matilda the Hun to everything in between.

Yeah, you're cute—but I'm *warm!*

—"Paula," an older biker gal;
Commenting on the skimpy "fashion statements"
of some of the younger girls
during the annual (often-chilly) fall Love Ride

Regardless of the style or station of these gals, the media has always pretty much relegated the male biker's treatment of "the chicks" to the same status as a can of oil or beer; something to be used, consumed, and then trashed.

The ingraining of this attitude began—like so many other parts of The Image—with Brando. His rough on-screen romance with

"Kathie" in *The Wild One* helped to sensitively demonstrate just how much "ladies love outlaws."

Kathie's gentle view of life, with activities like "picnics," seemed, *at first*, very different from Brando's.

"A picnic? Man, you are *too* square," Brando tells her. "I'll have to straighten you out. Now, listen, you don't go any one special place. That's cornball style. You just *go*…the idea is to have a ball. Now if you gonna stay cool, you got to wail. You got to put somethin' down. You got to make some jive. Don't you know what I'm talkin' about?"

She *did*.

She reluctantly loved his strength, his independence, and everything else that made him the antithesis of her small-town, less-than-screamingly exciting environment.

Then the attitude got hotter and nastier.

As the years passed, gender sensitivity went completely out the window. Salivating movie-marketing guys loved to add prurient punch when mentioning the "ladies" in their trick-tease trailers and on their soft-porn posters.

Take the 1968 surprisingly non-Emmy-winning film, *Hell's Bloody Devils*, whose ads promised "female love slaves."

That same year coughed up the equally compelling *Angels from Hell*:

> *When he wanted a town…HE <u>STOLE</u> ONE!*
> *When he wanted a girl…HE <u>GRABBED</u> ONE!*
> *When he wanted a cop…HE <u>BOUGHT</u> ONE!*
> *He's a CyclePSYCHO…*

Audiences received another treat in 1971 with *Angels, Hard As They Come*: "Big men with throbbing machines and the girls who take them on." "They ripped off his mama…so he tore chopper city apart!"

Well, of course he did. Who wouldn't?

That all may have been a few decades or so back, but like a long-abandoned fan site for a one-hit wonder band—law enforcement, painting with a very broad-badged brush, *still* insists that "women are chattel" in the MC world.

In all honesty, forty-plus years ago things *were* a bit different in this lifestyle. Hunter Thompson's "sex scene" in Chapter 17 of *Hell's Angels* and descriptions of the "Monterey Rape Case" coupled with the bad flicks to tattoo bikers as out-of-control high-pressure fire hoses of extremely potent and misdirected testosterone.

Another non-Emmy-winning example of discarded "gender sensitivity."

From the beginning, the male American Biker was seen as a stampeding deviant, slave-trader, and insatiable stud. All three labels may have had a *pinch* of truth; but large drops of these drooling traits can also be applied to a fair share of clergymen, business tycoons, Hollywood stars, politicians, and plenty of others. But the severity and impact of hits like these always revolve around the size of the target; and—as we've seen—the American Biker is a *damn* big and visible one.

Forty-plus years ago, a lot *was* going on. "Free love" (and the ever-present punch bowl of potential paralysis) was a party standard—at biker busts and everywhere else. In those forty-plus years, however, a lot has changed in virtually *all* facets of life in America.

But somehow, while other strata of society are seen as naturally evolving and progressing, time has evidently stopped when it comes to bikers. One of the '60s' most visible and vocal radicals, Tom Hayden, became a duly elected and suit-wearing politician; rocker Alice Cooper washed off the spooky make-up, put on a standard-issue golf shirt, and teed off on the pro-am circuit; and a United States president talked about his underwear and grass-smoking on MTV, and got head from a young woman in the Oval Office. Our society just shrugs off all of *that*. But when bikers "want a girl," it's expected that they'll *still* "just grab one." An' de Lord only knows they remain as "big men with throbbing machines" bent on rampage; using bullwhips and their Gene Simmons–like tongues to torment (and, yes, much more) "the girls who take them on."

But steamy quotes on sticky movie posters of the past are one thing. An "official document" from the Connecticut Gang Investigators Association of 2007 is another. With all due respect, if Bob Hope were still alive, it's a safe bet he'd still be doing the stale "hippie" jokes that he did long after that little sub-phylum had died away; but when it comes to law enforcement, we kind of expect them to be a bit more up with the times.

(Author's note: in the always-honorable tradition of continually striving for truth, this piece has not been edited for spelling and grammatical errors. And keep in mind, *this is from 2007!*):

Women and the Outlaw Biker

Outlaw motorcycle gangs are male dominated and highly chauvinistic. Women are treated as playthings and property. Women are generally victimized by forcing them into prostitution or street level drug traffickers, and quite often physically and sexually abused. In the outlaw biker's society women are bought, sold, traded or given away within the club.

Selling drugs in the mid 1960's teaches the outlaw biker the basics of supply and demand. When they learn men pay to rent the empty space between a woman's leg, they put their women to work. In the violent, profit-oriented society inhabited by the outlaw biker, that's all a woman is—a hole, a piece of property to rent or trade.

Women take up with outlaw bikers for different reasons: some are hungry, some need a warm place to stay, and others feel safe in a crowd. While outlaw bikers abduct and rape many women, most attach themselves voluntarily to the club and everything it stands for—drugs, alcohol, parties, fast bikes and cars, cheap thrills and sex. Horny women want endless sex every way it comes, the club becomes their outlet. Rebellious teenagers who strike back at their parents numb their minds with drugs and screw their brains out on the clubhouse floor. Bored business women take a walk on the wild side with macho men who lead dangerous, exiting lives. Women without education become somebody when they attach themselves to respected and feared outlaw bikers. Shiftless girls like the freedom from responsibility. The unloved and homeless confuse sex with affection and cherish the arms that hold them.

A woman's main value to an outlaw biker, aside from sexual gratification is daily income. She must give all her money to her old man. Bikers put their women to work in massage parlors, topless bars, cocktail lounges and strip clubs. Most are covers for prostitution. Prostitution is the bikers' most lucrative source of income after drugs. Another area where the women are used effectively is intelligence gathering. They will go into the community and take jobs at city, county and state offices where they have access to blank birth certificates, drivers licenses and other useful documentations. Other areas of employment the women will seek is that of police records clerk, telephone operators, employees in welfare offices and position within prison institutions. They will even sleep with cops to compromise them or gather intelligence. Women of motorcycle gangs mainly fall into three categories:

Mama or Sheep – *A mama is the sexual equivalent of a public well. Anyone can dip into her, at any time, as often as he wants. These are woman who belong to the club at large. They belong to every member and are expected to consent to the sexual desires of anyone at anytime. They perform menial task around the clubhouse, however do not attend club meetings. Some clubs permit these women to wear "colors" with the inscription "Property of (club name)", embroidered on the back.*

Old Lady – *These are the wives or steady girlfriends of club members. An old lady is the property of one biker and can't be used or abused by other club members. An old lady is not a club member and like sheep are not permitted to attend club meetings. They also will in some clubs wear "Property of" colors; however, with the name of the biker she belongs to on the bottom rocker.*

Broad – *A female who's sole use is being used as a sexual object. This would be similar to the way most men view one night stands. A common method of bikers is to pick up a female hitchhiker, gang rapes her and then toss her aside.*

Women are always helping the outlaw biker to get ahead. An example—several Hell's Angels have their old ladies turn tricks in topless bars in North and South Carolina. The bars are near military bases and the old ladies get all the weapons the club needs. The Cleveland Chapter got three light antitank weapons (LAW) rockets through their old ladies. Other chapters have gotten .45 caliber pistols and hand grenades from their women.

—Connecticut Gang Investigators Association;
ctgia.org

Okay, I give up. They must be right. Why, I remember back in 2009, when I "traded" my ol' lady for a 24-pack of Pabst and a slightly used Pingle petcock…Holy Christ!

But…

For all of the reality-distanced and horribly dated cartoonery in *Women and the Outlaw Biker*, I'll give the writers of this "lesson" to law enforcement *this*: they were right—or at least *sort of* right—about at least a couple of things.

When the writers claim "Women take up with outlaw bikers for different reasons," they're right. Women do. In 1972 the late Waylon Jennings recorded a country classic called "Ladies Love Outlaws." He was right, too.

But maybe, just maybe, the women who "take up with" bikers are not *all* hungry, horny, "shiftless," and living on the cold streets alone. Maybe their "different reasons" are a lot more "positive"—and fairly simple to understand.

> *You're just dating this guy*
> *'cause you like to kick ass and wear leather…*
> *and now you can wear your leather outside of the bedroom!*
>
> —"Julie," talking to "Jennifer";
> After Jennifer "took up with" a biker

It's possible that—in some circles—there's just more estrogen-fed appeal for denim and leather than for Banlon and polyester. Maybe it's more fun riding on the back of a big Harley than it is being strapped into in the shotgun seat of any one of a million nondescript little roundish cars. Maybe an experience-lined bearded face beats an untested baby-butt-smooth mug drenched with Polo.

Again, of course, in *some* circles.

And those circles have apparently expanded:

The Allure of the Biker Guy

We've all heard that women want a guy who's tall, dark and handsome, But maybe it's time to update that to "tall, dark and handsome—and on a Harley." Because it seems that since the days of the flicks The Wild One *and* Easy Rider, *a guy on a bike has held a special kind of bad-boy appeal. In fact, in a recent Match.com survey, "motorcycle" was the second most-popular term that women used when searching through online profiles...Guys with motorcycles have a little extra oomph...There's no doubt about it: A motorcycle signifies a little extra ingredient in a guy—a little extra testosterone in a world of sensitive men. Hey, sensitive metrosexuals are great, but some women still like a little cave with their man.*

—Amy Keyishian;
msn.com

"Bad-boy appeal," "extra oomph," and a little "cave with their man." Fine, but is all this really that new?

I don't expect that soft-sponge wimps in three-hundred-dollar shoes have ever *really* been the overall dreamboats of the ladies—even long before someone came up with the word "metrosexual" to take the sting out of being, well, a soft-sponge wimp.

Some of the prehistoric and bad-movie-inspired "intelligence" in *Women and the Outlaw Biker* had a very obvious bogus-quotient. But the mention of "Property of..." patches (and the underlying concept behind them) is another of those "couple of things" that touch on the truth. The "chattel" element is another story.

Everybody calls it a biker woman, a mama,
and that's really rather an insult to most of us
because a mama is somebody that goes around
and screws everybody...
Some of the women were just totally
as terrifying and scary as the guys...
You had to accept that sometimes the club was first,
you know, and accept it and respect it...
The only girls that lasted in the Hessians
are the ones that had guts.

—Linda B. Moncrief, Widow of Hessian "Mac";
Interviewed in *Hessians MC*

"Property of..." patches *are* still worn by the women associated with many clubs. Ladies *do* love outlaws, and most—if not all—are proud of it. For the most part, the "Property of..." patch doesn't brand the gal with subservience or the necessity to be laid out like a sexual buffet. No. It's an outward sign—like a wedding ring; but with a lot more implied power. Plenty of women with wedding rings are hit on by geeks and goons who have no respect; but you'd have to be a complete idiot, have a death wish, or at least be more hammered than God's own drunk to hit on a chick with something like "Property of Knuckles" on her back.

At first I was, "I'm nobody's property," but I took it wrong.
Then after awhile it was good to have that on my back...
to be part of the club and the family
and have my husband's name back there.

—Ibid.

You'd have to be more hammered than God's own drunk to hit on a woman with "Property of Knuckles" on her back...

Connecticut's LEO "lesson" was fairly accurate about one more thing. In spite of hype-reactionary comments like, "In the outlaw biker's society women are bought, sold, traded or given away within the club," their opening line about male domination in the clubs *does* bear truth. In major clubs, men can be members; women cannot.

That *is* the truth.

It's also true that even within the most happy, compatible, and copacetic relationships, the club often comes first.

> *You know, there's a lot of girls out there that*
> *just don't, you know, know how to take it, you know,*
> *and they don't last very long a lot of times*
> *'cause they expect to be number one all the time*
> *and when they get with the club or a patch holder*
> *there's certain obligations and priorities they have*
> *that some women just can't take second to, you know.*
> *It's definitely a breed of woman that's different.*
>
> —Robin Osborn, "Wild Bill's" daughter;
> Interviewed in *Hessians MC*

When the Boozefighters Motorcycle Club was formed in 1946, a set of by-laws was drawn up. By-law #11 states: "There will never be any women in any way affiliated in any way shape or form with the Boozefighters Motorcycle Club or its subsidiaries."

But Teri Forkner—wife of BFMC founder Wino Willie—formed the Boozettes (also in 1946) to supply support and assistance to their men, as well as establish a sisterhood of their own. The Boozettes still exist and *still* provide a strong support team for the club's events and members. Of course, over a half-century later they remain a *support team*, never *members*.

Virginia "Dago" Day began hanging around the club when she was just in her mid-teens. When you talk with Dago—when you simply *listen* to Dago—you are pulled "through the looking glass" into a history book that draws you into the actual lives and experiences of the men—*and women*—who were truly "the original wild ones": the pioneers of this entire lifestyle.

As men like Wino Willie, J.D. Cameron, Jim Cameron, Johnny Roccio, "Dink" Burns, Vern Autrey, Gil Armas, Jack Jordan, Jack Lilly, and the rest of the "pioneers" rode the early streets of Los Angeles, there was a female component as well. Teri and Dago and the other women around the Boozefighters formed their *own* bond.

Dago eventually married one of the original BFMC members, "Fat Boy" Nelson. Fat Boy was killed in a motorcycle accident in the late '50s.

When Dago celebrated her seventy-seventh birthday in 2007 surrounded by bikers and BFMC members (most young enough to be her kids—or grandkids)—it wasn't a celebration of just one day; it was a celebration of the entire era that has brought all of us to where we are today.

Dago's party was appropriately held at a true old-school bar; a throwback joint just nine and a half miles from where the original Boozefighters' hangout—the All American (or "the Big A," as it was affectionately called)—stood in the 1940s.

> *I love places like this! It's comfortable, man. It's all a part of that "other era" kind of a feeling. It's the kind of place that Toby Keith must have had in mind when he sang "I Love This Bar."*
>
> *You know, just last week I tried to go into this new bar they put in at the mall down the road. I had met this girl who told me she worked there, so I figured I'd go down and see her...maybe have a drink or two. Well, they just rebuilt the back half of that damn mall and they put in all these "upscale" joints. I was met at the door with a sign that reminded me*

of the "No Dogs Allowed" signs in the Snoopy cartoons. The warning read like a fuckin' legal brief, describing—in fine detail—the dress code that these bastards want you to follow while you drink their expensive fuckin' booze. Shit, there was a very specific section that "prohibited" "motorcycle apparel of any kind." Fuck 'em! That was never an issue at the All American and it's sure as fuck not an issue at a friendly dive like this!

Hell no! The issue here—especially today on Dago's birthday—is fun, celebration, honor, love, and respect. Hell, Johnny Roccio is here today, too! He was one of the "originals." Talking with him, listening to him, just shaking his hand is an honor for all of us who genuinely appreciate the men and women who led—and still lead—the kind of lives that gave us what we have today: a lifestyle that's based on real living, strong living— not the kind of weak politically correct cowering bullshit that dictates the kind of shirt we have to have on so we can drink a fuckin' overpriced beer in some scared, fancy fuckin' bar.

—Current Member of the BFMC;
"Expressing himself" at Dago's 77th birthday party

The 77th birthday party for Dago (as a young Boozette [left], and at her 77th [right]) was a celebration of an entire era.

It was the early '90s. My uncle had been dead for several years and my aunt was beginning to slow down. She looked all of her eighty years, but she could still get around pretty well. I took her and my mother on what would be turn out to be a final Thanksgiving trip to my cousin's house up in the Pacific Northwest.

As I sometimes do when I'm in a different town, I looked up the local Harley dealer. I figured I'd visit the shop and buy the obligatory t-shirt or some other gizmo or doodad.

I asked my aunt if she'd like to go.

"Sure," she said.

I knew that would be her answer.

She had ridden behind my uncle for the entire of the fifty-plus years they'd been married—and before that when they were just dating. She had ridden on his Indians and Harleys; his Flatheads and Knuckles and Pans. Being from the east, she had gone with him many times to Laconia when it was still just races and hill climbs. She had comforted him in 1957, the morning he discovered that some bastard had broken into their garage during the night and stolen his beloved Police Special. She'd gone with him into rural roadhouses long before the term "biker bar" was coined—and she could match all the guys drink for drink.

She was everything that a lady in this lifestyle should be. (My uncle *never* would have worn one of those *"the bitch fell off"* t-shirts.)

We headed to the Harley dealer. I felt naked without my bike. It's always pretty impotent to drive a lame little rental car to a motorcycle shop, but we had no choice.

This particular dealer's store was typical, right out of the new-age H-D boutique mold. At least a little homage to history was being paid, however, by a kind of mini-museum of antique bikes on display. I left my aunt alone to wander while I checked through the racks of shirts—sifting through the bright yellows, powder blues, and tie-dyes for something more "traditional," trying to remember the last time I had bought a piece of clothing that wasn't black or some shade of my clubs' colors.

When I looked around for my aunt, I noticed she had the ear of a young salesman. They were standing in front of a coolly restored VL, elevated a few feet off the floor on a shrine-like platform. I heard her telling this guy that her husband—my uncle—had once owned one just like it. He had. Then she pointed at a similarly presented big-seated U model. She told him her husband once had one like *it*, too. He did. The same went for an old 45 and virtually all the others.

But I could tell that this kid was just humoring her with a condescending "Do tell?" kind of attitude. Because she wasn't nineteen with a big rack, and big eyes for the latest big fuel-injected six-speed, he was dismissing her—and her life on a bike—as the ramblings of an old blue-hair, just a step above a bag lady.

He was smiling and shaking his head as he finally walked away from her. Then he intercepted me. He didn't know I was with her.

"How you doin'?" he asked me; hoping, I suppose, to sell me something like a brand new FLHTCU or another alphabet model that essentially spells "T-H-I-R-T-Y-G-R-A-N-D."

"Fine," I replied—waiting for the comment that I knew was coming.

"That old lady!" he said. "Man, how'd *she* get in here? Talking my ear off about 'the good old days'…geez! Telling me that her old man had all kinds of bikes like these relics!"

"He did," I said.

His smile was gone. So was mine.

I explained to him—calmly and rationally, of course—just what my relationship was to that "old lady"; and that my uncle did indeed have more motorcycles in his lifetime than this kid had ever even *thought* about selling here on this sterile showroom floor. I further explained that my aunt and uncle logged more miles in any given year—on bikes that didn't have belt drives, rubber mounts, CD players, ambient air

temperature gauges, intercoms, or "hands free security systems"—
than this clown would ever be capable of riding on any kind of bike. *Ever.*

I put the t-shirt back on the rack, and my aunt and I left.

I looked over at my aunt and my smile came back, as we headed
south on I-5 back toward my cousin's place, in our little round,
non-threatening rental car.

She smiled back.

I didn't share the details of my conversation with the salesman in
his homogenized button-down "work shirt."

She had really enjoyed her afternoon around bikes once again—
old bikes; the real deal. Bikes like the ones she had enjoyed for so
many years. Real steel that reminded her of my uncle and all the good
times they had and all the places they went on his ancient Harleys and
Indians. Back when it was more about riding and less about a show.

I looked at her and smiled again. She may have been eighty and
wrinkled and a lot slower than she used to be, but she had truly lived
this lifestyle. There was nothing left that she needed to prove to me—
nothing she *should* have needed to prove to anyone. The truth is the
truth and she told it very clearly.

She was the ultimate biker babe.

My aunt (far left) logged more miles a year with my uncle (second from left) than most folks ever could. She was the ultimate biker babe.

Chapter 12

Politics

External & Internal

[Helmet law opponents] *keep telling me
that it's your and my constitutional right if we want to
bash our heads in and die with our heads up against a curb.
I don't argue with that. I think that's marvelous.
Only problem is, the bastards don't die. They live.*

—Richard "Dick" Floyd,
Former California Assemblyman (D);
Interviewed by *Easyriders* magazine, May 1986

Freedom.

—Jesse Ventura,
Former Governor of Minnesota (Reform Party),
Answering why he opposes helmet laws;
Interviewed by *Playboy* magazine, November 1999

Politics: External

It was the night of November 6, 1990.

It was just before midnight, and I as I rolled south on I-5 in Central California, I was nauseatingly aware that my chosen lifestyle was about to be radically altered.

It was the night of California's election for governor. It had been a dull-sick campaign—a stumbling contest that was like a sack race for drunken gimps. Weak-tea Republican Pete Wilson against big-government control freak Democrat Dianne Feinstein; regardless of who won, we knew that *we* were going to lose.

For the past eight years, tough Republican Governor George Deukmejian, had refused to join the incessant State Assembly jackal, Democrat Richard "Dick" Floyd, and put mandatory helmets on the heads of California's motorcycle riders.

Before Deukmejian, then-Governor Ronald Reagan had taken the same hard stand.

All that was about to change. Wilson and Feinstein were full-face peas in a chin-strapped pod, regardless of their party affiliations.

This particular year had already started out on a depressing, suppressive note; with the suffering that comes when bad omens fly down your throat. Senator John Chafee (R-RI) and Representative Jim Cooper (D-TN) were peddling federal bills that would require helmets nationwide, and many states already had lid laws in place.

But this was California. This was where *it* all began. This is where The Image was locked in. This is where you can ride 365 days a year and be truly and comfortably "in the wind." This is the home of God's own Route 1 and more than eleven hundred miles of blue Pacific coastline. The Sierras, the Siskiyous, and the Mojave Desert are here. Capping all of this with a helmet would be like caging an eagle.

But a lot of wings have been clipped and a lot of cage doors bolted, under the color of authority by those who "know best."

On May 20, 1991, the winner and new governor, Pete Wilson, signed the latest incarnation of Floyd's bill into law.

Just three days before, on May 17th, the *San Jose Mercury News* published an article by investigative reporter Bernard Bauer. Bauer's piece attacked the statistics that Floyd had used to make his "public burden" case—the burden allegedly laid on taxpayers by injured bikers who supposedly require public aid and care after an accident.

Bauer wrote that Floyd had "won legislative support for his bill by saying that a law requiring motorcyclists to wear helmets will save the taxpayers from $65 million to $100 million a year in medical costs for head-injured motorcycle crash victims. However, both sources cited by Floyd denied that they provided those numbers to him. In fact, they said, accurate medical cost figures—or even reliable estimates—do not exist."

"He just pulled [his statistics] out of the air," said Senator Don Rogers, an opponent of the bill.

When Bauer confronted Floyd about the statistical discrepancies he used to push his bill, Floyd's reported response was: "Who gives a fuck?…I don't care what the figures are."

Simple *and* expected. Floyd didn't care about the taxpayers. And he certainly didn't give a Democrat rodent's ass about motorcyclists' safety. Throughout his entire crusade, Dick Floyd was very outspoken about his dislike for bikers. With the passing of his bill, Floyd's personal face-off with the biker community had finally ended; culminating in a self-pleasuring legislative ejaculation for ol' Dick.

Prior to Wilson and Floyd teaming up to care for bikers' heads, the fatality rate per one hundred accidents was 3.22 in California. In 2006—fifteen years later—the fatality rate was 3.84. "If helmets were effective in reducing fatalities and injuries," reads a portion of the 2006 attempt to amend the state's helmet law (SB 969), "this rate would be markedly lower instead of slightly higher. No matter how you slice it, mandatory helmet use has proven ineffective in saving lives."

What helmet laws *have* proven is that they are as incendiary in this lifestyle as abortion is in mainstream politics. They are Number One. A symbol and a statement for both sides.

And the endless debates have been a hell of a lot more heated than the very *worst* confrontation of religious zealots at your door—the ones who form entire religions around one or two biblical passages, loudly condemning you to eternal damnation if you don't kiss snakes, drink strychnine, or betroth your fifteen-year-old daughter to Elder Caleb.

Our side of these debates has used the big ammo of statistics, monetary facts, and the offer to purchase voluntary insurance riders to pretty much blow the public-burden theory and the "saved lives" theory out of the water.

But it doesn't matter.

The debate has expanded *way* beyond a single law or group of statistics. It's the ultimate "us versus them." It's the expression of the mainstream's desire to clip the wings and bolt those cage doors on something that—to them—is scary and intimidating. And it has come to epitomize the way the biker world sees the outside: as non-understanding and imposingly restrictive of the absolute essence of this lifestyle.

The Helmet Law is that big sacred stone at the top of the mountain, which will provide so many magical answers to the ultimate conquerors who finally turn it over one way or another.

"Who gives a fuck?" say the Dicks of this world.

"Freedom," say the Venturas.

Accompanying the helmet beast is a herd of other snorting, sharp-toothed biker issues that are also reined in and paraded around under the political Big Top: modifications to bikes, emissions controls, noise restrictions, lane restrictions, parking restrictions, special licenses and endorsements. There's required clothing (in Minnesota you can't ride a motorcycle without a shirt on); age restrictions (in Idaho Falls, Idaho, it's against the law for anyone over eighty-eight years of age to ride a motorcycle); and a hell of a lot more.

Where I live, the latest LEO harassment itch is the decorative leather braids that some riders have attached to their clutch or brake levers; affectionately known as "bitch whips."

Originally used as "attention-getters" if a car cut you off or got "in your space," these days they are usually hung on the bike simply for fun or aesthetic purposes. Club members often have them, with the woven strands of leather matching their club colors.

But now these "colors" can get your ass thrown in jail. Quick. With no discussion of the First Amendment.

I came up to a red light. Another bike rolled in beside me—a patch holder from another club. He yelled over, asking if we could talk for a minute. Sure.

He told me to warn all my club brothers—and anyone else who might have these things hanging off their bikes—to get rid of them. Now. He had been stopped, arrested, convicted, and incarcerated in the county jail for thirty days for the one he *used* to have on his bike.

And this guy was no spring chicken: late fifties—sixty maybe. And he'd just spent a full month of what remains of his life, behind bars—for a decoration. A fucking *decoration*.

The legal reason was that the metal clip at the end of the leather braid is considered a bona-fide *lethal weapon*. If you extend that little nugget of "logic," a Hello Kitty Light-Up Yo-Yo in a Girl Scout's pocket is a potentially lethal weapon (and a concealed one at that).

I tried to spread the word, but even the biker version of the "coconut telegraph" isn't perfect; I found out a short time later that one of our brothers down from Northern California had suffered the same fate with the local decoration police on the L.A. / Ventura county line.

289

Ringmasters are needed in circuses like this.

Virtually every special interest group in America has employed lobbyists and formed coalitions and organized into political demonstrations. Gays, vegetarians, unions, peacock farmers, pig hunters, pedophiles, prostitutes, coin collectors, smokers, acupuncturists, automakers, rock 'n' rollers, and every other energized collective you can think of uses blogs, pressure camps, and highly paid representatives to gain lawmakers' influence.

Bikers are there, too.

They have been for a long time.

As early as 1971, bikers decided to lock and load and begin fighting for their rights, which even then were being shot down legislatively by the states and the feds. The roots of arguably the most powerful political voice in the motorcycling community—ABATE—began in October of that year.

ABATE is an acronym that now stands for American Bikers Aimed Toward Education. But in the beginning it stood for words that were a bit more harsh—a bit more *direct*.

It was back in just the third issue of *Easyriders* magazine when then-editor Lou Kimzey started to organize and ask—to plead and pressure—the biker world to come together, to utilize our strength and numbers against "the other side."

His work and pleas became an organization.

The first name for this new army was the National Custom Cycle Association. But like when pro-wrestling's WWF had to change its name to WWE due to an acronym conflict, the NCCA was forced to change its name entirely. Kimzey changed his organization to: A Brotherhood Against Totalitarian Enactments—the *first* meaning of the letters in ABATE.

In 1974, *Easyriders* began to issue ABATE state charters, with Keith Ball as National Coordinator.

And ABATE wasn't alone.

Ron Roloff had already founded the Modified Motorcycle Association (MMA) of California; modified bikes being one of the *first* targets of "safety police" legislators and "people for a perfect world." The MMA went to war—on paper and in the streets.

People began to react.

The huge, towering sissy bars on that era's choppers, for example, were a direct sarcastic response to a law passed then, requiring "grab bars" for motorcycle passengers. We have the same sarcasm today, on our heads: helmets covered with raccoon skins; shaped like Nazi WWII buckets; or embedded with impaling spikes—all designed to make their own little "go fuck yourself" statement to those who made them mandatory.

But before the MMA and ABATE—before any organized resistance was formed—it was essentially the territory of the clubs to fight the fight for bikers' rights.

"As the rights movement grew," says biker-author and NCOM officer Bill Bish, "Don Pittsley, a member of the Huns MC in Connecticut, convinced his congressman, Rep. Stewart McKinney, to introduce HR 3869 to end the federal authority to withhold highway funds from states without helmet laws (i.e., the 'National Helmet Law').

"In July of 1975, Rob Rasor of the AMA, Ron Roloff of the MMA of California, and Ed Armstrong of ABATE of Chicago presented the House Sub-Committee on Surface Transportation with convincing testimony to repeal the helmet mandates.

"Later that year, with California being sued by the DOT because Governor Ronald Reagan refused to comply with the federal helmet law mandate, Roloff helped convince California Senator Alan Cranston to offer the language of the bill as an amendment to the 1975 Federal Highway Act. The Act passed—with overwhelming support from the California delegation because of the impending lawsuit—and was signed by President Gerald Ford on May 5, 1976.

"Not bad for a ragtag bunch of bikers with little or no previous political ambitions!

"In the previous decade," Bish adds, "before the MMA or ABATE came into existence, people like the Hells Angels MC and Ralph 'Sonny' Barger had succeeded in keeping California helmet law–free; even though Congress had passed legislation in 1966 requiring every state to pass a helmet law or lose ten percent of their federal highway funds—sound familiar?

"Rumors still circulate around Sacramento about a thousand Hells Angels on the Capitol lawn—well, it seemed like a thousand— and more HAs camped out on the doorsteps of legislative opponents. But the old intimidation tactics were wearing thin; club leaders realized that they needed to legitimize their efforts by creating a more sophisticated political lobbying arm—in this case, the MMA of California."

That's exactly what happened.

Throughout America, chapters of ABATE and the MMA and other motorcycle rights organizations (MROs) have worked and fought and defeated countless restrictive legislations.

But ultimately, the individual and local grass-roots actions are just as integral to the fight to retain our freedoms.

Inducted into the Sturgis Museum's Freedom Fighters Hall of Fame in 2005, John "Rogue" Herlihy is one of the most ruthless fighters for bikers' rights this country has ever seen. For over thirty years, he has dodged political bullets and has met every showdown for freedom with a steel determination and a will that just won't "let them get away with it."

Speaking Out

by John "Rogue" Herlihy

When Lou Kimzey contacted me about working for Easyriders, *I was International President of the Huns MC and I was putting on helmet law protests all over the East*

Coast. The problem was that the people in these states were having trouble letting each other know just what was going on—and more importantly, spreading the word to others who might want to get involved.

Bob "Bob Bitchin'" Lipkin came to the rescue with his BIKER *News. Most states began adopting names the way the Connecticut Motorcycle Rights Organization had, just by changing the first word to their state name.*

Many years after its founding, Lou Kimzey changed the name of ABATE from A Brotherhood Against Totalitarian Enactments to its current name: A Brotherhood Aimed Towards Education. He did this because those in the organization felt it was less offensive to the politicians they were working with.

I and many others feel that this is when these rights organizations began to become friendly with the politicians and in some cases take money from the government. Then, the problems actually increased. We all know the government does not give up money without expecting something in return.

Many laws have been passed with these new ABATEs at the helm; in most cases by making compromises instead of defeating laws. This is very controversial and the excuse is usually: "It's the best we could do." In many cases I do not agree, and though I still recommend that people join MROs, I also recommend that they contact their legislators directly as opposed to having a group speak for them. It is a fact that many of these groups' leaderships are not relaying what the majority of their membership wants.

Many people spoke before that House committee in July of '75 [arguing against helmet mandates]*, and I was the last person to speak. When I spoke before the committee I was Rev. John Herlihy of Bikers Church—not "Rogue," International President of the Huns.*

293

My opening statement was: "Since I am from
Connecticut, The Constitution State, I have only one question,
and that is: When did the federal government start condoning
federal blackmail and extortion?"

You could have heard a pin drop.

When the foreman finally got his wits back, he asked me
to explain.

I told him that the citizens of the State of Connecticut
had lobbied a bill through the House and Senate that would
repeal that state's mandatory helmet law. It was sitting on
Governor Ella Grasso's desk, but she had stated to me she
was reluctant to sign it because the federal government had
threatened to withhold highway funds if she did so.

The speaker told me that was very hard to believe—
to which I answered, "Sir, I actually held that letter [from the
federal government] in my hands and read it."

(Quiet Again.)

He said, "With all due respect, Reverend, I would like the
same opportunity to read the letter. Can you make that happen?"

Of course I said yes.

Now this had to happen by the next morning, so I
phoned Ella and told her of the situation. After some firm
conversation with her on my part, she agreed to send a copy
of the letter and a note explaining the situation; but stated
that she did not know if it would get to Washington in time.
I informed her that I would have someone pick it up.

I called the clubhouse and told a member to get it and
have it to me in Washington in the morning, no matter what
he had to do.

Well, the next morning we were back at the hearing and
I had not received the letter yet, when there was a commotion
out in the hall. I told the chairman I expected it was for me.

Here was one of my brothers, wearing his colors and fresh off the road, with the envelope in his hand. I took it, gave him a key to a hotel room, and told him to go get some well-deserved sleep.

As the chairman was reading the letter, I started to speak, and when he said, "Reverend, you can stop beating a dead horse," one of the others at the hearing grabbed me by the sleeve and said, "Let's get the hell out of her before they change their mind!"

Ella signed the bill to repeal Connecticut's mandatory helmet law and was followed by many other states.

—John "Rogue" Herlihy

Of course, this doesn't all stop with the tangible things like helmet laws, loud-pipe crackdowns, and handlebar height limits.

There is also *discrimination*.

I remember rolling into Prescott, Arizona. It was 2004 or '05. I was there for an event taking place just east over the hill in Prescott Valley.

This place—this area—is *made* for bikes and riding. It's perfect. It's warm, it's scenic, and it's rustic in that old-time Wild West way that connects on just so many levels with this lifestyle.

I parked the bike and walked down the main drag; a street that reminded me of the six-gun towns of Deadwood or Spearfish, with more than its fair share of wood-front bars and small restaurants and cafes.

Whenever you're alone in a place like this—walking down a street like this—damned if you don't *become* Clint Eastwood.

You're a nameless stranger, dusty and tired from the ride and in need of a drink—just like he always was when he rode into towns like Lago and Big Whisky.

But this time the comparison didn't stop with the romanticized fantasy. No. This time had that same looking-over-the-shoulder feeling of tension that Eastwood always had to put up with before he could get that leisurely drink.

The first bar I came to had a sign—*the* sign. The one that said anyone wearing "motorcycle apparel of any type" wasn't welcome.

The second bar did, too.

And there were more.

This was like not being allowed to be naked in Eden—not allowing Stetsons in Nashville.

I finally got my drink, twelve miles over the hill in Prescott Valley. They *did* let me in—but Applebee's isn't exactly my idea of a biker bar, and they cut me off after three Stoli and tonics.

The sign—and the attitude behind it—has made its appearance elsewhere, too.

> *We need a biker discrimination law.*
> *We don't have but about three states that has that.*
> *I can't even go to a mall down here wearing this bandana—*
> *but I can go in that damn mall and* buy *this bandana!*
>
> —Jim Owens,
> President, Shreveport, LA, Chapter of the Bandidos MC;
> Interviewed in *Bikers: The Inner Circle*

And the discrimination has expanded beyond the mall and even the bars where we were once welcomed. *The sign* is getting more omnipresent.

In September of 2007, a large group of members of the Hells Angels Motorcycle Club were not allowed to enter the Santa Cruz County Fair wearing their colors. Ironically enough—like Jim Owens' bandana—*inside* the fair, the Santa Cruz chapter of the HAMC had a vendor booth *selling* their support merchandise! The apparel could be purchased but not worn.

George Christie, President Emeritus of the Ventura HAMC chapter, was denied entry to the Ventura County Fair while wearing *his* colors, for two consecutive years (2002 and 2003).

In a court case that lasted over seven years, members of the Top Hatters MC sued the city of Gilroy, California, and its annual Garlic Festival because *they* were kicked out of the event in 2000 for wearing *their* colors.

It gets stranger.

The sign has even appeared at large, long-running, well-established motorcycle swap meets, like the one at Veteran's Stadium in Long Beach, California—prompting a series of protests by members of many different clubs.

A multi-club protest at the Long Beach swap meet united bikers against the bureaucratic threats to our way of life.

Discrimination Alert

*It has come to our attention that business establishments
in Arizona may still be discriminating against motorcyclists.
Please carry copies of this form* [an information card for
lawyers, detailing the discrimination] *with you at all times.
Discrimination can range from a sign stating "No Colors"
or "No Motorcycle Parking" or "No Motorcycle Attire" etc.,
to simply being asked to leave a place of business,
just because you are on a motorcycle
or because of your riding apparel.*

—From a recent MMA bulletin

The list of discriminations has become endless.
Thankfully the MROs remain relentless.

Politics: Internal

As in any "family" setting, along with protecting the clan from the pangs of the *outside*, there is a need for introspection—to look *inside*.

Both began to happen on January 27, 1986, in Las Vegas. Internal *and* external diplomatic bridges were erected when a gathering of motorcycle group leaders all across the country—along with activist attorney Richard Lester—formed the National Coalition of Motorcyclists (NCOM).

Bringing the clubs together created a strength-in-numbers power base to fight external political battles. But the need for clubs to be "brought together" in the first place said something: It exposed the obvious need for organization—and a group-grip on *internal* politics, as well.

As a result of NCOM, in 1988 the Confederation of Clubs (COC) was created in Southern California to begin this internal process; to take a direct look inside, creating a leather-wrapped forum for keeping peace in the sometimes volatile MC community, with the goal of directing energies at the *real* enemy.

The multi-color COC patches represent the spectrum of clubs that have united to fight against the common enemy— the true *enemy.*

We don't need to be fighting over territory.
We need to be sitting down with COCs and NCOM
and working on the laws,
things that's goin' on [unfair and restrictive legislation],
and what we can do to stop that stuff.

—Jim Owens;
Interviewed in *Bikers: The Inner Circle*

A lot of battles and wars have been lost when one of the engaged armies is surrounded or outflanked. It's bad enough having a battalion of legislators on one side, sterilizing our bikes and telling us how we have to "dress"; but it's especially draining to have to battle our peers, too.

But rivalries are a part of this lifestyle.

With this much strength, lock-willed independence, and genuine commitment to "family" in one place, there are bound to be those *"Family Feud"*—or even Cain and Abel—moments.

On the surface it's easy to think about comparing the COC to the United Nations. But that analogy just doesn't work. The two hundred or so countries represented in the UN are apples and oranges; cats and dogs. Their little show is more about pomp and circumstance than results. They don't speak the same language, eat the same food, dress the same way, look the same way, or share an affinity for operating the same type of vehicle.

The biker brotherhood is nowhere *near* this inherently and genetically diverse. *Except* when it comes to allegiances and fierce loyalty to particular families within particular clubs.

The trick has always been to make the common ground the priority, so that our families *within* that common ground can get along and can train our sights on—and *against*—the ones who want us in jail or sliced into eunuchs, as opposed to fighting among ourselves.

The COC has done a damn nice job of adding mellowing hops to some really tough brews.

It was the first time some of the brothers had brought their ladies to a COC get-together. A barbeque out in San Bernardino.

The formal meetings are not designed as companion-accompanied social events. They are business meetings. Business meetings where serious issues are discussed, hashed out, debated, and generally solved. Outsiders or casual observers belong elsewhere.

But this was different.

This event was open. It was a time for a lot of different patch holders from a lot of different clubs to get together on easier—*neutral*—ground and express some mutual love and respect.

Most of the women who have been around awhile have a good understanding of the motorcycle world and the world of clubs. They *have* to.

But to reach that "refined" stage, there are those moments when innocence becomes experience.

I overheard one of my brothers explaining to his newest lady just where we were going and what the event was.

"Oh, so it's like a *mixer!*" she said with innocent sorority-girl perkiness—reminding me of Rachael Ray in a studded collar and leather chaps, stuffing a roasted duck.

The whole thing was like a movie trailer for *Legally Blonde*.

"Well…" he said thoughtfully. "I guess so. I guess it's a…*mixer*."

Actually, it was. Sort of.

It's always such a rush to see a gathering—a *mix*—of so many patches in one place; legendary symbols of legendary brotherhoods all together. It's also such a rush to see the new clubs. Clubs that have dedicated so much to getting to know the right people, and obeying the proper protocol—so that they, too, can enter into this elite, double-barreled world.

But elite worlds and empires can be overrun and destroyed—not only from the outside, but from the *inside*.

So either you keep fighting, or you lie down.

Every person here—every *patch* here—obviously felt that the preservation of this lifestyle was important enough to invest time and effort into. Very few want to spend every second of their lives struggling through a vicious range war. And it's for damn sure that no one here wanted the core of their souls and personalities molded and dictated to by clueless politicians.

We fight the external and we negotiate the internal.

We battle arrogant, ignorant, and power-crazed officials; and we are learning to compromise with brothers who are just as tough, pig-headed, and stubborn as we are. And considering the freedom-draining alternatives, it's certainly worth the effort.

God, it's worth it.

The Springer Mantra

by Keith Ball

This country was built by rugged individualists; hard-charging warriors and creative thinkers.

It was constructed on freedom and the creative premise.

The Declaration of Independence was written by men who

owned slaves, but who knew what the right words were. It's nuts—but for generations, mainstream Americans believed there was an accurate world order, a notion of right and wrong, and freedom for all. As bikers, we were allowed to feel the wind, the open road, and all the elements in a solitary manner.

No one understands or represents the biker spirit like us Yanks. We grew up with freedom branded on our souls. Right or wrong, historically correct or scrambled—until this last generation—we were the bastions of freedom worldwide.

Did we carry the scrolls with pride and respect, treating them with the honor they deserved? Only history will answer that delicate question.

Did greed and lust play a role? Unfortunately the answer is, yes; too many times.

Still, no one represented the wildness of the West like John Wayne. No one lit up rock 'n' roll like Elvis. No one made movies like Sam Peckinpah and Clint Eastwood. No one represented the biker culture on-screen like Dennis Hopper in *Easy Rider* or Marlon Brando in *The Wild One*. No publisher represented the biker spirit like Lou Kimzey when he created *Easyriders*.

That's not to say Americans do it right *every* time or *all* the time. It's not to say we understand the oblique and abstract nature of freedom, or the code behind the American Biker spirit. But fortunately, we've enjoyed the freedom to express that nature in our machines, actions, words, film, and photographs.

We also—up until 2004—experienced almost total freedom to build whatever we wanted and roll our glistening dream down the middle of a freeway.

In 1971, a handful of American custom industry representatives, including Mil Blair and Joe Teresi from D&D Distributors and *Easyriders*, met with the Department of Transportation (DOT) and proved that long front-ends and raked frames were as stable as, or more stable than, stock bikes. The DOT dropped any proposed regulations against the custom market and we were free to go.

For thirty-five years, we built whatever our drug-induced brains dictated. Then we chased chicks with our chromed steel-swords. There's nothing particularly practical about custom motorcycles; but they represent the very essence of our being free.

More than ever—in the midst of the twenty-first century— we need everything that custom motorcycles represent. In an era of regulation, global warming, and preconceived notions of sanctity, we need out-of-control loud-piped choppers to remind the public that this country was built on freedom; not safety, security, and selfishness.

Few understand the desire, the expression, and the nature of the metalflake angel or the chrome god; few understand our lane-splitting mantra. Who in their right mind would spend all winter in a below-freezing garage to build an inefficient, less-than-economic, unprotected two-wheeled art object? We devote every last dime, ruin our marriages, and build something so jewel-perfect it should be housed in glass and displayed in the Smithsonian.

Then what the hell do we do?

At the first spring thaw, we roll it onto the pothole-strewn streets, packed with thousands of careening two-ton automobiles piloted by unfocused maniacs full of financial and family woes, and we attempt a test ride at over a hundred miles an hour.

We carve through traffic like a wire through cheese, bolts loosening, brackets cracking. In a flash of dual coils and electronic ignitions, our dream is a reality, aboard fifty-year-old technology and untested welds.

But to us, it's all part of the perfect life, wrapped in a history of freedom, creativity, and sex. What more could anyone want?

We'll fight to our last breath to keep the spirit alive.

America needs us.

Those Who Ride

by Rogue

Bikers are an endangered species;
motorcycle riders are a dime a dozen.

In the fifty-plus years that I have been riding motorcycles, I've seen a lot of changes—not only in the motorcycles themselves, but also within the society that rides them. There is a definite difference between a "biker" and a motorcycle rider or enthusiast; and how that is determined depends on many factors and standards—and just who is doing the defining.

Who is right, and who can and should be able to call themselves bikers, is not a decision to be made by me. If you *are* one, you know it—and if you're not, you're not fooling anyone but yourself by saying you are.

Owning a motorcycle does not make you a biker; it makes you a motorcyclist.

There are many sayings among riders, but the one that states "Thirty thousand dollars and three hundred miles does not make you a biker" really rings true.

To be fair, many people have jobs and lifestyles that restrict them from living the biker lifestyle to the fullest.

They do it when they can.

There is nothing wrong with that, as long as when you hop on your ride, you do not try to project yourself as something you are not.

I'm not really sure when the changes to the lifestyle started, but I think saying in the '70s would be close enough.

One of the first major things was the federal government deciding to make motorcycle helmets mandatory. This brought people together who were tired of having the government telling them how to live their lives.

Enough was enough.

Even bikers in favor of wearing helmets got involved. It never was *really* about the helmets; it was about people wanting to make their *own* decisions about what was best for them. This was as good a place as any to make a stand.

Another major change came in 1983 when Harley-Davidson started the Harley Owners Group (HOG): Buy a Harley and become a member of this "club." Wear a back patch. Call each other bro. Go to some great parties. The organization has grown to include chapters from around the world; and they *do* put on great events.

During the '70s is when motorcycle magazines started to really become popular and to promote riding and the lifestyle; and that continues to this day. They cover every aspect you can think of, though much of it is about the fun, parties, and events.

Today, major events are held around the country, and on any given weekend there are so many local events you cannot make them all.

Fun, fun, and more fun!

It seems that of those who ride now, many are in it for the fun and aren't paying attention to all the other aspects of the lifestyle.

But one *good* thing about the increase in riders is that motorcycles have become a more dependable source of transportation. Aftermarket companies are supplying a large assortment of quality parts, which has produced jobs and more money for more people.

The bad thing is that everyone wants to jump on the bandwagon and get in on the money—and this includes government and other agencies who say they are for "safety."

Granted, with the increase in riders—many with no prior experience—collisions and deaths have gone up. I am sorry to say this is bound to happen. Those pushing for mandatory helmet laws are still at it, and they continue to push for all kinds of things to protect riders when they crash. This has never been successful, and there's no reason to expect that to change.

The logical thing would be to try to eliminate the wrecks in the first place. The Motorcycle Safety Foundation (MSF) was started some years ago by motorcycle manufacturers. Together with the AMA, they saw a need to have schooling for the many new riders.

I was one of fifty people invited to the first Meeting Of The Minds to set up a safety program. Motorcycles were donated to schools around the country, and courses made available at little or no fee.

Over a period of time things changed, and prices kept rising. Now the MSF is pushing to make motorcycle riding courses mandatory before an operator's permit can be issued. Thus, MSF becomes the only business in the world that wants to manufacture a product and then force you to pay for a course on how to operate it.

Plus, when people complete one of these courses, they get a certificate that—in some states—allows them to get an operator's permit without taking a state-issued test. Duh…the agency issuing the permit is taking the opinion of *another* agency: an agency that wants to sell a motorcycle!

I see some big liability issues here.

With the ever-growing number of riders, a good part of the motorcycle world has become a fashion show and a big party; with many buying motorcycles as a means to attend events and increase their numbers of friends (not that I find any problem with that, as I also get to attend a lot more events and meet new people!).

Some motorcycles in bike shows and on television now are works of art and display incredible new technology (though I personally would not want to ride most of them any distance!).

So there have been a lot of changes.

All in all, I would say they are for the better. But with growth, there are going to be problems, and hopefully "those who ride" will make the decisions that are best for *themselves* and not let groups or government agencies do that for them. That is part of being a *biker* isn't it? Making your own decisions about what is best for you, while letting others live their lives as *they* see fit, as long as it doesn't affect *you*!

Enjoy life and the time you spend riding, but also make time to ensure the enjoyment is still around for our children.

Through the years, bikers have lived by an unwritten code. This code includes—in part:

Be proud of yourself and
don't hide your chosen lifestyle from anyone.

Respect and learn from those
with more experience or knowledge,
and pass those teachings on to others.

Your word is your bond and must always be kept.

Help others when you can.

Never say die and never give up, no matter how bad it gets.
You will always come out of it.

Chapter 13

We Ain't Goin' Quietly

The Past, Present, and (Possible) Future of Major Events

In 2006, my documentary film crew
traveled to Echo Basin Ranch in Southern Colorado
during the Labor Day weekend to make a film about
what should have been one of the best biker parties ever.
Instead, bikers were cheated and bikers' freedom was stolen.
What went down does *matter and we ain't goin' quietly.*

—Jeff "EZJ" Kraus,
Filmmaker, South Bay Biker Productions

Durango.

Riding through this area of Southern Colorado is like taking a tour of heaven; it's an asphalt orgasm that becomes multiple with every cool new turn and bend in the road.

313

I remember rolling south out of Lightner Creek. I turned my head and told my lady on the back that right that second, there was nothing on earth I'd rather be doing.

I meant it.

Still do.

It was perfect.

Always is.

Even when the churning mountain weather turns sour, there is still a humbling magnificence about being open and exposed on that bike, cradled by the San Juan Peaks—wet, dry, hot, or cold.

Route 550 will take you from Durango to the 1870s mining town of Silverton; it's a forty-nine mile ride north over Coal Bank Pass—a nice little 10,600-foot rise where I've seen snow before summer has officially ended.

But that didn't matter.

What *did* matter, again—as always—was the ride. And the feeling you get when you connect two of the last slices of the old and wild Western frontier with yourself and an old and wild two-wheeled vehicle—a vehicle that exists because *some* people truly get off on feeling everything nature has to dish out, without the anti-climax of insulation or shield.

Back in Durango you can park your bike along Main Avenue, walk to the Strater Hotel, and fall directly back into the 1880s. You can get a drink in the Strater's Diamond Belle Saloon and talk to the ghost of Louis L'Amour as he tells you how he wrote his classic series, *The Sacketts*, in room 222 right above the bar. Look toward the door as the honky-tonk piano plays, and imagine the miners, gunslingers, bawdy chicks, drifters, grifters, and hustlers who have shared the bar's heavy glasses and helped stain the worn wooden tables.

And now it's you.

And now you're a part of the new frontier—maybe the *last* frontier in terms of rejecting restrictions, relishing rebellion, and feeling genuinely fast in a world that wants to slow down and snuff out anything with even the slightest hint of more rugged times—times when not *everything* was belted in, muffled, holstered, and neutered.

Durango will do this for you.

Durango is also the center of the troubled rally that has been known as the Four Corners Run, the Iron Horse Run, the Rally in the Rockies, Ignacio Bike Week, and others.

The word "troubled" has to do with the *politics* of this event, *not* the partying. And it's a "trouble" that has crept into other big-time get-togethers as well.

"Troubled" is a word seldom used when talking about the simple enjoyment of a whole bunch of bikers coming together to ride and share brotherhood; to eat, drink, camp, parade, and party.

The idea of *anything* being "troubled" in the mix of bikes, bikers, and the beauty of this area is like a massive zit popping up on the nose of Miss Universe.

But it happens.

If one pretty nose can get red and gooey, so can others.

Big events of *any* type require big planning and big organization to make them work. Sure. But almost from the start, the yearly Labor Day run in Durango had behind-the-scenes problems. While the people attending just enjoyed the ride and relaxation, the organizers continually struggled—for control, for money, for recognition.

The center of the actual run was ostensibly the fairgrounds in the town of Ignacio, twenty-four miles southeast of Durango; with the "big parade" taking place in downtown Durango. But it didn't really matter. Like any other major run, people spread themselves out over the whole area, absorbing and enjoying it all, not really caring about the "official" promoter's name on the "official" programs next to the "official" t-shirts at the "official" merchandise booths.

Ultimately, the most "official" thing to true bikers is simply having a good place to go and good people to enjoy it with.

When the "good place to go" is "officially" closed off to bikers, however, is when the real "trouble" starts.

Since its 1993 beginning, the Durango rally has changed its name and promoters and venues several times. The run was even "officially" cancelled in 2002, with those in charge citing that year's drought and fire danger in the area.

But there was also the little factor that the rally had no major venue for things like vendors and entertainment. The Ignacio fairgrounds—The Sky Ute Events Center—is on tribal land, as is just about everything else in Ignacio; and the relationship between the promoters and the Southern Ute Indian Tribe was on a warpath from the beginning. In 2002, the arrows really rained down and the Durango event had no "official" place to call home.

But the bikers came anyway.

They had "a good place to go" regardless of whether it was "official" or not.

Four years later, in 2006, it was a whole different story.

With a new promoter and a new venue in the spiffy Echo Basin Ranch, it appeared that all the right hoops had been jumped through—that this event might actually get an "official" identity *and* some consistency.

No.

A last-minute court ruling to drastically limit the number of people allowed at the main campground essentially pulled the plug on the latest incarnation of the Durango run.

Bikers Roar as Judge Limits Rally
ONLY 600 CAMPERS ALLOWED

The Four Corners gathering could draw 100,000 and organizers had expected several thousand to stay at the Echo Basin Ranch. The ruling is being appealed.

—*Denver Post,* August 30, 2006

It's one thing when backstage hassles change the name of an event or cause the vendor tents to go up in another part of town; it's a lot more frightening and intense when outside authorities come armed with legislation, badges, and a cavalry of court rulings.

Thousands of people were headed to Durango in '06. Thousands of people saw the light-up signboards telling them to go home.

Jeff "EZJ" Kraus documented the "trouble" at the 2006 Four Corners run in his film, Showdown in Durango.

The main "justification" the court came up with for "limiting attendance" in Durango was that the new organizer, Dan Bradshaw, had not provided enough security. This particular "reason" has been a tool commonly used by courts and authorities who want to shut down or stall an event.

It was used in 2005 to close down the Viet Nam Vets MC's Annual Mardi Gras—also at the last minute. You could literally smell the food starting to cook at the vendor booths behind the fence, even as Los Angeles County Sheriff cars lined up to block the entrance to the run.

It was used in Hollister. Twice.

Before the Durango "massacre," the year 2006 saw the first modern-day cancellation of the Hollister Rally. But like Durango '02, people came anyway. It was an ironic display of forcing the officials to bring in the very legions of law enforcement that they (supposedly) were trying to avoid paying for in the first place; and now it was without the benefit of the revenue an "official" event would have generated.

Hollister's "official" rally was reinstated the following year, but was axed again in 2009. The "Birthplace of the American Biker" again fell into a bureaucratic, legislative, and just plain mean prohibition, akin to not allowing the consumption of chocolate in Hershey.

Bikers (and their revenue) were once appreciated in the Birthplace of the American Biker.

Hollister in happier days.

The slime-slip tug o' war between event coordinators and authorities—including police, city fathers, city councils, and other politicians—has polarized entire communities. On one end of the muddy rope are merchants and proprietors who make millions of dollars from the biker trade; they are joined by city, state, and federal brass who rake in tons of tax dollars. But holding tight to the opposing greasy knot, digging in their heels, are law enforcement and others in high places who simply don't like bikers—regardless of financial gain.

San Benito County Sheriff Curtis Hill's focus isn't on the everyday goings-on of the [Hollister] *rally, but of outlaw biker gangs who could cause problems at it, he said.*

319

Between 30 to 40 officers from sheriff and police departments throughout the state will arrive Friday to assist deputies, with the sole purpose of monitoring the activities of biker gangs attending the event, Hill said.

"Some groups are here only to conduct criminal activities—it's a part of any biker rally," Hill said. "Whether they're laundering money, dealing dope or dabbling in prostitution...For me it's all about criminal activities going on and if we see it we're gonna address it."

—*Hollister Free Lance,* July 1, 2004

Part of *any* biker rally?

Really?

I've been to a million motorcycle events. I've been a simple attendee *and* I've worked behind the scenes. And in all honesty—trust me on this—I haven't laundered even one red cent at any of them. I've never picked up (*or* pimped) any skanky mini-skirted pros, either.

Drugs? Maybe.

Sort of.

I *have* been offered plenty of smoke that would make even Bob Marley's spirit proud. But no one has ever tried to *sell* me anything. Ever. No commercial offers of pure opium, jars of ecstasy, or little plastic bags of white powder. Not one. Yes, lots of big, twisted smiles from friends and acquaintances wanting to share a brotherly hit off of Maui's finest with me; but sharing some reasonably potent herb in that context just doesn't fit with the classic and technical definition of "dealing dope."

I *have* experienced times, however, when *real* trouble sets in.

The aforementioned ripples from the deadly tidal wave that was the 2002 Laughlin, Nevada, River Run shootings are still being felt. To say that the Laughlin run was never the same after that is a heavy understatement.

No event in the West was the same after that.

A club-friendly event that had been well-attended by many MCs for the past two decades immediately became a minefield for anyone with a patch on their back.

It's worth a recap. It's worth a few more looks at Laughlin when considering what the future may hold for the major events:

On April 27, 2002, at around 2:15 a.m., the bar at Harrah's Casino became a "bloody battlefield," as the press continually called it, when members of the Hells Angels Motorcycle Club and the Mongols Motorcycle Club faced off in a sudden shoot-out that resulted in three deaths—two members of the Angels, one member of the Mongols. A fourth body, that of Hells Angels member Christian Tate, was discovered about an hour later out on I-40, about a hundred miles west of Laughlin. Police speculated that he was actually murdered closer to 1:30 a.m., forty-five minutes *before* the chaos exploded at Harrah's.

I was there in Laughlin.

I was there for the lock-downs, for the shake-downs, for the questions, for the speculations—for the most massive rage of rabid cops against the biker machine *ever*.

Every person there could probably tell you *exactly* where they were the moment they found out what was going on. *And* how quickly they knew what the ramifications would be.

This one wasn't going away anytime soon.

I didn't go back to Laughlin in 2003.

I didn't *plan* to go back *ever*.

I guess I just wanted to remember it as it was—*before* the shootings. I knew damn well that every cop in the state, and probably the feds too, would be there—from now on.

Over the years—*overall*—Laughlin had been a pretty cool event. I had been to all of them. I had dealt with the good years and the somewhat less-than-perfect years. I had dealt with the windy and dusty rides. I had dealt with the heat, the occasional desert rain, and the Year of the Butterflies and the Year of the Grasshoppers. I had dealt with it when the rooms in every hotel in the whole town were taken over by a promoter who forced everyone to buy at least four days of overpriced accommodations, even if you couldn't get out there until Friday or even Saturday.

But it was generally worth it.

Some great concerts were held in that amphitheater at the Flamingo. The Flamingo always held a lot of Angels as well; it was their headquarters for the weekend, which provided a high-proof atmosphere. And the event always had free live music, too—blues and classic rock in the tents down around the front of the Edgewater and the Colorado Belle.

There was the yearly ride over the dam, through Bullhead City and out to the nostalgic Route 66 town of Oatman—until local law enforcement put up sobriety check points on either end of the only road in and out of the place. That ended the ride out there—for me, at least.

We used to look forward to watching the impromptu "parade" along Casino Drive—crazy bikes and crazier chicks. But that was stopped, too.

It got so that once I parked my bike in front of the hotel, it didn't move again until I was ready to head home. Even *that* was bearable. There was still plenty to see and do.

But when 2002 blew up, I knew it was over.

For me, at least.

When 2004 rolled around, one of my closest friends asked me to help him out with his two vendor booths. I would have rather pulled out my own front teeth with rusty channel locks, but he and I go way back. I agreed to help him out.

The River Run "officially" begins on Wednesday or Thursday (I've lost track), but I decided to get out there on Monday. I wanted some time alone. I wanted to re-absorb all of it after the shootings. I wanted to watch the town fill up with bikes, like a fast-forwarded time-lapse film. After a "year off," I wanted to see if I could even handle being back there.

And I was going to wear my patch—even though I knew I'd be greeted at places with "No Colors Allowed" signs. But I figured, "Fuck 'em!"

I wasn't disappointed.

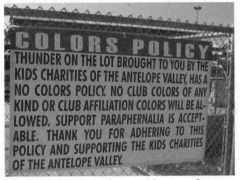

No Colors policies have become disturbingly prevalent at events.

The first things I saw when I rounded the bend toward hotel row were a signboard and a vinyl banner—both telling me that colors weren't welcome at that particular inn.

I was staying at the River Palms. Luckily, they had no signs and I felt fairly comfortable.

My friend arrived on Wednesday. By Thursday we were set up and selling.

I stayed to myself, not really even enjoying my "off time." When we wrapped up the booths at night I just went back to my room and drank by myself. No bars. No fun. Just doing my job, looking forward to heading west as soon as we cleaned things up on Sunday night.

Things were fairly uneventful—until Saturday around noon.

It started off with my going to a convenience store to buy a case of water and some ice. The smiling little girl behind the counter rang up a bill that came to sixty-one dollars and some change.

I was polite.

I told her that there must be some mistake; she needed to *recalculate*.

Again, sixty-one bucks and change, for a five-dollar flat of water and one fucking bag of ice.

What the hell…?

I was stunned. Leaving the water and the ice in front of her register, I walked out without causing a scene—but I have to admit, even as a devout free-range capitalist, that kind of gouging makes me nuts.

A bit later I was making my way from one of my friend's booths to the other by cutting through the Terrible Herbst gas station.

The first thing that startled me was a helicopter swooping in to hover low, right over the station. Then the cop cars started to move in. Lots of them. From different agencies.

I hadn't been much paying attention, but I was surprised to see a big group of Angels fueling up. The cops pounced immediately and in force; and I had walked right into the middle of it.

Frankly, I was shocked to see any of the Red & White in town at all—post 2002. Evidently the cops were, too. One cop told me to "get your ass out of here!" I quickly took his suggestion. Meantime, the Angels were being searched and questioned—and, in a couple of cases, cuffed.

I couldn't wait to get out of that town. Sunday night couldn't come fast enough.

The 2005 rally came fast, too.

Along with it came another request from my friend—and another capitulation. He had only one booth this time, further north on Casino Drive than before.

Again I was met with signs. More of them. But—again—the River Palms seemed cool with me and my colors.

Las Vegas Metro wasn't as cordial.

Friday night looked like a war zone along the boulevard. Three years after the shootings, and the law enforcement heat was just getting worse.

Cops swarmed in cars, on horseback, on bicycles, on motorcycles, on foot, in helicopters. Flatbed tow trucks were staged everywhere to impound and load up the bikes of anyone accused of "getting out of line." I have no idea how I made it unbruised and unarrested from the vendor area back to the River Palms, less than a mile south. I guess I was lucky.

The prohibitions in Laughlin have become a joke. Sadly, they're no laughing matter.

The next night, I wasn't so "lucky."

On Saturday, we wrapped it up at about ten p.m.—a lot earlier than most of the other vendors, but we were beat. I was on my look-at-me purple-flamed FXR and I needed to head south from the vendor area; but there was *no* way I was going to try to make a left turn across Casino Drive. There were more cops and horses and helicopters and law enforcement stuff than even on Friday night.

I felt sick and doomed, but I'd be damned if I was going to take off my cut.

I turned right—north—and went a half-mile or so before I could legally make a left turn into a parking lot (there's no way I was going to try a U-turn, either) and get myself turned around. I was heading south now, in sight of the River Palms.

I stopped at a red light behind a car. When the light turned green, the car didn't move. I was about to swing around it, when I noticed that this car was a Ford Crown Victoria. With a small antenna on the trunk.

I felt like an idiot.

I had let my guard down, and there was no excuse. I suppose I could rationalize that I was exhausted and my observational instincts were dulled and crippled. But, again, *that's no excuse*. Fatigue is a rationalization I hate. That kind of slip in the jungle or even "the street" will get you killed or eaten. Or worse.

In that second I knew I was completely fucked.

Another unmarked car pulled up behind me. Two more came up on either side.

The expected red and blue lights began from all angles. A loudspeaker told me to shut off the bike, park it, and get off with my hands up.

I'd been through this drill more than once, but this time I was legitimately worried. Not because I had anything that might show up as a "problem." No. I was as clean as a Catholic schoolgirl before prom night. I hadn't even had *anything* to drink all day—and that's rough for me; most nights by ten, I'm already extremely *comfortable*. But not tonight—not here. I wasn't *that* much of an idiot.

The reason I *was* worried is that I didn't know just how "dedicated" these boys (and girls) were. This rally—this environment—would be a great springboard for whatever it might take to climb up the status ladder in their world. I wasn't anxious to be that last rung.

The first cop to approach was from the car directly behind me. He was a little guy—maybe 5'4" or so—with an obvious complex about his stature. He told me to lean facedown against the lead car and put my hands behind me.

I did it; but in the process I asked him—casually and respectfully, of course—just why I had been stopped.

He told me—somewhat less casually and respectfully—that I had made an illegal lane change.

I told him—still casually and respectfully—that I had made *no* lane changes at all.

He told me—now with *zero* casualness and respect—that if I wanted to argue with him, I'd be going to jail and my bike would be impounded.

Okiedokie.

At least we both knew where we stood on all this.

I also knew that this night had just begun. None of us were going anywhere any time soon. I was already draped over a brown four-door Ford with my hands locked behind me, so my expectations of any kind of apology or quick redemption and release were relatively low.

"Napoleon" asked me where my license, registration, and proof of insurance were. I told him that everything he needed was in the small leather bag strapped to the sissy bar.

He told me not to look toward my bike.

This bothered me a bit. Not that I for a minute believed he wasn't a fine upstanding citizen and an honest protector of the peace, but... for the most fleeting of moments, I just happened to think: *Gee,* what if this officer had just made a big drug bust in, say, an urban area of 'Vegas or somewhere close; and, *gee,* what if some of the confiscated contraband got "caught" in his sleeve; and, *gee,* what if said contraband just "happened" to fall into that bag on my bike; then, *gee,* I'd be looking at spending pretty much all of my sunset years in a senior citizen's suite at a Nevada State Penitentiary.

Stranger things have happened.

While going through my wallet, Officer Diminutive found my State of California Department of Justice Basic Firearms Safety Certificate: a valuable piece of paper, without which you cannot legally purchase a gun in the Golden State.

Now, he had *already* asked me if I had any firearms or weapons on me. And I had *already* told him no—as if he wouldn't have found any I might have had stashed, during his search of me and that little tool bag on the FXR anyway.

But now he stood me upright, off the Ford's trunk, and asked me again.

My answer hadn't changed.

"No."

"I mean, do you have any firearms at all?!" he shouted at me. "Do you *own* any guns?!"

"Yes," I said. "Many."

Bang! I was slammed back on the now-familiar trunk lid of the Ford.

I heard him make a radio call that eventually connected him to some agency in Los Angeles: the county in which I reside.

After an expectedly long delay, I heard the reply call.

An *Adam-12*–type, echoing radio voice told Officer D that I had no wants or warrants in California and that the guns I owned were all legally purchased and registered; but "the voice" concluded by saying that I was a "person of interest" in something or other.

This was marginally damning, but apparently not concrete enough for my little buddy to "take me downtown" and earn some stripes for himself.

It *was* enough, however, for him to bring in the "gang specialists."

Another car showed up with a man-woman officer team. After the pair put me against a chain-link fence and took pictures of me from the front and the back, they began asking me questions about my club.

I was concerned about their ignorance.

But after spending many minutes giving them a history lesson, I finally stopped myself. I suggested to this team that while I didn't think it was ethical or healthy for me to continue this seminar on the history of motorcycle clubs in America, there were many sources "out there" that they could pick up and read, view, and/or listen to that might help them in their quest to become legitimately schooled in the field that they had already been deemed experts in.

My patience was wearing thin.

I was tired, angry, and needed a drink.

I asked them if our relationship here was nearing an end; if perhaps our collective activities of this evening were coming to a conclusion?

Almost.

The Munchkin with the badge had one more shot. He wrote me up for the invisible illegal lane change.

I didn't say a word.

I got back on my bike and rode straight to the River Palms. On Sunday I *walked* to and from my friend's booth.

It would be the last time I would ever visit Laughlin—for the River Run or for any other reason.

My experience in Laughlin and the heavy-handed atmosphere there isn't unique. It simply goes with the territory anymore. Whether the 2002 shootings were the *main* catalyst for the increase in law enforcement at so many motorcycle events, and for the imposition of more and more regulatory ducks to be precisely aligned in a row, can be debated.

Maybe just the sheer increase in people who want to be a part of these gatherings is what did it.

Maybe it's still the fear.

Maybe it's still the envy.

In any case, the big events are still the big events. There is nothing—*nothing*—like the feeling of being a working part of thousands of bikers with thousands of bikes all gathered together because, well, *they're bikers!*

There are the traditional and biggest events like Sturgis, Laconia, Daytona, and (on again, off again) Hollister. There are the others—too many to count—like the Lone Star Rally, Arizona Bike Week, Biketoberfest (Daytona's pre-Halloween bash), the Las Vegas Bike Fest, and Rolling Thunder in the nation's capital. There are the annual one-day events like L.A.'s Love Ride and the massive Christmas toy run in the Dallas–Fort Worth area every December.

And then there are the one-off runs like the Harley-Davidson 100th Anniversary in Wisconsin in 2003:

We passed through seven states on our ride there along the northern route; we went through seven *different* ones on the way home along the southern route. Of the fourteen, nine of them had no helmet laws—at least for adults—so we were able to enjoy our ride even more.

I don't think I've ever felt more *connected*—more like I was going to a real *celebration,* rather than just another event.

Milwaukee has hosted "anniversaries" for their mechanical hometown hero before, but this was the *100th.* The idea that people were coming from all over the world made it feel like a pilgrimage—a hallowed Harley hiatus.

The ride was everything you'd expect. Weather that changed by the minute. Heat in California, Nevada, and Utah. Hail and cold along I-70 in Colorado's White River National Forest.

But then the *real* heat hit in Nebraska.

We had been spoiled by being helmet-free through Utah and Colorado; but we had to put the lids back on at the Nebraska state line, near the junction of I-76 and I-80. And it was hot, *damn* hot.

In temperatures like that, helmets become crock-pots that cook your brain.

We had been trying to run at night during the worst stretches, but our timing had gotten a little off. Despite the heat, we really wanted to make some time so we ran with it.

We stopped at a rest area somewhere in the middle of nowhere along I-80. Another small group of bikes had stopped there, too; all of us trying to escape the screaming solar attack for at least a little while.

In the men's room was one of the other group's riders; an older guy. He was leaned over the sink, soaking a bandana with water and wiping his face and head, trying to cool down a few degrees.

The man was as red as the core of the sun. I figured that if this ol' boy went even another mile he'd seize up with heat stroke and fall off of that bike like a rock.

I offered some advice and he took it.

He told me that they'd already talked about just hanging there at the rest stop until they—and the day—cooled down a bit. Then they'd find the nearest motel and pack it in.

It was a good choice.

We wound up doing the same.

But in a weird way, this kind of suffering and dedication added to the near-religious nature of all this; like the pilgrim with shredded elbows and crippled hands who crawls on his belly to his particular Mecca.

People—myself included—may complain now and then about some of the corporate arrogance and failings of the Harley-Davidson Motor Company. They may lament about how their dealerships have become more like supermarkets than the good old friendly oil-stained neighborhood shops; or about the high prices of parts; or about anything else that people always find to bellyache about. But in their hearts, every biker realizes the impact of this machine and this company and its history.

For the 100th, a hell of a lot of people made a hell of a big effort to make it to *this* lifestyle's particular Mecca.

For miles around the Milwaukee area, every city and community had special events planned. A huge group of concentric circles of fun pulsed out from the Juneau Avenue epicenter. It was the snazzy centennial that the mothership deserved.

But the finale was weird.

In a way, it showed a little of that corporate "disconnect" that people talk about—*bitch* about.

After *so* many people had made their way *so* far to get here for a *connection*, someone made a blunder.

A quarter of a million people—give or take—were primed and ready for a raging last blow-out party. And as always, music served as the centerpiece for the fun.

The Doobie Brothers, Tim McGraw, and Kid Rock opened the show.

It was a mix that worked; the party had started.

But the headliner had been kept a secret.

A surprise.

All week long the local radio stations had been speculating. Teasing. Names were tossed around: The Stones, maybe? Skynyrd? Springsteen? Who would take this crowd to rock 'n' roll heaven as this holy hoopla reached its climax? Who would send them on their journeys home with a "freebird" in their souls and "heavy metal thunder" still echoing in their heads?

Five years later, at the Harley 105th, "The Boss" *would* be the musical headliner—but not this time.

This time it was…

…*(drum roll please)*…

…Elton John!

Elton John. Elton John?
He's not American, certainly not very manly,
and far from hard rock.
The last rocking song from John
came at a time when H-D was still owned by AMF.

—Andy Tarnoff,
Publisher, OnMilwaukee.com

I'd play you a song about motorcycles,
but I don't have any.

—Elton John;
Performing at the Harley 100th Anniversary

In a toxic-purging kind of way, it was okay. Maybe it's *good* that some people—even those who manufacture the machine we have become one with—*still* don't have the inside track directly into what makes us tick.

It's good that there's still a mystery here.

It's good that who we are and what's truly inside us isn't just a demographic or a statistic.

In the end, I'm glad there's still a lot to this lifestyle that can't be second-guessed or simply *marketed* to—that there's still a lot that is simply a part of some people and not a part of others.

Elite.

As we rolled south out of Milwaukee, about to cross the state line into Illinois, the last couple of weeks kept running through my head. A lot had happened on this trip—a lot happens on *every* trip. That's why we do this.

But that last night in Milwaukee cropped up—the Great Elton John Fiasco.

I started to smile—laugh, actually. I loved the thought that if nothing else, no one—*no one*—will ever know exactly what goes on in my mind, or the mind of any biker, as we lose ourselves in the solidarity of the ride. It's such a precious solitude; sacred and impenetrable.

I considered it a pretty safe bet, however, that not *many* who have "headed down the highway," cranking on the throttle, have matched the roar and the beat of the road with the lilting strains of "Tiny Dancer" running through their heads.

While things like the Harley 100th are unique and schedule-special, the "annuals" have become as permanent a part of many of our calendars as our mothers' or kids' birthdays.

Of the three biggest and most well-known yearly runs—Laconia, Daytona, and Sturgis—Laconia is the oldest; with an origin that dates back to a fairly large gathering of motorcyclists at Weirs Beach in 1916.

As with most of the solid and venerable rallies, in the beginning the New Hampshire event was all about things like racing and hill climbs and all the other activities associated with the various Gypsy Tours. The Loudon Classic was—and *is*—the race that Laconia centered around; it is now the longest-running motorcycle race in America, held every Father's Day.

In 1923 (some sources say 1917) the Laconia rally was "officially recognized" as part of the Gypsy Tour by the Federation of American Motorcyclists (later to become the AMA). Unfortunately, the Weirs Beach riot of 1965 truly burned the event. Post-riot pressure from officials and a decline in attendance cut the event to just a three-day affair, down from a week.

It took many years for Laconia to regroup. Attendance finally began to increase in the '80s. In 1990, hoping to build the numbers even more, local business owners contacted the AMA, asking for their endorsement once again, and for them to restore the run to a week in length. In '91, the businessmen teamed up with the Lakeside Sharks Motorcycle Club to form the Laconia Motorcycle Week Association.

Their efforts worked: Laconia Motorcycle Week now runs every year from the second Friday in June through Father's Day, with a party crowd that ranges between one and four hundred thousand people.

In the beginning, before wet t-shirt and "big belly" contests, rallies were about venerable things like racing.

Daytona Bike Week began in 1937—again, as an event centered around racing. The Daytona 200 was the main event, run on a 3.2-mile course of both pavement and the beach.

From 1942 to 1947, the race was canceled due to World War II. But—like Durango in 2002 and Hollister in 2006—people showed up anyway. They had "a good place to go and good people to enjoy it with."

When things officially restarted in 1947, the Daytona 200 was promoted by NASCAR pioneer Bill France. And just as those noisy little stockcar races became a "smashing" success, so did Daytona.

Each early spring, a half-million winter-weary bikers thaw out in Florida, spending ten balmy days riding and whooping it up along the beach in Daytona.

In 1938, a year after Daytona kicked off, J.C. "Pappy" Hoel and his Jackpine Gypsies Motorcycle Club had a small get-together in the Black Hills of South Dakota. Around two hundred riders showed up for the first "Black Hills Motor Classic." They raced, hill-climbed, and did a little partying.

Pappy and his wife Pearl had an Indian Motorcycle dealership on Junction Avenue in Sturgis. Riders camped in the Hoels' backyard and were fed Pearl's "weenies, sloppy joes, potato salad, and watermelon for dessert."

This little party led to one of the biggest and most famous of all biker parties: the monster mash that we all refer to simply as "Sturgis."

The number of bikers who roll to Sturgis is about the same as those who make it down south to Daytona, but Sturgis is really the defining rite of passage—not only for the *American* Biker, but for bikers all over the world who come to be ordained into the Sturgis/American Biker experience.

South Dakota's Black Hills and the Badlands provide the perfect stage for this August drama—for this life-changing attitude assault. It's all about endurance and fun: a commingling of will and soul and sand and rocks, of mountains and plains and fast motorcycles and the complete forgetting that big cities and time even exist.

The crowds and brotherhood at the Buffalo Chip; the swinging doors and Wild Bill's ghost in Deadwood; Mount Rushmore; Sundance; the eerie monolith of the Devils Tower; the streets and the people along Main Street—*this* is Sturgis.

So is the ride there.

As always.

More epic journeys have probably been made on the way to and from Sturgis than to and from any other motorcycle event. Just the idea that you're *riding to Sturgis,* from just about *anywhere,* indicates an "epic." Among life's initiations, it's right up there with your first beer, your first time drunk, your first bike, or maybe even your first dose of non-solo intimacy.

The weather, the breakdowns, the people along the way, the towns along the way—*this* is also Sturgis.

This *is* a rite of passage.

For American Biker Rich Halmuth, it was even more:

At Least It's Not Raining

by Rich Halmuth

Remind me never to go camping in polar bear country.

My trip to Sturgis was…interesting.

I leave my house at 6:00 a.m.

No rain. Cool.

Well…until I get five miles out of town—then it starts to pour.

I meet my club VP at 6:30 and ride over to meet my probate, "A.J.," at 7:00. We need an early start; today is the club's summer mandatory run—about three hundred miles— and then I'm on my way to Sturgis.

We stop for breakfast to meet up with the rest of the chapter. Pretty soon here they came: "Bud," our Prez, leading; Lovey an' his ol' lady, Martha; "Ezyrider"; "Rickus"; an' "Oh Bill" an' his ol' lady in the sweep vehicle. We head down the road and stop for gas, an' here comes "Showtime"; now we got a nice-sized pack.

With Bud in the lead, we take off on the I-77 West, headed for Columbus, Ohio. We follow our Prez, an', yep, he gets us lost (typical Prez) in the dark section of Columbus.

Back on the road. More directions.

Okay, we are on the right track now. Well, sort of. Bud sees a bar an' waves us in.

Hmmm...

Well, the air-conditioning is cold. An' the beer is cold. An' my brother Oh Bill is giggling. Now he's hysterically laughing. I say, "Wahtz up?" He says, "Go look at the pictures on the wall." Somebody shouts out: "Put some Johnny Cash on the jukebox!" Oh Bill says, "Shit! We should have picked the other bar."

Yep, our Prez had led us into a gay bar.

Oh well, at least the beer was cold, an' we were the only ones in it.

So after a few beers we decide to leave.

Rickus is out in the parking lot soaking up some rays when this fire truck drives by, blows the horn, an' whistles at him. Rickus waves back. I about fall off my bike, I'm laughing so hard. I say, "Shit, right out of The Village People!"

Well the run site is about twenty miles up the road. We're early, an' we meet up with Skillet; his ol' lady, Patty; an' Ginseng. Pretty soon other members of the club started arriving. Twos an' threes, tens an' twenties...more an' more. Pretty soon the entire parking lot is filled with members of every chapter. And we have twenty cop cars there to escort us on our run. What a sight!

Pretty cool. The cops stop traffic for us, an' four hundred–plus of us roar through Columbus, Ohio, on a seventy-mile 75-mph ride to the party site. They have big banners for us, an' people everywhere are filming us. The party is great. The band sucks, but the food isn't too bad and the beer an' wine are ice cold.

The next day, three of us leave for Wisconsin so one of our brothers can spend some time with his son up there. We make it to the Indiana/Illinois line the first day, then through Chicago an' up into Wisconsin. Stop off at a cool H-D shop before heading into Green Bay.

About an hour north of Green Bay, the shit hits the fan. Fuckin' cager puts on his right blinker, an' I go to go around him an' he whips a left in front of me. I slam into his left front fender with my running boards an' blow his left front tire. Then the bike flips over on its side, skidding me under it for thirty feet.

Helllllllllloooooooooooooo! Road rash.

My bike smashes into a ten-ton water-pumping station, used for drilling pipe under the ground. Cute, huh?

Well, two construction workers are there, an' they tell me not to move. I tell them get this motherfuckin' bike off me! As they're lifting it off me, this asshole comes up an' says, "Look what you did to my car, man!"

Couldn't shoot him—I didn't have my piece on me (good thing, huh?).

Well, they manage to get the bike off me: What a mess! No, not me—the bike. I'll heal.

No floorboards, no oil filter, no regulator, no pipes, no carb an' air filter. Saddlebags destroyed, seat destroyed, tweaked handlebars, busted-off spotlights, no windshield, paint job shot to hell. Both fenders an' both tanks: dents and scratches in them. Plus all my gear—all over the road.

Well, the first-aid guy comes up an' I decline any attention. Like I said, I'll heal. But look at my bike! I'm so pissed off, I could spit razor blades.

Now this bitch cop arrives on the scene, an' she wants to give me a fuckin' ticket. I just say "Fuck it!" an' go sit against a tree.

About five minutes later, my two club brothers show up an', man, are they pissed! I calm 'em down and tell 'em I'm cool. Probably a broken leg or shattered kneecap, but see if you can get a truck an' get my bike outta here before the vultures start scavenging parts off it.

So they split, an' another cop shows up. He comes up an' asks me if I'm all right. I say we'll deal with that later; right now I'm only worried about my bike.

Well, he talks to the bitch for fifteen minutes, arguing with her, an' basically tells her to leave. Then he goes over an' talks to the driver of the car and tells him he can leave. Then he walks over to me an' asks me if I can walk or hobble over to the accident scene. I tell him I can.

We go over there, an' he asks what the fuck happened. I tell him the dude put on his right blinker, an' I go to go around him without crossing the line, an' he whips a left at the last moment. Bang! The rest is history.

The cop says, yeah, that's what he figured happened. Then he tells me he's the other cop's supervisor an' that he wasn't going to let me get a ticket 'cause he rides an' he sees this shit all the time. He asks if I'm going to be okay. I tell him, yeah, thanks for the help.

Then here comes the cavalry. They got a truck an' three strong boys; they load her right up in the truck, and we take it up to Russ's Cycles in Oconto, Wisconsin.

Then I go to the hospital.

No broken bones but, man, did I have one swelled-up knee an' foot an' leg! Good case of road rash, an' a third-degree burn on my right leg.

These boys at Russ's Cycles are miracle workers: for fifteen hundred dollars parts an' labor, they're able to put me back on the road again.

Well my two club brothers had split for Sturgis on Wednesday, 'cause we'd made an' agreement if one goes down an' it ain't too serious, the other two keep going. Well, I go to Russ on Thursday, give him a grand, an' am reachin' into my wallet to give him another five hundred, when he stops me an' says, "When you get home an' get your shit together, send me a check for the rest of it." Hot damn!

Back on the road again, so I decide to buzz up to Michigan just to see if I can ride. Yep, no worries. Forty-five miles up an' forty-five miles back. I'm leaving for Sturgis in the morning, an' I stop back at Russ's shop to thank him. He asks me if I have a lawyer. I tell him no, so he gives me a card for bikers' lawyers. I call this firm an' they sent a biker four hours from Milwaukee up to me. He takes forty pictures of my leg an' thirty-five of my bike. I tell him what happened an' he says, don't worry about a thing, he'll handle everything. Tells me to have a safe trip an' to call him.

When I get back next morning, 5:00 a.m., I'm checked out an' on my way to Sturgis. Well...after getting turned around a few times...now I'm on my way to Sturgis.

Pick up a riding partner just as soon as I hit 41 South. He's also on a Heritage, a 2003. We jump on 21 West an' ride together for awhile. We cross the Mississippi into Minnesota, then we jump onto I-90 West. I split from him at Albert Lea, 'cause I want to ride over to Iowa just to say I was there.

Okay, I was there—an' there wasn't much to see.

Back onto I-90 West.

Here come the bikers: first in ones an' twos, then threes an' fours, an' then packs of them. Sometimes up to a hundred in a group. Bikes on trailers, trailers pulling bikes. Seen a few patches, also; Invaders out of Indiana, a few 81s, a few Outlaws.

Cross into South Dakota without a hitch—except wind. Damnnnnnnnn. You have to ride your bike on a 45-degree angle. Never felt wind like this.

I ride within 170 miles of Sturgis. I'm beat. Stop into a KOA campground. Have ya' ever tried to put up a tent with one leg, with the wind blowing? Enough said. Had an Indian taco for supper an' two ice-cold Bud Lights.

Next morning, 5:00 am, I'm on the road again. Stop into Wall Drug for breakfast. Holy shit—look at the bikes! Every kind you can think of and all packed down as heavy as me or heavier. There are Volkswagen trikes, Harley trikes, Harley trikes with Volkswagen backs, all kinds of choppers, British bikes, German bikes, Jap bikes. All kinds of bikes. Well, I had a good breakfast—five slices of French toast, a pile of bacon, coffee, an' OJ for five bucks.

All kinds of cool shit to see! The problem is, I can't walk around. Can only walk on my bad leg for about fifteen minutes before I have to rest. So I say fuck it, an' ride out of town— back on I-90 West for Sturgis.

Well, I arrive at Elkview Campground. Fuck, it's hot: 118 in the shade. I figure my brothers have been waiting for me, but surprise, surprise, I beat them. The gimp on the busted-up H-D beat 'em. Hahahaha.

I go an' set up camp in the only tree site, then ride down to the campground bar. Put six beers away so fast it should make my head spin, but it just goes right through ya'.

I'm sitting there around 6:00 p.m., workin' on my twelfth beer an' eating a steak dinner, when in walks my club brother, Showtime. He says: "Man, you're a sight for sore eyes." I ask him, "Where the fuck you guys been?" He tells me Ezyrider got a flat an' he stopped an' took off his front brakes at least twelve times. I ask why the fuck he didn't just leave them off till he got here—he didn't need front brakes on this flat prairie anyhow.

Well, they eat and say they want to go into Sturgis. I tell them to go ahead; I'm going to bed. I crash about 9:00 p.m. an' sleep to the sounds of roaring Harleys all night long.

Wake up at 5:00 a.m. My brothers are out cold. I say, fuck this shit, and ride down to Rapid City. Have a good breakfast at Denny's then head off to see Mt. Rushmore. Fuckin'-A, that is one cool thing! Just imagine hanging off a rock face an' carving faces in the stone with dynamite and air hammers!

Ride out of Mt. Rushmore and through the canyon to where you can only see George Washington's face. Then ride over to the Crazy Horse Memorial. Man, this place is awesome! The video about how he did it is unreal. I want to get a copy but I'm afraid to spend any money, as I'm short on funds because of the wreck. But I decide to splurge an' take a bus ride to the base camp of the memorial.

Fuck me. I can't get my leg up on the fuckin' stairs of the bus.

I'm just about ready to say fuck it, when this big bearded face looks down at me an' says, "What's the problem, brother?" I tell him I can't get my fuckin' leg on the damn step. He reaches out a giant bear paw an' pulls me up on the bus. Tells me his name is "Wizard," Sgt. of Arms, Iron Men MC in New Hampshire. Tell him my name is "Lucky Yank," Sgt. of Arms of my club's Mountain Chapter. Just add water an' become instant friends.

Well, me, him, an' his ol' lady have a good time B.S.in' an' telling road tales. I tell him all about the wreck. He's concerned about my leg an' tells me I need to keep a eye on it an' make sure the lines keep running sideways an' not up an' down. I tell them both I'll keep an' eye on it.

Well, the ride to base camp is about fifteen minutes long, an' we stop an' look up at it, an' the driver says, "Okay folks, that's it. Hope ya' enjoyed the trip."

Wizard an' his ol' lady look at each other an' say to me, "Fuck, that was a shitty deal for two hundred and fifty bucks." I say, "What two hundred and fifty bucks? Man, you two got on the wrong bus! This is the four-dollar bus ride!"

We get back to the Memorial Building an' I tell the driver what happened. He says no worries, gets on the radio, an' tells the other bus driver he found the missing couple. So they go all the way up to the top. While I wait for them down below, I go an' check out Wizard's bike. It's an Ultra Classic with a supercharger on it. Real fancy paint job with murals o' wizards an' demons. Lots of chrome. Even has an' auxiliary starter button. And air-ride suspension.

I'm sittin' on the steps, an' some old lady slips an' falls an' lands on—you got it—my bad leg. She asks if I'm all right. I tell her, "Yeah, I'm too old to cry." She says, "Let me see your leg, son. I just want to make sure you're okay." I pull my pant leg up, an' I just about give her a heart attack when she sees how black an' blue an' swollen it is. I tell her, "Relax, ma'am. I had a motorcycle accident."

About a half-hour later, here come Wizard an' his ol' lady with big smiles on their faces. Tell me they got lots of pictures an' that they'll send me some when they get back home to New Hampshire.

*We are all dying of thirst and decide to get a drink.
We stop off at this small bar and I buy them a round. They say
they are heading for Sturgis. I'm going to Deadwood. Well, we
say our goodbyes an' Wizard shakes my hand an' gives me a big
bear hug. Then the big motherfucker slips two hundred dollars
in my vest. Tells me it's just a little travelin' money, an' that if
I ever get a chance to help a brother, I ought to do it.*

*Well, we ride together for about an' hour then we split
at Deadwood. The place is jam-packed with bikes. They are
motioning me into this parking lot. I ask the guy how far is the
Number Ten Saloon? He says about a six-block walk. I decide
fuck it, I can't walk that far, an' ride off. Well, I get gas an'
decide to ride to North Dakota.*

Phewwwwwwwwwww.

On the 85 North. Winds blowing 70 mph. Talk about crazy!

*Finally arrive at the North Dakota border, 5:00 p.m.
Have to ride on into Bowman and get gas. Fuck it—never
been to Montana! So I hang a left on 12 West an' ride over to
Montana. Ride all the way over to Miles City. It's 9:00 p.m.
Decide to get a room for the night…Ninety dollars for a room.
Fuck that shit. Which way to Wyoming? Down 59 South, close
to three hundred miles away.*

Phewwwwwwwwww. Gonna be a long ride tonight.

*So I'm on 59 South an' my headlight goes out. No biggie.
I can just use my spotlights.*

*Shit—what the hell is that? It looks like someone put
antlers on a horse. Damn mule deer. Okay, deer, stay right the
fuck where you're at. Now what? Prong-horned antelopes?*

Okay, better slow it down some.

*Down to 50 mph. Now it's really going to be a long
ride to Wyoming. Welllllllllllll…might as well just sit back an'
enjoy the ride.*

At least it's not raining.

Shit, SOB, spoke too soon. Guess I'm gonna get wet.

At least the wind quit blowing—shit!

I need to learn to keep my mouth shut about things.

So I ride in the rain and the wind for about 150 miles, then I come to this one-horse town called Broadus. Manage to find a gas station that's open and fill up. Then I ride back out of town, back into the wind an' rain, mule deer an' antelopes.

Okay, so I'm wet, cold, hungry, there's deer everywhere, an' antelope.

Can't get any worse, right?

Wrong. Now it starts thundering—but in the distance. Watching a thunderstorm dance across the prairie, I say to myself, "Man, am I glad I'm not in that fuckin' shit."

When will I learn to not even think of these things?

Here comes the lighting an' thunder. Okay, so I'm the highest thing on this road. Damn bolts are getting closer an' closer. Shit, that was too fuckin' close! Lightning bolts comin' out of the sky at ten to fifteen a shot, ten feet away from me—this is getting a little hairy.

SOB, it can't get any worse than this!

What the fuck? Sign pops up: Wyoming state line, 12-percent grade ahead, drivers use low gear. Shit. Up we go, now.

We are having some real fun! Rain, wind, lighting, mule deer, antelopes—What the fuck? Shit, a badger just ran out in front of me!—an' a 12-percent grade.

Now I know it can't get any worse.

You got to be kidding me! HAIL?! Nooooooooooooo… ouch, ouch, ouch, fuckin'-A ouch! An' nowhere to hide from it.

Okay, I finally reach the top of it.

Man, what a view! Hey, the hail stopped! An' so did the rain, an' the wind died down some, an' no deer for awhile.

Lookin' at that storm throwing lightning bolts, wind, rain, an' hail—an' to think, I rode through it!

Rich Halmuth's blustery brick road to Sturgis: *Lightning and hail and mule deer—oh shit!*

Okay, down the mountain we go. Sixty miles to Gillette, Wyoming. I don't care if a motel room costs a 110 dollars a night—I'm getting one! Ah, Motel 6: "You won't pay a lot an' we'll leave the light on for ya"'! Yeah, right. Some fuckin' raghead owns the joint: 250 bucks a night. Fuck you, ya SOB.

Back on the road. Ah, I-90 East. Fuckin'-A, here comes the wind again. Only a few miles an' I'll be back in Sturgis.

You got to be fuckin' kidding me: 180 miles to Sturgis. It's 2:00 a.m. I see a sign up ahead for Moorcroft. No vacancy. Shit. Okay, more gas an' I'm on the road again. Hey, a truck stop an' three bikes. Well, I go inside an' get some real hot, bold coffee, an' I look around the corner an' find three bikers. Well, actually one biker, one wannabe, an' one, well…let's just say he's an' educated asshole.

Me an' the other biker start talkin'. He tells me he took off from Oklahoma, rode to California, then up to Oregon, then Washington. Then over to Idaho, over to Montana, then to Wyoming. He's been on the road for twenty-one days.

He was heading for Sturgis tonight but the fuckin' wind was killing him, so he stopped here for the night. Been here about four hours.

The wannabe was on his way back from Sturgis. Says he stayed at Buffalo Chip Campground an' couldn't get any sleep. An' women kept asking him to fornicate with him. An' they wanted to do other things to him too. Me an' the old grizzled biker both says to him at the same time: "Damn, boy, what are ya, gay?"

Then I find out the age of my friend: seventy-four years old. Seventy-four years old an' he's been on the road for twenty-one days. Damn, now there's *a real biker. I tell him what happened to my leg, an' he tells me, better keep an' eye on it so you don't get a blood clot in it.*

Now the educated asshole starts in.

An' the old biker goes, "Oh Christ, not again."

First he asks me how much my Harley's worth. I tell him thirteen grand. He says, "You know how much my *bike is worth?" I ask him what he's riding. He says a 1986 Goldwing. I say, "Probably about two grand." He says, "Yeah, that right? Two grand—an' I just paid six grand for it three weeks ago?" I say, "Well, ain't you the smart one?" I tell him he got fucked.*

Then he starts on this shit about how many carbs do I have, an' coils, sparkplugs, and all kinds a stupid shit.

Then he asks me how come you guys ride those big Harleys? I tell him I guess 'cause we don't want to ride that Jap crap. Then he starts telling us he has a Ph.D., Bachelor's Degree in this an' that, an' that he's cuma-sum-motherfucker-stupid-asshole, or something like that—as Arlo Guthrie would say.

He talks for forty-five minutes an' nobody understands a word he says.

Well, after about two hours of that shit, I decide to put it back into the wind. So I buy the old biker a cup o' coffee an' a Danish. I shake his hand and say, "Old man, it's been real an' it's been fun, but it ain't been real fun."

I tell the wannabe he should take up skateboarding.

An' to the educated asshole (who, by the way, informed us he didn't have any insurance, no registration, an' no driver's license—don't you just love 'em?), I say: "Best thing you could do is go back to school. An' leave the motorcycle riding to real bikers." He then says to me: "You can't go out into that wind; it'll kill ya'." I say, "Yeah, well maybe. But at least I won't have to sit here an' listen to your B.S."

The old man comes out to my bike, gives me a bear hug, an' tells me, "Ride safe, bro." He thanks me again for the cup of coffee an' the Danish, and then tells me to go fuck myself an' laughs out loud for me making him sit there with those two assholes again.

It's 6:00 a.m. I arrive back in Elkview campground in South Dakota.

Phewwwwwwwwwwwww. What a ride. Seven hundred and fifty miles!

My two brothers are just crawling out of their tents. "You up already, Yank?" they say to me. I grin an' say, "Yeah, but not for long."

I ride down to the bar an' get me some breakfast, an' then go to bed.

What a day an' a night.

—Rich Halmuth,
Adventurer Extrordinaire

That, brothers and sisters, is Sturgis.

That is a rite of passage.

The Journey

by Cole Alan Bieler

I have had the good fortune to travel many miles down many different roads.

It all started when I was a kid and my parents wanted to make sure that my brother and I had the chance to see this country and its people. It took years, but one thing I learned was that certain people have an attitude and outlook about life and living that causes them to stand out in a crowd. And often, they feel a sense of loneliness while in that crowd. They have a look on their faces and a tone in their voices that seems to reveal that they're always looking ahead, looking down the road; not just to a destination, but to the journey.

They enjoy the moment, but live for the journey.

These people are filled with self-confidence and self-reliance. They revel in the challenges of planning, preparing, and traveling; of being "out there." The Captain Kirks of the world can—with confidence and joy—look out into the vastness of time and space. Even with all of its challenges and dangers, with a casual wave of the hand they can order the ship forward…out there…somewhere.

American Bikers are among these travelers.

351

One such biker was a guy I met on my way to Sturgis a few years back.

I was running with a friend. My friend had never been to Sturgis before—he had never been on this kind of a trip before. Before we left, he wanted to know what kind of clothes to bring. I told him about the rapidly changeable weather and terrain that we'd cross. I told him about the extremes in the heat and cold. He told me he was more interested in what was the coolest fashion to wear.

We finally got on the road. After several hours of riding, we stopped in a rest area to stretch and have a quick sandwich. This guy pulls up on a well-used Harley; one carrying the scars of many road trips. After a quick acknowledgement and hello, it didn't take long to strike up a conversation. We didn't have much to eat, but we shared what we had with him.

The guy's name was Jim. We talked about past trips, the greasy spoon about 250 miles further up the highway that we had both stopped at in the past, the people we looked forward to seeing at Sturgis, and future travels we intended (or hoped) to take. The conversation was relaxed and easy, as if we had known each other for some time.

My friend who was riding with me chimed in with talk of some new gadgets he'd bolted on his bike, his plan to get a *new* bike, his new riding gloves, and asking whether he'd see some *real* partying and "gratuitous nudity" once we got to Sturgis.

My friend was clearly looking to impress and convince Jim that he was a true "biker."

Sitting with these two men, the difference was clear. Everything we talked about was of mutual interest and all part of the experience of such a trip. Other than some wear and tear, our clothes and appearance were similar. But the priorities were so different.

Jim was dressed for the road, while my friend had dressed to fit in. Jim was also looking forward to some partying and eye candy, of course; but his focus (and mine) was the journey.

Jim finished his break and prepared to get back on the road. He said goodbye to my friend and then stepped over to me and paid me a great compliment. Shaking my hand, he said, "Thanks, I'll see you down the road, brother."

While I have not seen Jim since, I know that if he's alive, he is still out there on The Journey. The chances are I *will* see him again, as I remain on The Journey as well.

Chapter 14

The Dave Mann Image

The Look, The Last Ride, To Hell and Back

It's like how Alberto Vargas painted all those pictures of chicks for *Playboy* magazine. They were perfect. They weren't *actual* women to most guys; they were their fantasy. They were deep in their minds, their dreams.

Dave Mann did the same thing with the American Biker. Every one of his classics—"Ghost Rider," "Sunset Boulevard," "Won't Start," "Run Heat"; all of them—this is how the American Biker is supposed to look: doing the things he's supposed to do, acting the way he's supposed to act.

But you know what? There *are* women out there who *do* look like the Vargas babes; and there are plenty of bikers out there who look and act like they just walked out of the paint in "Hollywood Nights."

This lifestyle has many ideals that the mainstream thinks either don't exist or are unattainable. They settle for dreaming and never even try. And that's fine with me—that leaves just that much more for those of us who want to wring every drop out of these few short years that we've been given.

I don't ever have to be reminded just how real this lifestyle is. But occasionally there are *those moments*; sharp slices of time and place that melt on the tongue of truth—revelations and sensory experiences to be savored.

I was on the set of an internet TV series called *Sturgis Rider Live*, a production that evolved from the combined talents of biker musician Charlie Brechtel and "Woody," the owner of the Sturgis Rally's world-famous Buffalo Chip Campground.

We were in the town of Copperopolis in California's gold country, surrounded by hills and mountains and places like Yosemite, Angel's Camp, and the historical settlement of Murphys, where Wild West outlaw Black Bart used to hide out.

The set was made to resemble a saloon.

The ambience was set and thick.

The cameras panned to the bar in front of me. Parked there was a custom '49 Harley FL, built by respected custom-builder Keith Scarboro as a tribute to the most observant and brilliant biker artist of all, the late Dave Mann.

In the background, we could hear the voice of Jim Elrite. Jim is the show's announcer. He is a thirty-five-plus-year member of the Hells Angels Motorcycle Club and former president of the San Jose chapter. Hearing his voice is like hearing the low-pitched growl of a mountain lion just outside your window at midnight; hungry and fearless, with big impact.

Jim also hosts our DVD series, *Bikers: The Inner Circle*. The show's reviews have referred to Elrite as "edgy."

He is.

Jim Elrite is also *that guy*. He is a true American Biker. His look, his demeanor, his image, shine with Vargas-like perfection; but he's as real and genuine as it gets.

Thankfully, he is not alone.

Dave Mann took *that guy* and gave his portrait to the world. It was a portrait not designed to *prove* that the essence of *that guy* was real—Mann didn't have to do that—but rather to finely detail every aspect of this lifestyle and the image that goes along with it.

Mann began painting his canvas of the biker culture for *Easyriders* magazine during the publication's inaugural year of 1971; his creative work continued until his health began to fail in 2003. Dave eventually passed away in his hometown of Kansas City, Missouri, on September 11th of 2004, one day after his sixty-fourth birthday.

Dave Mann laid bare our good along with our bad. The sheer and unparalleled glamour times, as well as those "uncomfortable" times: times when we grit our teeth, freeze, sweat, or just plain have to *literally* ride out some brutal wave. That "riding out," however, ultimately always proves to be less harsh than the alternative of sitting safely "behind the fences" lamenting about what might have been.

Mann's work was a mirror of our lives—our *full* lives. And a full life is one in which each detail is relished; either enjoyed or at least learned from. Mann captured every detail, large and small, of the biker lifestyle with the precision of a siege-trained sniper—never missing his target, even by a hair.

A searing example of Mann's accuracy was featured in the center spread of the November 1985 issue of *Easyriders* (an especially interesting issue in that the cover girl was the *very* young, lovely and talented—and soon-to-be-famous—Traci Lords, who used a fake ID to make more than a hundred porno films while underage. She used the name "Susie" in this layout). Nighttime was Mann's setting for this issue's work. A group of bikes were rolling—obviously fast; his bikes always seemed to be flying—along a dark street in front of a joint called the "Harbor Lights Bar." Above the street and the bikes and the bar was the barely discernible outline of a huge suspension bridge.

I remember looking at this painting for the first time. Like all of Mann's work, its effect doesn't stop at just your eyes or at the edge of your basic response lobes. No. It goes deep, ripping and shredding, like a bullet constantly rerouted by bone and flesh and muscle— careening crazily, touching every nerve.

I immediately thought of San Pedro and its rough waterfront and the giant specter of the Vincent Thomas Bridge. I thought of the many times I rode there as a kid, sitting behind my uncle; even when there *was* no bridge, just the road in front of the old ferry building and a seemingly endless row of bars and grills, where attitude and balls of carbon steel were required for entry.

Then I thought of 'Frisco and the Golden Gate and the ancient neighborhoods that dot The City, with streets packed tight by ornate homes and storefronts like that which housed the original shop of Harley dealer pioneer Dudley Perkins.

I felt the presence of the bridges and waterfronts of Seattle and Portland, and the southern passage along I-5 that I traversed during hard rides to and from Canada.

The bikes in the painting were pure Mann: rigids, Shovels, kick-starts, fenderless, with 21-inch front wheels, classic peanut tanks, and flamed Fat Bobs—all gaugeless and taste-filled. The riders were all-Mann as well: full beards, long hair, shades, bandanas, leathers flowing in and with the wind, strong gloved-hands on the throttles, black jeans, blue jeans, and the always-prevalent heavy boots. They rode in close formation; implying good and trusting riders, good and trusting brothers.

Vargas-like perfection...

Mann loved the real stuff.

The sheer and unparalleled glamour times, as well as those "uncomfortable" times...

Mann reared a particularly ugly and cold head in *Easyriders'* January 1989 issue when he stormed the magazine's centerfold with the horror, discomfort, and simple pain-in-the-ass nature of being a biker in winter. The frigid shock of coming out of a bar to find your bike covered with snow—and worse, your front wheel frozen to the pavement in a mound of ice—is seen so dead-on in the sick wince of Mann's biker in the painting; so is the "oh no, the shit's about to hit the snowy fan" look on the face of his ol' lady.

The risks necessary to enjoy this way of life demand a price. That, of course, is the truth. And Dave Mann always spoke the truth through his art.

"Roadtrip Come Undone" first appeared in the September 1990 *Easyriders*. Anyone who has ever set out on a road trip with *way* too much stuff can relate to the mess and the hassle and the danger and the aggravation that "bungee cord failure" can produce:

> *I had to take a cage to Hollister this year because I had just had a wreck. It was a hit-and-run…the guy hit me and left me by the side of the freeway. Anyway, it worked out okay because I was able to take Dago with me. At seventy-seven years old, Dago is still wild and crazy and active. She's been around since the beginning, and she* knows *this lifestyle.*
>
> *Well, we were going up the I-5 with a big pack of our club members. We got ahead of them when they stopped for gas. We're rollin' along when we see this guy alone on a bike, stopped by the side of the road.*
>
> *Dago immediately says: "We need to stop and help this guy!"*
> *"Sure, why not?" I say, and I pull over.*
>
> *I back up to the guy, and it turns out that he's a weekend warrior who just bought a brand new Harley. Brand new helmet, brand new pants, brand new boots, brand new logo-leather jacket. Everything says "Harley-Davidson": this guy is like a corporate billboard.*

He's a little frustrated.

He has all his shit thrown off his bike, and it's all over the ground. I look at his bike, and I see a jacket sleeve hanging out between his tire and his fender.

"Holy shit, that shouldn't be there!" I say.

I ask him if he needs some help; and I'm looking at the sleeve and the jacket, and I ask him how that happened.

Turns out he had his jacket packed on the back of his bike, and it came loose and got wrapped around the whole rear wheel and tire. It nearly caused him to wreck.

We start rocking the bike back and forth, and pulling on the jacket and shit, but it's not doing any good. The guy is getting more and more frustrated. And I can tell he's scared to death…I'm wearing my patch and all.

Well, about thirty seconds later, this pack of about sixty bikes comes roaring up the freeway. I see it's my brothers, so I'm out on the road doing jumpin' jacks, wavin' to get their attention, tryin' to get them to pull over.

You shoulda seen the look on this guy's face! Now I'm in *real* trouble! *he was thinkin'!*

The pack pulls over and "Pretty Boy" comes up.

"What's the problem?" he says.

"Well, we gotta get this guy's jacket out of his wheel!" I tell him.

Pretty Boy just stares for a minute or two. I don't think he believed what he was seeing. Then he pulls out a knife about the size of a damn sword!

He goes over and starts cuttin' on the jacket. Bit by bit we hack it up and get it out of the guy's wheel. I offer to take what's left of it with me in the cage and give it back to the guy when we get to Hollister.

But this guy is so pissed off.

"Fuck that jacket!" he says. "Keep it as a souvenir!"
So I kept it!
I offered to give the guy my cell phone number, in case anything else happened to him or he needed anymore help, but he said, "No! No! I don't need anything else!"
He was just so happy that we were leaving, I think!

—"Zippo";
Hollister, 2007

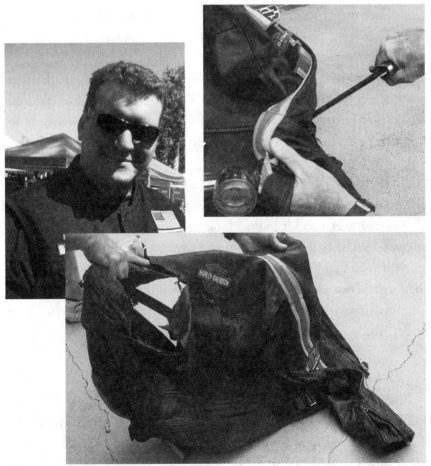

"Zippo," living out Dave Mann's "Roadtrip Come Undone."

More bleak reality—rain and storms—is seen throughout Mann's creations, exemplified in pieces like "Handlebars & Rain" and the ironically named "The Sunshine State."

The dank, sinking feelings generated by "Dark Roadside Repairs," "Daytona Zoo," and "Heavy Rain Breakdown" touch so many of us who have been there. These kind of "memorable" experiences have provided good subject matter for the "it's kind of funny *now*, but it sure as hell wasn't so funny *then*" barroom conversations.

There were no taboos in this man's art; just the truth. Just like the culture he represented.

The stinging reality of prison and jail life cuts through titles like the scorpion-starring "Mexican Burnout" and Mann's famous celebratory portrayal of a biker-inmate's release, and his welcome to freedom by his brothers and some boob-flashing babes.

Ah, yes, the babes—the women.

They, too, are perfect in a biker sense. More important than the universal drool-inspiring bodies that Mann crafted for them, the chicks all had that near-psychic look; a look that always said they *knew*. They knew so much. There was wisdom and strength behind the T&A. They let their men be men, and bikers be bikers, while never compromising their own status as important components of this life-lusting society.

At times, they are just blatantly smarter and more grounded in reality; study "His and Hers."

Ben Nighthorse Campbell talked about bikers being "kindred spirits" to heroes and legends. Like a shaman with a direct line to the other side, Dave Mann conjured up those kindred spirits and integrated them into the soul of the American Biker. His ghost images haunt.

His juxtapositions show the biker and the machine as conduits for all that is muscled, mystical, enduring, and exploding with awe. He summoned up the leather-tough Pony Express riders; the Vikings; Native-American warriors; total eclipses; Santa Claus; and even Neptune, the Roman god of the sea—complete with a hot mermaid riding in a slightly unorthodox fin-dictated position, side-saddle on a p-pad.

One of Mann's more intriguing works is an untitled piece he created with another true legend, Ed "Big Daddy" Roth. This particular painting features Loki, the Norse god of mischief, in all his crimson glory—a portrait that is now the commanding centerpiece of the patch of the Vagos Motorcycle Club.

Mann gave his respect to biker history with renderings like "Wild One" (homage to Hollister '47) and "Seattle Cossacks" (a tribute to the famous stunt team, established in 1938).

He often shared the highway with America's truckers—the other "road dogs" of this country—with paintings like the bike/big-rig night-shot in *Easyriders'* February '96 issue.

In January of 2004, Dave Mann's final original center spread for the *Easyriders*/Paisano group of magazines was published in *BIKER* magazine. His last artistic ride was called "To Hell and Back"; it depicts a classic Mann-style biker—but on a new-style scooter— surrealistically meeting *himself* on the fiery, experienced-laden journey to, and from, Hell.

Again, more perfection. More crosshair-accurate detail.

It was a *flawless* last ride for Mann; for his work, and for his observations of the American Biker. The red-sky painting screams out that to live this lifestyle to its hilt is indeed to go to Hell and back; to be cleansed and educated with revelations that never stop. The rider is facing himself; confronting his own fears, thoughts, and innermost feelings—something that every one of us does, and *has* done, on those long solo rides, far from the mental diversions of a car or any other form of cage.

We *are* "edgy."

Damned edgy.

This entire *lifestyle* is edgy.

It's dangerous, with a colorful history and the wildest cast of characters in the universe. It's based around a machine that's quick, slick, and loud. We see wrecks and death. We feel the sun and the wind and the forces of nature like no one else. We feel the strong bond of brotherhood like no one else. We are looked at by society like no one else.

We *are* like no one else.

Ultimately, the most poignant thing about Dave Mann's art is that he *didn't* create The Image. He didn't dream up the look, or the lifestyle. The great composers didn't invent the tonal scale; but they took the notes and made them dance. Dave made *us* dance, too.

Dave Mann lived in the very real inner circle of this way of life. He observed what and who we are (and who *he* was) and used a rare talent to express it, showing us a reflection of ourselves that—depending on the circumstances—makes us cringe, makes us laugh, makes us cry, or makes us stand tall with pride.

In *that* reflection, within *those* emotions, surrounded by *those* experiences, and glowing with *that* image, the American Biker is defined.

And *that's* what instills that "fear and envy" into those on the outside.

True and real American Bikers like Jim Elrite, and like those given life through the brushes, pens, and strokes of Dave Mann, really *do* exist.

The ideal and the fantasy in all their thunder-fast glory is *actually* there to be enjoyed and experienced: You just need to twist that throttle far enough and hard enough.

If you dare.

Source Notes

The information in this book obviously came from a wide variety of sources. Thankfully, much of it came from my own hands-on, "I was there" experiences. The remainder came largely from those of close friends, acquaintances, business associates, and unique souls I have met in my travels.

Every source has also been identified in the book's context so that the reader knows immediately where a quote or reference came from. (I have always found footnotes too clinical and distracting!)

We are extremely grateful to all who contributed their stories and wrote original pieces to help develop the depth and breadth of this ambitious undertaking.

We would specifically like to thank Dave Nichols, Kim Peterson, Mark Dodge, and the rest of the staff at *Easyriders* magazine for their blessings in using the following reprints from their publication (the media chapter wouldn't have been the same without Clint Armentor's classic piece about biker movies!):

The news sources and other objective sources referenced and/ or quoted from are used either with direct permission from the originator or by invocation of the Fair Use Doctrine of United States Copyright Law, which allows for the use of copyrighted material for such purposes as commentary, criticism, news reporting, research, teaching, or scholarship—all of which are done in the most honest and straightforward way possible in *American Biker.*

Photo Credits

We're proud of the photos in *American Biker*. Most are original and have not been published or seen anywhere else. Like the personal recollections throughout this book, many were garnered by myself and my partner, Jennifer Thomas, while at gatherings of bikers who were simply doing what they do—being a part of this lifestyle.

Our deep appreciation goes to the people and organizations who have provided us materials from their sacred collections. We also extend thanks to Randall Wilson for the still captures from his brilliant documentaries, including *American Biker*, the film—the inspiration for this book.

Included also are images from my *personal* sacred archive—a large gallery comprised of material sent to me by a wide variety of sources, in hopes that it can and will be used to further the legacy and history of the *American Biker*.

We believe that has been accomplished!

p. xiv: Capture from *American Biker,* the film.
Used courtesy of Guerrilla Docs.

p. 11: Photo by Jennifer Thomas.

p. 21: Courtesy of Oshkosh Aces MC.

p. 24: Photo by Jennifer Thomas.

p. 31: Photo by Bill Hayes.

p. 33: Courtesy of Boozefighters MC.

p. 35: Courtesy of Boozefighters MC.

p. 48: Courtesy of Jack Jordan.

p. 54: Capture from *American Biker,* the film.
Used courtesy of Guerrilla Docs.

p. 55: Photo by Barney Peterson.
Used in accordance with the Fair Use Doctrine.

p. 56: Photos by Jennifer Thomas.

p. 60: Courtesy of Jim "JQ" Quattlebaum.

p. 68: Capture from *Bikers: The Inner Circle, Vol. 1.*
Used courtesy of Big 7 Productions.

p. 71: Capture from *Bikers: The Inner Circle, Vol. 1.*
Used courtesy of Big 7 Productions.

p. 73: Capture from *The Wild One.*
Used in accordance with the Fair Use Doctrine.

p. 74: Courtesy of Flash Productions and Outlaws MC.

p. 86: Capture from *American Biker,* the film.
Used courtesy of Guerrilla Docs.

p. 89: Courtesy of The Chosen Few MC.

p. 91: Photo by John "Ghost" Wagner.

p. 96: Photo by Bill Hayes.

p. 102: Photo by Bill Hayes.

p. 103: Photo by Jennifer Thomas.

p. 104: Courtesy of Billy Warlock.

p. 108: Courtesy of Oshkosh Aces MC.

p. 109: Courtesy of Tom Skoglind and Oshkosh Aces MC.

p. 113: Photo by Jennifer Thomas.

p. 116: Photo by Bill Hayes.

p. 130: Photo by "Uncle Watts" and "Uncle Hoss."

p. 132: Capture from *Hessians MC*.
   Used courtesy of Guerrilla Docs.

p. 141: Photo by Bill Hayes.

p. 155: Photo by Jennifer Thomas.

p. 156: Photo by Jennifer Thomas.

p. 161: Photo by Jennifer Thomas.

p. 162: Photos by Jennifer Thomas.

p. 163: Photo by Jennifer Thomas.

p. 164: Photo by Jennifer Thomas.

p. 170: Courtesy of Gene Long.

p. 172: Courtesy of Gene Long.

p. 199: Courtesy of J.J. Solari. Special thanks to Cecily Solari.

p. 202: Photo by Jeff Kraus.

p. 215: Photographer unknown (from the "personal sacred archive").

p. 229: Courtesy of Jennifer Thomas.

p. 239: Courtesy of The Chosen Few MC.

p. 241: Courtesy of Kara Grace.

p. 245: Courtesy of Steve Boyd.

p. 247: Photos by Jennifer Thomas.

p. 251: Courtesy of Steve Boyd and Yuriko.

p. 254: Photo by Jennifer Thomas.

p. 256: Courtesy of Paul Jamiol.

p. 277: Photo by Jennifer Thomas.

p. 280: Photo (left) courtesy of Virginia "Dago" Day;
Photo (right) by Jennifer Thomas.

p. 283: Courtesy of Bill Hayes.

p. 297: Capture from *American Biker,* the film.
Used courtesy of Guerrilla Docs.

p. 299: Photographer unknown.

p. 305: Courtesy of Keith Randall Ball.

p. 309: Capture from *Bikers: The Inner Circle, Vol. 1.*
Used courtesy of Big 7 Productions.

p. 317: Courtesy of Jeff Kraus.

p. 318: Photo by Bill Hayes.

p. 319: Photo by Bill Hayes.

p. 323: Photo by Bill Hayes.

p. 325: Photo by Bill Hayes.

p. 335: Photo by Jennifer Thomas.

p. 347: Courtesy of Rich Halmuth.

p. 351: Photo by Bill Hayes.

p. 361: Courtesy of "Zippo."

p. 365: Photo by Jennifer Thomas.

Bibliography

A wealth of media is referenced in *American Biker*—books, magazines, films, television shows, news sources, and more. As mentioned, each source is identified immediately in the book's context.

The purpose of this bibliography is to allow the *American Biker* reader to further explore the always "interesting" and ever-moving world of the motorcycle culture. Some sources listed are *directly* referenced in *American Biker;* others are by writers and personalities who have contributed to the content of this book.

Bear in mind that we don't necessarily *endorse* the content of every work listed (the infiltration books, for example) but we at least recognize that they are important to the study of the many facets of this compelling and unique lifestyle.

Books

Ball, K. Randall. *Harbor Town Seduction*. 5-Ball Incorporated, 2010.

Barger, Sonny. *Hell's Angel: The Life and Times of Sonny Barger and the Hell's Angels Motorcycle Club*. HarperCollins, 2000.

Caine, Alex. *Befriend and Betray: Infiltrating the Hells Angels, Bandidos and Other Criminal Brotherhoods*. Thomas Dunne Books, 2008.

Caine, Alex. *The Fat Mexican: The Bloody Rise of the Bandidos Motorcycle Club*. Random House Canada, 2009.

Carroll, Lewis. *Alice's Adventures in Wonderland*. Macmillan, 1898.

Cavasos, Ruben "Doc". *Honor Few, Fear None: The Life & Times of a Mongol*. HarperCollins, 2008.

Coyote, Peter. *Sleeping Where I Fall*. Counterpoint, 1998.

Davis, Miles. *Motorcycle Yoga: Meditative Rides through India*. International Institute of Indology Incorporated, 2003.

Dixon, Martin. *Brooklyn Kings: New York City's Black Bikers*. powerHouse Books, 2000.

Droban, Kerrie. *Running with the Devil: The True Story of the ATF's Infiltration of the Hells Angels*. The Lyons Press, 2007.

Hall, John. *Riding on the Edge: A Motorcycle Outlaw's Tale*. Motorbooks International, 2008.

Hayes, Bill. *The Original Wild Ones: Tales of the Boozefighters Motorcycle Club*. Motorbooks International, 2005.

Jamiol, Paul. *Bikers Are Animals: A Children's Book on Motorcycling*. Dog Ear Publishing, 2009.

Krebs, Dennis. *When Violence Erupts: A Survival Guide for Emergency Responders*. Jones and Bartlett Publishers Incorporated, 2003.

Levingston, Tobie Gene. *Soul on Bikes: The East Bay Dragons MC and the Black Biker Set.* Motorbooks International, 2003.

Lyon, Danny. *The Bikeriders.* 2nd Edition. Chronicle Books, 2003.

Queen, William. *Under and Alone: The True Story of the Undercover Agent Who Infiltrated America's Most Violent Outlaw Motorcycle Gang.* Random House, 2005.

Roberts, Beverly V. *Portraits of American Bikers: Inside Looking Out, The Flash Collection II.* Flash Productions, LLC, 2010.

Roberts, Beverly V. *Portraits of American Bikers: Life in the 1960s, The Flash Collection.* Flash Productions, LLC, 2008.

Shaylor, Andrew. *Hells Angels Motorcycle Club.* Merrell Publishers Limited, 2004.

Solari, J.J. *When Bikers Meet Humans.* J.J. Solari, 2007.

Stein, Michael. *Born to Be Wild: Harleys, Bikers & Music for Easy Riders.* Edel CLASSICS GmbH, 2006.

Thompson, Hunter. *Hell's Angels: The Strange and Terrible Saga of the Outlaw Motorcycle Gangs.* Ballantine Books, 1966.

White, Amy. *Wicked Bitch.* Lulu, 2009.

Winterhalder, Edward. *Out In Bad Standings: Inside the Bandidos Motorcycle Club, the Making of a Worldwide Dynasty.* Blockhead City Press, 2005.

Films and DVDs

American Biker. Guerrilla Docs, 2005.

Bikers: The Inner Circle: Vol. 1. Big 7 Productions, 2006.

Easy Rider. Columbia Pictures, 1969.

Gimme Shelter. Maysles Films, 1970.

Glory Road: The Legacy of the African American Motorcyclist. Guerilla Docs, 2002.

Hessians MC. Guerilla Docs, 2005.

The Long Ride Home: Run for the Wall. Guerilla Docs, 2006.

Showdown in Durango. South Bay Biker Productions, 2006.

Wheels of Soul. Guerilla Docs, 2002.

The Wild One. Columbia Pictures, 1953.

Publications

Easyriders. Paisano Publications.

Thunder Press. Affinity Media.

Index

American Biker
> Birth of xiii, 2, 34, 41, 49–56, 88
> Birthplace of 102, 318
>> *See also* Hollister (CA)
> *See also* books, *American Biker*
> *See also* films, *American Biker*

AMF (American Machinery and Foundry) 250, 333
Armas, Gil 48, 279
Atkins, Susan 187
Autrey, Vern 279

B

Baldwin, Irl 71
Bales, Vivian 256
Ball, Keith Randall "Bandit" xi, 218, 222, 290, 305–307
Bandidos Motorcycle Club. *See* clubs, Bandidos
Barger, Ralph "Sonny" "The Chief" 2, 41, 70–71, 121, 122, 138, 146, 174, 175, 176, 179, 186, 206, 208, 233, 246–247, 292
Bass Lake 121–122
Battey, Sumpter 20
Bauer, Bernard 287
Baxter, Sheriff Tiny 121
> *See also* Bass Lake
Beers, Tom 219, 220
Beerup, George 34
Bieler, Cole iii, xi, 12, 351–353
Big Four 66–67, 75, 77, 87, 101
Bigsby, Paul 30, 31
BIKER News 293
Bikers: The Inner Circle (DVD series) 68, 96, 296, 301, 356

C

D

E

F

films (cont.)

L

M

T